THE CHRISTIAN MEANING
OF HUMAN SEXUALITY

PAUL M. QUAY, S.J., PH.D.

The Christian Meaning of Human Sexuality

Expanded and Revised Edition

EDITED BY REV. JOSEPH W. KOTERSKI, S.J.

IGNATIUS PRESS   SAN FRANCISCO

Original 1985 Edition
Credo House Books
Evanston, Illinois

Imprimi potest: J. Leo Klein, S.J., Provincial
Chicago Province

Nihil obstat: William B. Smith, S.T.D.
Censor Librorum

Imprimatur: + Joseph T. O'Keefe, D.D. [1985]
Vicar-General
Archdiocese of New York

Cover photograph by FlairImages

Cover design by Riz Boncan Marsella

First Ignatius Press Edition © 1985 by Paul M. Quay
Expanded Edition © 2017 by Ignatius Press, San Francisco
All rights reserved
ISBN 978-1-62164-123-0
Library of Congress Control Number 2017931747
Printed in the United States of America ∞

CONTENTS

INTRODUCTION TO
THE EXPANDED EDITION

Joseph W. Koterski, S.J.

At his death in 1994 Father Paul Quay left an incomplete manuscript on the theology of natural family planning (NFP). Mindful of certain questions that have been raised about this subject, especially in the minds of Catholics who want to live in accord with the teachings of Christ and his Church in regard to their fertility, he undertook to address those questions by extending to this topic what he had already done in his book *The Christian Meaning of Human Sexuality*. As before, he saw the need to consider the matter in the light of faith and not simply on the natural level. He made considerable use of such specialized disciplines as ethics and genetics as well as other pertinent domains of science and philosophy. But the central perspective needed here is primarily theological, and so above all he pursued these questions in the light that our faith shines on the meaning of the human person and especially on the meaning of human sexuality.

As his literary executor, I have long pondered how best to proceed. Let me apologize for the delay in bringing his reflections into print. The material that appears here as supplementary material to a revised and expanded edition of his book was in diverse states of readiness for publication. In some parts all that was needed was to supply citations for the references. But even in those places where the argument needed to be filled out or the style to be revised, I have tried to be faithful to his line of thinking and to make the needed changes without altering his intended meaning.

Becoming acquainted with Father Quay's approach to the Christian vision of sexuality will prove invaluable to anyone concerned about the various moral and theological questions that have been raised about NFP. In support of the guidance that he gives on various practical questions, the book provides a rich theological understanding of the natural and supernatural dimensions of the human being, with detailed application to the areas of sexuality, fertility, and procreation. Occasionally the notes make reference to yet another work from Father Quay's hand, *The Mystery Hidden for Ages in God*.[1] That masterful volume offers a yet more general framework for understanding the process of authentic growth in the spiritual life and in moral character and thereby provides a profound theological context for appreciating Father Quay's vision of the Christian meaning of human sexuality. To assist the reader in seeing these interrelationships, this introduction will first turn to a summary of the larger and more theoretical book and then to an overview of *The Christian Meaning of Human Sexuality* before offering a précis of the new material that is printed here.

The Hidden Mystery

Pondering a question posed by Professor Alfred Shatkin, the mentor of his doctoral dissertation in physics at MIT, Father Quay begins *The Mystery Hidden for Ages in God* by reflecting on why it is that the spiritual growth of most Christians is so slow, and why the moral lives of many Christians seem no different from (if not actually worse than) many of those around them. An important part of his extensive answer to this question involves a distinction between the learnables and the developmentals.[2] The emphasis that schools usually place on communicating vast quantities of information and teaching the various skills that individuals need to learn for their professions has often meant giving far less attention to students' personal maturation and spiritual development. The failure to provide the needed formation in faith, in the virtues, in sound friendships, and in whatever else may help a given person to mature as a man or a woman imperils the readiness to be a spouse, a parent, and a responsible member of one's community, let alone to gain eternal salvation.

---

[1] Paul M. Quay, S.J., *The Mystery Hidden for Ages in God* (New York: Peter Lang, 1995).

[2] Quay, *Mystery Hidden*, pp. 362–69.

The proper application of the distinction between the learnables and the developmentals to any given culture is, of course, complex. But, to take just one example that is especially germane to this book, the long process of acquiring the type of education that tends to be provided during the years spent in college, graduate school, and specialized training is often pursued at the expense of one's formation in character and faith. How many the stories that any of us could tell about young people who get involved in the sort of romances that lead to sexual liaisons well before they are prepared to commit themselves to marriage and family. They often feel that they must put off any life commitments until they have completed their formal education or their technical training. The surrounding culture may well present sex as a form of play and provide what is conveniently labeled "protection" from undesirable consequences such as pregnancy. As a result, these young people may well find themselves unprepared or ill equipped to resist the understandable urges for sexual pleasure, for pleasant company, and for experimentation with their newfound liberties.

Many cultures, of course, offer their own distinctive patterns of personal formation. The stronger the culture, and the more homogeneous the population, the greater the likelihood that the young will tend to mature at the rate that these structures of support are suited to encourage. Cultures that are in moral or spiritual regression, as seems to be the case in Westernized parts of the world today, do not provide much support for human formation and personal maturation. Hence, much depends on individual families, but family structures in this culture have been seriously weakened too. Their resources often pale beside the other forces to which young people are exposed. This is particularly true of our current electronic culture. Many of the most formative influences on the minds and souls of the young often run counter to what parents might wish for their children. The increasing accessibility and the vivacious allure of electronic media are pervasive, and many parents come under its sway without realizing the effect that it has on themselves, let alone their children.

In light of the regressive character of the West, it is no surprise that Christians are no better than their neighbors, and sometimes worse. The presentation of the faith can easily seem overly bookish, uninteresting, or even superstitious. For this reason, much of Father Quay's book is given to considering what our Christian faith can and should do to help a person mature according to the pattern that God has designed for us in Christ.

The issue that Father Quay has chosen for discussion is, of course, complex, but the main lines of his answer direct us to reflect on the consequences—individual and social—of not taking seriously the need to recapitulate the life of Christ in our lives. As the Church has always taught, we need to imitate Jesus. What differentiates Quay's approach from that of many other good volumes in the area of Christian spirituality is that he treats the call to imitate Jesus not simply in terms of discrete moments when we need to look to his example but holistically by showing how the pattern of our growth and development must imitate the pattern of the life of Jesus as he grew through all the stages of human development that are intrinsic to the human nature that he assumed.

In the course of recapitulating the stages of his life, we need to be sure that our lives follow his pattern, that our choices follow his teaching and his example. To make such choices well, we need the assistance of the sacraments that he gives us through the Church. Actively living as members of his Body is central to participating in his life. On the other hand, failing to follow his example and to grow in him according to the pattern that he established makes it likely that we will simply follow the trends in our culture and thus be no better than the nonbelievers among whom we live, and perhaps even worse, should there arise in us any sort of presumption that merely being Christian is enough, without having to take it too seriously.

The early chapters of *The Mystery Hidden for Ages in God* lay the theological foundation for this project by considering, first, the ways in which man is made in the image and according to the likeness of God, and, second, the damage to the image and the likeness of God in us that has been brought about by original sin. A crucial part of these early chapters is an explanation (well worth study in its own right) of the Church's long-standing commitment to the four senses of Scripture. The term "sense" here is intended as "level of meaning", as explained in the *Catechism of the Catholic Church* (CCC 115ff.).

In his trio of volumes entitled *Jesus of Nazareth* Pope Emeritus Benedict XVI likewise makes thoroughgoing use of this hermeneutic.[3] In addition to the often misunderstood literal sense of Scripture, there are three spiritual senses: the allegorical (perhaps better called the typological sense), the tropological (the one concerned with morality), and the anagogical (the one that deals with matters eschatological and sacramental). Despite serious neglect in recent times, the four senses remain crucial to the proper interpretation of divine revelation.[4]

The later chapters of the book make use of this foundation to lay out an understanding of the doctrine of recapitulation: the recapitulation by Christ of the life of his people and the recapitulation in Christ that Christians—as individuals and as members of the Church—need to undertake.[5] The term "recapitulation" comes from Ephesians 1:10, where Saint Paul uses it to describe the way in which Christ "sums up" or "unites" in himself all things. Saint Paul mentions this doctrine in the course of announcing the theme of the Mystical Body of Christ that is central to this letter. In fact, the notion is ubiquitous in the Pauline writings (for example, seeing Christ as the New Adam in Romans 5:12ff.). The doctrine of recapitulation by and in Christ is at the heart of the typological sense that pervades the Bible.

Put briefly, the way in which these four senses of Scripture work is this. The three spiritual senses are the levels of meaning that the Holy Spirit has intended for us and inspired in the biblical author, and the literal sense is what the human author under divine inspiration intended. The literal sense includes the "plain sense" of the text but is not simply reducible to it, nor is it always a claim about historical events. If the human author intends to communicate something of a historical nature, as in, say, the book of Judges or in the Acts of the Apostles, then the literal sense is historical. But if the human author intends some figure of speech, such as a metaphor or a simile, or deliberately uses some style of writing or some genre, such as a parable, an allegory, or a moral tale, then the literal sense is to be found only by grasping the significance of the figure of speech or the genre chosen for a given text.

---

[3] See Joseph Lienhard, S.J., "Pope Benedict XVI: Theologian of the Bible", *Homiletic and Pastoral Review*, September 1, 2011.

[4] Quay, "The Hermeneutic Problem" in *Mystery Hidden*.

[5] Part Three ("The Church, the New Israel"), especially chapters 17 and 18, focuses on seeing how the Church is to recapitulate in Christ the life of the chosen people and on how we are to undertake our own recapitulation of Christ within the Church.

The spiritual senses are not meanings that some human interpreter imposes on the text. To the contrary, at these three levels the meaning of the text and of the figures and actions recorded therein can be found only by obtaining a proper grasp of the literal meaning of the text, in the proper sense of "literal". This task is crucial for coming to understand what the Holy Spirit intended. In this respect, what we can come to understand through the spiritual senses differs entirely from any interpretation that is imposed on the text from without, whether of the sort favored by such contemporary approaches as postmodern hermeneutics, feminism, liberation theology, the social gospel, and so on, or of the sort often favored by various traditions of Christian spirituality, such as the applications that individuals reading the Bible often make for themselves or that retreat directors and spiritual guides may use as a lens for putting a helpful focus on some aspect of a person's life. To pray about our own hypocrisy, for instance, we might well use a text such as the parable by which the prophet Nathan gets King David to see the shamefulness of his having committed adultery with Bathsheba and of having arranged for the murder of her husband, Uriah (2 Sam 12:1–6). Valid and insightful as such applications are when done carefully, they should not be thought to be the meaning of the persons and events that are found in the Scriptures as intended by the Holy Spirit through his inspiration of the sacred authors. In the strict sense of the term, the spiritual senses are present in the text and await our discovery. They are not something imposed on the text by any reader, nor are they applications of the text to our situations.

As mentioned earlier, Tradition labels the three spiritual senses the allegorical, the tropological, and the anagogical, and one will find this usage in authoritative ecclesial texts such as the *Catechism of the Catholic Church* (for example, §§115–17). The traditional nomenclature, however, may not always be the most helpful. In our standard speech the term "allegory", for instance, generally names a literary genre, and thus most of the time allegory actually belongs to the literal sense, for the adoption of extended metaphors and the carefully crafted uses of one figure to stand for something else is a deliberate work of the human author.[6]

---

[6] As Jaroslav Pelikan explains in *Whose Bible Is It? A History of the Scriptures through the Ages* (New York: Viking, 2005), pp. 127–33, there was a widespread tendency during

One can even find Saint Paul explicitly using allegory in this sense in his discussion of Hagar and Sarah.[7]

As the genre chosen by a human author, allegory is not the focus of the first of the spiritual senses. Rather, as the *Catechism* notes, what warrants the use of the term "allegory" in the traditional enumeration of the spiritual senses is a specific type of correlation that is often outside the purview of the sacred writers, namely, the correlation of Type and Antitype (*CCC* 128–30). Adam, for instance, is the Type, and Christ is the New Adam, the Antitype. Likewise, Isaac is the Type, and Christ as the New Isaac is the Antitype, and so on. More generally, Christ is the Antitype who recapitulates the Type, such that in his lifetime he takes up certain members of his people and certain of their deeds. Yet the relationship is not simply that of fulfilling what had been prefigured. In each case, Christ the Antitype completes what was incomplete, perfects what was imperfect, and above all, sanctifies what was sinful. Abraham leads Isaac up the mountain to be the object of sacrifice, but an angel comes in time to prevent Isaac from having to die. In Christ, the Antitype of Isaac, however, the sacrifice is completed and perfected. Whereas Adam wimpishly joins Eve in sin, Christ is willing to suffer and die for his Bride, the Church, in order to render her holy and spotless.

At the heart of any interpretation of Scripture done according to the spiritual senses is the realization that the mission of the Word Incarnate is the redemption of humanity and the restoration of the damage that we have suffered—both the damage inherited by the human race as the result of the Fall and the further damage that actual sin does to us as individuals and to our families and societies. However many the possible ways in which our redemption could have been brought about,

---

the Reformation to reject the spiritual senses as allegorical interpretations imposed on the text during the Middle Ages. Given some of the wild allegorizations offered during the medieval period, one can well understand and sympathize with this reaction. But the resulting loss of the true typological sense is regrettable. In his *Biblical Theology of the Old and New Testaments: Theological Reflections on the Christian Bible* (Minneapolis: Fortress Press, 1993), pp. 11–13, Brevard S. Childs takes note of twentieth-century efforts to recover the typological sense and the attempts to disengage it from allegorical interpretations, and yet he himself does little with the typological sense in the remainder of his sophisticated study of the problems of biblical interpretation in the field of biblical theology.

[7] Gal 4:21–31; see also the discussion of Jacob and Esau in Rom 9:6–13.

revelation makes it clear that God chose to accomplish our redemption by the suffering and death of Jesus. The shedding of his blood atones for sin in the way that no animal sacrifice could ever have done (see Heb 9:23–28).

The restoration of the damage proves to be complex. It includes the tutoring of the human will, so that we learn to avoid sin and to do what is good and right (a task for which the moral sense is particularly needed). It includes the reorientation of our desires for our true home and the medicinal remedies of the grace of Christ (hence, the eschatological and sacramental dimensions of the anagogical sense). It also includes the provision of an example of rightly ordered life and the experience of coming to know Jesus as someone whom we need to love personally. Doing this will draw us toward union with the Father in the Spirit and toward maturation along the paths that God intends for us. For this reason the focus of the typological sense is on the recapitulation by Christ that perfects what is imperfect, completes what is incomplete, and sanctifies what is sinful.

The bulk of Father Quay's volume is dedicated to showing how these three spiritual senses of Scripture serve to help bring about our transformation in Christ. In the course of tracing out in detail the way in which Jesus recapitulates the life of his people, Quay shows us how we need to recapitulate the life of Christ. He reflects at length on the way in which man is made in the image and according to the likeness of God, and on the relation of original sin to the love that it negates. Doing this involves grasping the loves that are characteristic of each member of the Trinity and the creaturely analogues that God intends for us to have by the way in which he created us. This part of the project is accomplished by close reliance on the great Cappadocian theologians of the patristic period: Gregory of Nyssa, Gregory Nazianzen, and Basil. By considering their insights on the inner structure of uncreated love within the Trinity, Quay shows how to understand the abiding damage done to us by the Fall as well as the ways in which Christ, the new Adam, restores what is damaged in human nature and sanctifies what is sinful.

Stated in brief compass, the characteristic love of the Father is the love of free generosity that in eternity gives to the Son everything that the Father is and has (except the very relationship of Fatherhood). The special love of the Son is the love of free receptivity, for he is grateful in eternity to the Father for having so freely given himself and he is graciously ready to give himself freely in return. The typical love of the Holy Spirit, in this view, is the free delight that the Spirit shows at the perfect generosity of the Father to the Son and at the perfect receptivity of the Father's love by the Son.

Now, as creatures of the Triune God, our nature was made to exhibit the creaturely analogues of this free generosity, this free receptivity, and this free delight, but the Fall has damaged all this. Instead of freely bestowing goodness in a way akin to the Father's generosity, we tend in our fallen nature to give our love only to what strikes us as loveworthy. And instead of freely receiving goodness in a way that is akin to the Son's receptivity, we tend to operate as if we will be loved by others only if we seem sufficiently loveworthy (for we ourselves would only give our love to what seems to us loveworthy). The stronger among us then tend to be manipulative, trying to force love, while the weaker fear they are hopelessly unlovable and verge on despair. Finally, instead of freely taking delight in the giving and receiving that we witness and thereby displaying a creaturely analogue to the love, characteristic of the Holy Spirit, we are easily inclined to envy and jealousy. From these defects spring any number of actual sins and bad habits in those old enough to make free choices of will.

With this picture in mind, we can better appreciate the typological, the tropological, or moral, and the anagogical senses of Scripture. Through them the Holy Spirit provides us with what is needed for our salvation and sanctification. At the literal level the Scriptures present to us, among many other things, the historical deeds of Jesus that fulfill the prophecies and prefigurations of the Christ. At the typological level they show the recapitulation of Israel by Christ, perfecting what is imperfect, completing what is incomplete, and sanctifying what is sinful, for he is the Truth. At the moral level they show not only what is right and wrong but what we ought to do for love of Christ and why, for he is for us the Life. And at the anagogical level they present to us the way in which Christ shows us the hope of heaven and shares with us a strength beyond our own by which we can travel, for he is the Way.

The answer to Shatkin's question thus comes by understanding how we are slow to take the means that God intends for us to use in order to become mature, by growing in Christ and according to the model that he provides. That there was an eternal Son who is the very image of the Father is a mystery that was long hidden for ages in God (hence, the title of the book). But the disclosure of this mystery in the life of Jesus Christ gives us the knowledge of how we can be restored to the image and likeness in which we were made. The image and likeness in us have been shattered by the Fall and by actual sin, but in Christ we have the means to be healed, and with that healing comes growth in the spiritual life and in moral character, for God intends us to be perfect, even as he is perfect. At numerous points in the course of *The Mystery Hidden for Ages in God* Father Quay discusses sexuality in relation to the pattern of growth and development that is normative for the human person. In *The Christian Meaning of Human Sexuality* he makes that topic his central concern.

The Christian Meaning of Human Sexuality

To appreciate better the new material on the theology of natural family planning that can be found in part 2, it will be helpful to bear in mind what Quay explains in the main part of this volume on the Christian understanding of human sexuality. The purpose of divine revelation, according to our Catholic faith, is to disclose to us what we need to learn about God for the sake of our salvation and also to give us an understanding of ourselves as desperately in need of God.

Of the many dimensions intrinsic to human existence, some are clearer to us, some more opaque. The wonderful discoveries made by scientific research in recent decades have shed much light on numerous aspects of the process by which each human being is conceived and grows. But the meaning of our lives as well as the meaning of human sexuality and the activities that lead to the generation of children ever remain a question that is beyond the scope of technical discoveries. The answer to these questions in its fullness comes only from what God has revealed. To understand more about the intricacies of the processes of human generation is still not to grasp the meaning of marriage, of sexuality, or of procreation as God intends us to understand it. In faith, however, we can learn what we could otherwise never know.

Quay's approach to the Christian meaning of human sexuality puts the focus on what divine revelation shows us in this regard. His study is not only a consideration of what kinds of sexual behavior are right or wrong, but about why this is so for those who want to love Christ and to live in him. Abstracted from a living faith in him, a faith that calls us to conform every aspect of our minds and our hearts to him in love, much of what Jesus said about such things would be hard to accept. It struck even his disciples as unbelievably difficult to practice —that to look lustfully at a woman is already to commit adultery with her in one's heart or that remarriage after divorce is adulterous, or that in heaven there will be neither marrying nor being given in marriage.

In our day as well, much of what the Church teaches about sexual morality is sadly ignored by many Catholics, if not openly rejected, despite the unmistakable clarity of the Lord's teachings on these matters and the centrality of these issues to God's plan. We are created as male and as female, and will be so for all eternity. In taking our nature to himself the Word has shown himself the sole norm of what it is to be human. In suffering for us and embracing bodily death, and in his bodily ascent after his Resurrection, Jesus shows us the goodness of our bodies, to the point of including his body forever in his heavenly life with the Father and the Spirit. Mary's Assumption into heaven likewise shows us something about the glorified bodies that we are promised. Not only the rights and wrongs of sexual morality but also the very meaning of human sexuality in God's sight makes full sense only when seen as part of the mystery of our life in Christ.

By this concentration on divine revelation, Quay's approach bypasses (without in any way denying) the arguments frequently found in other spheres of Catholic discourse (for example, natural law argumentation). Quay concentrates instead on the mystery of life in Christ that is offered us through the Scriptures and the living Tradition of the Church. What Christ himself said about sexual morality perplexed many of the people who heard it, including his closest associates, but in time they came to see what he said about this subject to be essential for being his disciples. When Christianity moved out into the pagan world, the Christian stance on virginity and chastity was often misunderstood and resented, with martyrdom the frequent outcome for those who would not take part in the unchaste actions of others. Yet it was never for chastity itself that the martyrs died. Rather, it was their love for Christ, who wanted them to be chaste, that imparted to them such a complete determination to live in chastity. For them it was an integral part of their witness to the Lord, and it remained a part of their witness even when the period of bloody martyrdom ceased and such other forms as eremetical life and monasticism emerged.

The main focus of Quay's book is a consideration of the meaning that God has made known for human sexuality through two forms of symbolism—the natural symbolism of our bodies and the scriptural symbolism that is prominent in divine revelation. At various points in the discussion of natural symbolism the reader will find considerable overlap with the thought of John Paul II, whose Theology of the Body makes extensive reliance on this symbolism.[8] For instance, chapter 3 ("Sexual Intercourse: The Natural Word of Love") is similar to but precedes the thought of John Paul II.[9] In this section he distinguishes between the licentiousness of mere nudity and the expectations of trust and full acceptance of one another that is suggested by the nakedness of spouses before one another. Even though many of Quay's insights about the language of spousal communication were developed prior to the appearance of the English translations of the pope's materials, their views clearly ran along similar tracks, and anyone interested in John Paul II's Theology of the Body will find additional insights here.

The distinctive lens through which John Paul II set forth his understanding of human sexuality is the complementarity of male and female, seen especially in light of the nuptial meaning of the body.[10] The long series of Angelus addresses in which he articulated his Theology of the Body lays out the implications of this nuptiality for spouses as well as for those not married, those preparing for marriage, and those committed to virginity and celibacy. He accomplishes his project through careful theological reflection on three biblical sources in particular: (1) the original unity of man and woman, the theme of his catechesis on the

---

[8] John Paul II, *Man and Woman He Created Them: A Theology of the Body*, trans. Michael M. Waldstein (Boston: Pauline Books and Media, 2006). See also Mary Shivanandan, *Crossing the Threshold of Love: A New Vision of Marriage in the Light of John Paul II's Anthropology* (Washington, D.C.: Catholic University of America Press, 1999).

[9] Father Quay's book was initially delivered as a set of Lenten meditations at John Carroll University. The first edition of his work bears the copyright date of 1976.

[10] The text as originally translated into English can be found in John Paul II, *The Theology of the Body: Human Love in the Divine Plan*, with a foreword by John S. Grabowski (Boston: Pauline Books and Media, 1997). For an excellent introduction as well as a superior translation, see John Paul II, *Man and Woman He Created Them*. Among the many books on the Theology of the Body, see especially Mary Shivanandan, *Crossing the Threshold of Love*.

book of Genesis, (2) the purity of heart taught by Christ, the focus of his catechesis on the Sermon on the Mount, and (3) the joy of life in the Holy Spirit, the topic of his catechesis on the writings of Saint Paul, including coverage of the resurrection of the body, virginity and celibacy for the sake of the kingdom, and the sacramentality of marriage.

The last section of John Paul's work is directly concerned with *Humanae Vitae*. It is particularly noteworthy for its explanation of the intrinsic relationship between the unitive and procreative dimensions of sexual intercourse. Not only does it present a novel argument for the position that Pope Paul VI defended by a natural law argument in *Humanae Vitae* when reaffirming the Church's opposition to contraception, but it also gives a solid foundation for understanding so much else about the Christian vision of human sexuality. As his prepapal book *Love and Responsibility*[11] demonstrated, spousal communion, including sexual intercourse, involves a communion of persons. The proper assessment of what is good and bad, what is right and wrong, on any number of questions about sexual ethics can be clarified by thinking of the question in terms of the language of the body and the ways in which our bodily activities express the person.

For John Paul II, the moral problem with contraception is that it contradicts the language of total and reciprocal self-gift of husband and wife to one another.[12] In any form of contraception there is a discrepancy between what is being said with one's words (and perhaps even with one's mind) and what is being said with one's body. Contraception involves the severing of the unitive meaning of intercourse from its procreative meaning. The deliberate prevention of the very possibility of procreation means in effect that the desire for union is not a desire for union with the whole of the other person but the desire for a union that excludes the fertility of the other. Using this approach can give much insight into other moral problems that have recently emerged, such as in vitro fertilization, for it is a case in which procreation is being sought apart from union. In the current movement

---

[11] Karol Wojtyła, *Love and Responsibility*, trans. H. T. Willetts (New York: Farrar, Straus, Giroux, 1981).

[12] This view is reflected in *CCC* 2370, which cites John Paul II's Apostolic Exhortation *Familiaris Consortio*, November 22, 1981, no. 32. See also Benedict XVI's Encyclical Letter *Caritas in Veritate*, June 29, 2009, no. 28.

to give social and legal approval to gestational surrogacy and gamete donation the same logic is being applied, with disastrous results.

In his reflections on this topic Father Quay puts great reliance on the notions of sign, meaning, and symbol. These ideas are crucial not only for understanding the theology of natural family planning but also for grasping the Christian meaning of human sexuality in general. The Billings Method, for instance, teaches women how to observe and chart their mucus patterns, to understand better the natural signals that can enable them to know the meaning of these patterns and thus learn whether they are in a period of fertility or infertility. As Quay shows in great detail, all human sexual activity has an intrinsic meaning, but some ways of engaging in sexual activity will prove not to be in accord with our words and intentions, and some of our choices will have a meaning that is not in accord with the plan that God has devised for our behavior.

As Quay explains, in its most common usage a symbol is a type of sign that leads to knowledge of something else. Natural signs bear a meaning without any human intervention; smoke, for instance, is a sign of fire, and certain kinds of clouds are a sign of coming rain. Natural family planning, of course, depends on recognizing in mucus the natural signals of periods of fertility and of infertility. Conventional signs, by contrast, bear the meanings that they do only because of human choices. Words, for example, whether spoken or written, have the meanings given to them in a particular language, but (except perhaps for those that are onomatopoeic, such as "meow" and "woof") there is nothing in the word itself that will help anyone to learn its meaning. Some signs consist of images that in some way resemble what they signify (such as the use of ♡ to stand for a heart), and they may be regarded as symbols when the sign of a heart is used to point to something on another plane, such as love. What is distinctive of a symbol is that there is something about the sign (its structure, material form, activity, appearance, etc.) that is somehow like the immaterial or spiritual reality that it signifies. We can readily use fire as a symbol for love, for fire is warm, attractive, and endlessly fascinating, and yet (like love) it can become dangerous and even destructive if it gets out of control.

People use symbols all the time—not only consciously and deliberately in our art, literature, politics, and science, but also at deep levels of our being. Long before infants are able to express anything in speech, they use the bodily functions of which they have become aware to express symbolically such things as love, rejection, and aggression. As it turns out, sexual activity is symbolic, and recognizing the meanings carried by this symbolism is deeply important for the right ordering of things that are often too complex to be fully expressed by our words. We cannot distort or change the symbols that flow from our nature without doing great damage to ourselves and to our relationship to the rest of reality. One sees this, for instance, in the recent drive for legal recognition of same-sex marriage that has proceeded at breakneck pace in overturning the taboos that have been in place for the entirety of recorded history, with little concern for the evidence of how destructive homosexual activity is for those involved, let alone for the structures of society.

As part of his discussion of the pervasive presence of symbols in human life, Quay notes their presence in the Church's sacramental and liturgical life, not only for rites and ceremonies but for reenacting the great mysteries of God's acts within history—the many references, for instance, to the offering of the paschal lamb as way of representing the sacrifice of the Lamb of God on the Cross. In addition, there is a lavish use of symbols in the Scriptures that record divine revelation. These symbols tell us much about the nature of God as well as about morality.

In Quay's analysis, it is no surprise that God uses symbolism to reveal himself to us and to teach us more about ourselves. Our Creator knows how we regularly use symbols not only in our linguistic communication but also in our body language. To rectify those forms of symbolic activity that have been badly distorted by sin and yet make up so much of the natural religions of humanity, God did not forgo or obliterate symbolic action but corrected it, so as to make it possible for us to gain a right understanding of the material world and the true meaning of human life. In addition, by these symbols, he also gives us much knowledge about his own inner life, in ways that far exceed the normal range of our powers of intellectual comprehension. Such symbols do not exhaust the mystery of God, but the tremendous potential of their concreteness provides ways in which human minds can ponder the mystery of God more and more deeply and thereby come to have access to what transcends all times, places, and cultures.

To plumb the mysteries of the Christian meaning of human sexuality, Quay turns first to the natural symbolism of the body and of the marital act, and then to the deeper meanings of sexual actions that are made known to us in and through the Scriptures. Toward the end of the book, he examines the meaning of various corruptions of our sexuality as well as the rich symbolism of celibacy and virginity. In his investigation of the natural symbolism, he emphasizes the correlations between bodily and psychic structures, and in his review of the supernatural symbolism prevalent in the Scriptures he shows the way in which the natural meanings of sexuality are employed to illustrate something about God's nature and the relation of God to his creation.

Although Quay is committed to the position that our integral human nature is fully understandable only in Christ, he shows that there is much that we can grasp at the natural level. Even without revelation people of every culture can readily discover some of the meanings that God intended in these physical acts. The need for the stable union expected in marriage, for instance, can be seen in the very way in which our bodies are formed sexually for the procreation and rearing of children. Quay argues at some length against a reductivist view of sexuality that is increasingly popular in some circles. He shows that our bodies are not just sets of physical functions. They express in a visible way the natural and intrinsic meanings of ourselves.

Just as a man's genitals and the actions that he performs through them are largely external and outwardly directed, swiftly aroused but quick to subside, so too at the psychic level he tends to focus his interest spontaneously on things outside himself, and especially his interest in the larger world. In Quay's vision, male interiority tends to come from the mind, by which a man often thinks about how to build a world that will be suitable for himself and his family.

The body of a woman is very different. Her genitals are interior and hidden, her response more tactile than visual, her arousal is often slower but more long lasting. Her interiority is primarily linked to the empty space within her that only another person can fill—the children who may grow within her body and the husband who will love her.

These brief allusions to typically masculine and feminine traits give only a bare hint of the many dimensions of human sexuality that Quay discusses in chapter 3. He examines at length such phenomena as nakedness, intercourse, the physical and psychic union of spouses, and natural marriage. Those acquainted with John Paul II's Theology of the Body will find this entire section to provide fresh insights into otherwise familiar territory.

The fourth chapter considers sexuality and the Scriptures—not just through stories (for example, David and Bathsheba) and the moral directives (for example, the Commandments as given in Exodus and Deuteronomy, the detailed regulations given in Leviticus) but also through symbols of sexuality (for example, the rose, the snake). Far more important than symbols of sexuality, however, is God's use of the natural symbolism of sexual activity to describe much about himself and what our relations to him should be.

From the early chapters of Genesis we see the symbolic use of sexuality to discuss things that are on completely different planes. The sexual union of man and woman that makes them two in one flesh (Gen 2:20–25), for instance, represents the fullness of their personal union as a couple and as parents, united not just in their spousal embrace but in the flesh of their children. Unlike the majority of nature religions, which often take sexual union itself as sacred, the Bible presents sexuality as something that belongs only to creatures, not to God, who is pure spirit. Through the prophet Hosea the Bible does speak of Israel's relation to God by using the image of human sexual union, but when it does so, the pattern is quite distinctive. The people of Israel is here presented as the unfaithful bride of the Lord, for Israel has flirted with living according to the standards of her neighbors rather than remaining faithful to God's commands. The striking sexual symbolism that the book of Hosea uses (a wife engaged in prostitution) points not to something sexual in God but to something utterly spiritual, the horror of infidelity. Adultery is a sundering of the most intimate of human bonds and so is taken as a symbol of idolatry. Amazingly, the prophet then shows God as a husband who takes back to himself a wife whom he loves deeply despite her infidelity. In this way he uses the image of marital union and sexual infidelity to symbolize relations that utterly transcend the sexual, namely, God's own enduring love and fidelity as it corrects what is distorted and elicits a response of repentance.

By the use of sexual and marital imagery in this and other biblical books (for example, Ezekiel, the Song of Solomon) God inspires the sacred writer to show how God uses his own steadfast love for his people, even in times of infidelity, to teach his people how human

marriage ought to work. It should be monogamous, faithful, and fruitful, like his own love for Israel. In the New Testament we find the
same basic themes, changed only slightly so as to reflect that it is the
Church, the new Israel, that is the Bride of Christ. John the Baptist,
for instance, describes himself as the friend of the Bridegroom (Jn
3:28–30), and Saint Paul fleshes out the comparison in such texts as
chapter 5 of Ephesians and chapter 6 of 1 Corinthians. The book of
Revelation (especially chapters 19 and 21) points toward the marriage
feast of Christ and his Bride, the Church, in heaven as the consummation of all things. In addition, there is much about nonsexual actions
that also does so much to convey "I love you" to those whom we love
and to those with whom we want to grow in love (see Phil 2:4; Gal
6:2; Rom 12:10; 1 Jn 3:17–18).

In chapter 5 Father Quay discusses the wealth of such sexual symbolism as it appears in the Scriptures by following out such themes as the
maternity of the Church and the adoptive paternity of God. Jesus is the
Only Begotten Son of God, while all the rest of the baptized become
children of God only by adoption, and by this adoption we are made
the brothers and sisters of Jesus (see Gal 3:26–27; 4:5; Rom 8:23, 29–
32). Particularly striking in Quay's account here is his reflection on
the fact that nowhere in Scripture is Christ said to beget children of
his Church. He is not the father of anyone, and he does not enter into
sexual union with his Bride. Although Christ's love for the Church
is not sexual, the best symbol that we have for the quality of the love
that Christ and his Church share is the sexual union between husband
and wife. We become children of the Church by adoption, not by natural birth. Rather, the Church brings forth God's children virginally,
as Mary did, through the agency of the Holy Spirit (see Jn 3:5). From
first to last the Scriptures show us many and varied aspects of human
sexuality as symbols of the relations between God and his people, and
it is clear that God regards our sexuality as something good and fitting
for expressing the highest truths about divine-human relations.

In many ways the most practical chapter in this book is the sixth:
"Christ on the Cross—Sexual Lies and Counterfeits". Here Father
Quay again pairs a consideration of natural symbolism and scriptural
symbolism to set forth the reasons certain sexual practices are destructive for those who engage in them and for societies in which they are
common. In regard to the natural level, his analysis is quite close to

that of John Paul II. We misuse our sexual powers, for instance, when we use them to tell lies, as in adultery, for those involved are saying in the symbolic language of bodily intercourse, "I am wholly yours, yours alone, forever"—but for at least one of them that cannot be true, by reason of belonging to someone else already. Quay points out that there can also be falsehood within marriage when, for example, a husband forces sex upon his wife against her will, or when a wife deliberately chooses to be cold or without reason refuses to cooperate with her husband. In these cases what they mean by their act of intercourse is not what that intercourse means of itself.

Some forms of sexual deviance are not strictly lies but corruptions of the meaning of our sexuality. Masturbation, in Quay's view, is a symbol of withdrawal from reality and of frustration, often done in self-pitying loneliness. What was intended for fertility, children, and family becomes a mechanism for pleasure, relief of tension, or material for a sperm bank. Likewise, Quay finds the symbolic structure of homosexuality to suggest perpetual juvenility and adolescent ambiguity. There is no gift of one's self to another, no true receptivity, other than the total gift of self to the other in marriage. The symbolic structure of contraception, whether by a barrier method or a withholding of one's own fertility, involves sterilization, for the true symbol of love, of mutual gift, and of receptivity is excluded. As Quay shows in great detail in part 2, the symbolic structure of NFP is quite different from any form of contraception. Even when a couple knows of their cyclic periods of infertility as a couple, the couple remains essentially open to life.

In the second half of the sixth chapter Father Quay turns to the Christian understanding of sexual lies and sexual perversions. Here he turns to the use of sexual symbolism in revelation, where the symbol primarily shows something about God and his relation to his creatures and often discloses something of great importance about his creatures and the proper use of their sexual powers. Of special interest in this portion of the book is Quay's focus on what Saint Paul makes central to the fifth chapter of Ephesians. Husbands and wives are to love one another as do Christ and the Church. Seen in this perspective, those relationships between husband and wife that reflect the relations between Christ and the Church are sound and good. Relationships that are inconceivable between Christ and the Church, by contrast, show up the error involved in the ways in which there is one or another kind of abuse of our sexual powers.

Seen in this perspective, adultery would signify the inconceivable turning away of Christ from the Church to some other bride, or the idolatry of the Church in worshipping some foreign god. The sexual union of unmarried people symbolizes the old paganism. A man who fornicates tends to resemble one of the ancient deities who was thought to confer his favors capriciously as he chose. He can never thereby represent God's marriage to Israel or Christ's pledge of union with the Church. A fornicating woman might symbolically represent a people who worshipped such a deity as long as they thought they received divine favors, but she can never represent the unconditional devotion expected of Israel and the Church.

It is certainly possible for people to come to understand the errors involved in the use of our sexual powers regarding masturbation, homosexuality, and contraception from consideration of natural symbolism, but there is much further light that comes from considering the scriptural use of sexual symbolism on these questions. Again, Father Quay uses the fifth chapter of Ephesians as a central text. There he reflects on the fact that Christ did not come to please himself but to love his Bride—one whom he sought at great cost and with the risk of rejection. Unlike those who masturbate to try to please themselves, Christ is always intent on his Bride, whom he espoused on the Cross and whom he makes fruitful by giving her his Spirit. Similarly, the Church may never rest content with the gifts of the Spirit in isolation but must always have a missionary zeal that is eager to share them with those who do not yet know Christ. This insight in turn gives additional understanding of what is wrong about masturbation: it is an effort at pleasing oneself and fails to imitate Christ or the Church.

For Father Quay, male homosexual behavior symbolizes a man in love with one like himself and seeking to be his own savior. It is a refusal of the femininity of the Church in all her human weakness and a repudiation of the true otherness of God. Similarly, lesbianism symbolically signifies a Church turned away from the Lord to embrace what is like herself—one who is also a creature and dependent on union with Another who is decidedly not like herself. He notes that lesbianism symbolizes not a genuine church but nature worship, and that it is not surprising to find that in matters of spirituality lesbians often turn to worship of the Earth-Mother rather than Christ.

Contraceptive intercourse curiously symbolizes the notion that God might bestow his grace and pour out his Holy Spirit without allowing them to bear fruit, without granting the Church the power to bear him new children. It is as if God would not mind if his people were to enjoy the pleasures of his light and consolation while refusing to bear the fruits of grace in real faith, hope, and charity toward God and all his people. Instead of remaining open to whatever fruitfulness God may elicit and bless, there is a withholding of the gift of oneself and a readiness to use whatever barrier or sterilization is required.

The final chapter of the first part is dedicated to a consideration of natural and scriptural symbolism with regard to virginity, continence, and integrity. With the same penchant that was shown in the previous chapters for providing helpful practical advice, Father Quay here reflects on the ways in which young people need to learn genuine continence and to attain self-mastery in the area of sexual drives and desires before they will be ready to give themselves totally in marriage. He notes that sexual intercourse is a symbol of the loving self-gift of one spouse to the other. If a person does not already have this sort of self-possession and self-control, it will prove impossible to give oneself entirely to one's spouse or to show the appropriate restraint when required by situations such as illness, emotional upset, or childbirth.

The Theology of Natural Family Planning

The distinctive contribution that the new material contained in part 2 of this book makes is an understanding of the theology of natural family planning (NFP). Father Quay's manuscript does not address the much discussed question of the various methods that have been devised.[13]

---

[13] The tireless work of such pioneers has produced a number of methods. The story of John and Evelyn Billings is recounted in Tess Livingstone, *The Billings Enigma* (Ballan, Victoria, Australia: Connor Court, 2013); there is a fine account of the Billings Ovulation Method in Evelyn Billings with Anne Westmore, *The Billings Method: Using the Body's Natural Signal of Fertility to Achieve or Avoid Pregnancy* (South Yarra, Victoria, Australia: Ann O'Donovan, 2011). Among the approaches related to the Billings Method are the following. Teen-STAR (Sexuality Teaching in the context of Adult Responsibility) is a developmental curriculum developed by Dr. Hanna Klaus, M.D., that informs teenagers about fertility patterns and teaches responsible decision-making and communication skills in sexual behavior. Dr. Thomas W. Hilgers, M.D., Director of the Pope Paul VI Institute for the Study of Human Reproduction in Omaha, Nebraska,

Instead his interest is in considering NFP in light of the meaning of human sexuality through reflection on the natural and scriptural symbolism discussed above. In his view, attending to the fullness of divine revelation in Jesus Christ shows us the meaning of bodily life and human activity and thus allows us better to understand the true meaning of human sexuality. In the course of these chapters we can not only find reliable answers to such frequently raised questions as whether NFP is morally licit and whether there is some obligation to have all the children one can, but we can also get a better sense of the goodness and beauty of God's design in creating human sexuality and marriage in the way he did.

What makes NFP possible at all, of course, is the existence of natural cycles of fertility and infertility. Infertility, Quay reminds us, should not be mistaken for sterility. The periods of infertility are stages in the cyclic process that makes procreation possible. They are times of preparation for the ripening of a healthy ovum. As such, infertility is the natural condition of all individuals during childhood and the natural condition of adult women during the larger portion of their menstrual cycle, and thus it is quite unlike sterility, which is the lack of biological ability to procreate. Infertility, properly understood, is natural in the strongest sense of the term and in fact required for fertility to be of full value to a species. For Quay, the continuous and rhythmic (but seldom completely regular) alternation between fertility and infertility

---

is responsible for the Creighton Model FertilityCare™ System and NaPro Technology, which has standardized the terminology describing mucus observations and has its own rules concerning the use of the cervical-mucus biomarker to achieve or avoid pregnancy. The Sympto-Thermal Model was pioneered by Dr. Josef Roetzer and further developed by Dr. Konald Prem of the University of Minnesota. Based on the realization that the three phases of the menstrual cycle are the result of four hormones that are observable in various ways, this method involves attentiveness to cervical mucus, the condition of the cervix, and temperature patterns. The Marquette Model developed by Professor Richard Fehring and his colleagues uses the ClearBlue Easy Fertility Monitor for home-measurement of hormone levels in urine to estimate the beginning and end of the time of fertility in a woman's menstrual cycle. This information is intended to be used in conjunction with observations of cervical mucus, basal body temperature, and other biological indicators of fertility. Under the leadership of John and Sheila Kippley the Couple to Couple League has promoted the Sympto-Thermal Method of NFP in conjunction with moral and psychological formation. For a more detailed account of the various NFP methods, see Michael D. Manhart, Marguerite Duane, April Lind, Irit Sinai, and Jean Golden-Tevald, "Fertility Awareness–Based Methods of Family Planning: A Review of Effectiveness for Avoiding Pregnancy", *Osteopathic Family Physician* 5 (2013): 2–8.

symbolize, at the minimum, human oneness with the natural world and its various cyclic rhythms. For those who seek without success to have children, it may seem akin to the season of winter, but even this least promising season of our lives still gives good grounds for hope in the hidden growth of a fertility that leads to new life.

In this connection, Father Quay's reflections on the meaning of postmenopausal sterility will be welcome to many, for a better understanding of the symbolism of the dying out of the power to give new life allows us to recognize that a woman is much more than one who bears children. Much as a man's ongoing fertility symbolizes his never finished task of caring for his family, so the laying down of the burdens connected with pregnancy and childbirth opens a woman to new possibilities for the service of her loved ones, of the larger community, and of the common good, especially by the communication of the wisdom she has acquired about the rearing of children and the care of a family.

Relying on the amazing discoveries that have been made, especially by those working on the scientific basis for NFP, Father Quay reflects at length on the theological significance of the processes of human procreation. Among the points of special importance here are the distinctive features of the process that results in the union of human gametes and thus the actual generation of a new child from the act of intercourse. He notes, for instance, that the time of human fertility is not correlated with the period of interest in intercourse in the way that is typical for other mammals, but with providing conditions that are advantageous for the health of the women who conceive and of the children who are conceived. In animals, estrus is not only the external sign of fertility but normally the sole inducement to copulation. Thus, even considered biologically, the distinctiveness of human cycles of fertility and infertility is fundamentally at the service of the family. They help to preserve the health and the physical strength of the mother as well as to guarantee a suitable spacing of the siblings. Although not every peak of fertility will result in a child, each peak offers a capacity for procreation. Each one constitutes a pledge and promise of God's ongoing work of creation.

Biologically considered, all the aspects of human sexuality exist for the sake of the union of the gametes and the nurturing of any children who are conceived. But the act of intercourse, even during a fertile period, does not by itself accomplish the fertilization. Formed in the bodies of fertile women and men, the gametes are completely dependent on these bodies for the conditions that allow them to survive, but they are independent organisms, each one living with a life of its own. The fusion that results in a child takes place at some point after the act of intercourse. There is a fascinating hiddenness to the union of the gametes, for their fusion is brought about by processes independent of the knowledge and will of the parents. The genetic diversity (from little to great) between parents and their offspring (as well as among siblings) manifests at the macro level the independence of the gametes at the micro level.

For Quay, this independence has its own symbolic importance. Recent biological discoveries about the processes of reproduction make it possible for us to see far more clearly than previous generations could that, strictly speaking, the parents of a child have not created or made the child, and that the child is not something that they own, not something that is in any way their property. Rather, every child belongs to God, who designed the remarkable processes by which we come to be.

Further, the child who is conceived is an independent entity, even though completely dependent on his mother if he is to grow to maturity within the womb for long months. Even after birth he remains dependent on the care of his parents for a long time. Symbolically this represents ongoing dependence as well as independence, for at every stage of human maturation we can speak of the normal growth and development of an individual only insofar as that person remains both in radical dependence on others and in radical independence of them. Only by the total self-gift of ourselves to others can we develop fully our potentialities, and yet only by living in proper independence from others will we have character enough to be able to give them anything. All of this interdependence begins with the process of procreation: none of us could have come to be without the contribution of gametes from our parents, and yet the union of those gametes already shows an independence of those parents.

NFP gives us a way to enter into the symbolism of the fertility cycle, and for Quay this has a profound theological significance. So long as a couple has not intrinsically altered the nature of their act of intercourse through contraceptive interventions by poison or blockage, the marital act continues to symbolize the fullness of spousal love, even if no union of the gametes occurs and no child results. The intrinsic meaning of sexual intercourse includes the procreation of children, but it does so in a different and less direct way than it signifies love and personal union between the spouses. The act of spousal intercourse means marriage, the union between the spouses themselves at all levels of their being. It does not directly mean the actual union of gametes, but only the possibility of their union. Rather, the fertility of each spouse (whatever its condition) has to be included without reserve in the gift of self that constitutes each act of intercourse. But it is not the case that this gift will always bring about conception, and often it will not do so.

For Quay, this aspect of the meaning of the symbolism of sexual intercourse helps us to understand one of the most significant differences between NFP and any form of contraception. In contraception, the woman (or, less often, the man) is made sterile, but neither one is made sterile through natural family planning. In natural family planning there remains the promise (and for some the hope) of conception and new life. As those who practice NFP know, there is need to consider the situation not only physiologically with regard to days of fertility and infertility but holistically with regard to the needs of the family that, after all, provide the valid reasons for using natural family planning in the first place. In contraception, by contrast, as Quay says, the result is only death—dead ova or dead sperm or (in some contraceptive methods) the suppression of growth.

The structure of the treatise on the theology of NFP reflects the same pattern found in the more general account of the Christian meaning of human sexuality: first, a consideration of the natural symbolism, followed by a consideration of scriptural symbolism. Applied to the question of the temporal patterns of fertility, this method permits Father Quay, first at the natural and then at the supernatural level, to consider such topics as the significance of the deep hiddenness of the union of gametes that begins the process of conception and the way in which NFP makes possible a special form of cooperation with God's plan.

The nature and activity of the gametes, he notes, are in large measure hidden from our observation, even with recent advances in science and technology. Other aspects of sexuality are not so deeply hidden. In both men and women the signs of sexual maturity are obvious. Even though menopause is not as easily evident, Quay says it is not long before it is possible for anyone to recognize that a woman has lived beyond her power to conceive. But the fertility cycles are hidden, and only with the scientific research that led to reliable NFP methods have we discovered signals reliable for knowing where a woman may be in her cycle—fertile mucus, a slight rise in body temperature, the relaxation of the cervix, changes in electrolytes, magnesium, and hormonal levels, and perhaps some shadow of estrus. These signs are largely invisible for any woman not trained to notice them. Even when noticed, their connection with fertility has been overlooked or misinterpreted by entire cultures for centuries, and our own culture is largely ignorant of this connection.

What the Scriptures see symbolized by the hiddenness of fertility, however, is that conception is not of human doing but something divine. Well aware that a man's seed must act within a woman to beget a child, Israel saw conception as brought about by divine power, however dependent on the cooperation of human action. Despite our increased knowledge and despite such morally questionable techniques as in vitro fertilization, there remains much that is mysterious in the union of gametes. The more we learn about the intricacies of the processes of human conception, the more reason to insist on God's direct act of creation of every person.

Quay also notices that there is an adoptive aspect that can be discerned in all human procreation. In the case of any child who is conceived, the parents are called upon to accept the child. Even though the baby comes from them, it is at the deepest level not theirs but God's. The child is begotten and borne by them from their own bodies, and yet genetically different from each of them and, hence, to some degree a stranger at birth. In some cultures one sees a hint of the need for accepting the child in the way that a child is given a name related to his father. In these sad days, when abortion and infanticide make clear that what is natural to us is not always acknowledged or accepted, we see parents returning to his Maker an infant who is not what they wanted, perhaps because they see the child as "damaged goods" or just not the "model" they desired.

Another part of Father Quay's investigation of this topic comes with his reflection on the way that sexual desire and the power of its enjoyment can continue into old age, long outlasting fertility. Noting the uniqueness of human sexuality in this regard, he finds that it symbolizes that personal union is a good that may be sought through sexual intercourse indefinitely, even when children cannot be expected. Desire for physical union, he argues, is something that can readily be expressive of other levels of spousal love, levels not tied in any evident way to fertility. The situation here is entirely different from that of any other form of life. What largely takes the place of estrus in man is human speech. The expression of love and passion through words, he notes, is a far more potent stimulus to copulate than estral pheromones or even provocative glances or touches. And, he observes, couples whose sexual union finds its sole pleasure in the mere physical act cannot usually stay together very long. The personal character of human sexuality makes all the difference for understanding the many particular questions that arise, including the distinction between NFP and contraception.

Relying on the same sort of distinction that Monsignor Robert Sokolowski has promoted in his efforts to clarify certain distinctions that are important for natural law theory,[14] Quay shows the relevance of distinguishing our natural ends from our consciously chosen purposes. Following this approach in the area of marriage and sexuality, Father Quay urges that, so long as one does not fall into the error of supposing that some chosen purpose may ever legitimately contradict a natural end by blocking or poisoning the powers of procreation (what normally happens in contraception), it is legitimate and praiseworthy to pursue a purpose that is important to marriage (for example, mutual love and union) even when there is no biological possibility of seeing one of the natural ends of marriage (procreation) come to fruition. He discusses this approach at length as one way of considering the moral legitimacy of NFP.

Finally, Father Quay offers a sustained reflection on the way in which the Scriptures use the natural meaning of cyclic fertility to signify symbolically something of the supernatural mysteries. The cycle of human fertility is, of course, just one among the many cycles of nature. They are all the result of the way in which the Lord created the world and declared it good. From what we can learn in revelation, the cycle of fertility is also good and in fact, a sign not merely of natural hope for the continuation of the race but also of God's fidelity even amid the havoc that our sins work. Like such natural cycles as those of the moon and the sun, the cycle of fertility is not itself religious, but it serves

---

[14] Robert Sokolowski, "What Is Natural Law", in *Christian Faith and Human Understanding* (Washington, D.C.: Catholic University of America Press, 2006).

as the framework within which God acts, first by the creation of new and immortal beings, and then by his great interventions, his deeds of redemption and salvation that bring his Church to be, and those further deeds of grace that constitute her the fertile mother of children spiritually by baptism.

All considered, what we have from Father Quay is new material on a question of tremendous importance, much worthy of our study and prayer.

PREFACE TO
THE FIRST EDITION

This little book attempts to sketch, without learned apparatus, the understanding of human sexuality that divine revelation offers us.

It is intended primarily for Christian adults who wish not only to know what kinds of sexual behavior are right or wrong but to gain true insight into *why* such behavior is right or wrong for those who seek to love and live in Christ. Sexual morality is part of the mystery of our life in Christ and makes full sense only when seen as such.

The approach taken here bypasses, without denying, the usual ethical and natural law types of arguments. Since understanding of the Christian mystery, so far as we are given access to it, is offered us through the Scriptures and the living Tradition of the Church, my effort has been to show what sexuality means for the Christian in terms of the Scriptures and a most important part of the Tradition, the teaching of the Fathers of the early Church.

The Fathers were at one in teaching, in an endless variety of ways, that sexual activity by Christians is meant to mirror the relations between each of the divine Persons and the Church, and that these relations constitute the most basic meaning of any right sexual activity.

Theoretical justification for this approach can be found in other things I have written, listed in the Other Readings on page 233. But all of that is left aside here, where I wish simply to set forth the deep reasons given us by God in his revelation for the moral teachings of his Church on sex.

Finally, I wish to thank the host of people who, over the years, have selflessly supported and urged forward the writing and publication of this book. Many have offered me their ideas, experience, and suggestions, have commented on or zealously promoted what was written already, have given financial support, have heartened me by their interest and gracious encouragement, and have prayed for the Lord's help and blessing. It is my fault alone that this mountain of goodness has brought forth such a small mouse of a book. Please accept my gratitude and be assured of my continuing prayers.

PAUL M. QUAY, S.J.
Loyola University of Chicago
Feast of Saint John Bosco, 1984

I

THE MEANING
OF SEXUALITY

CHRIST: THE IMAGE AND LIKENESS OF GOD

The Uniqueness of Christian Sexual Behavior and Its Social Import

From the time of our Lord, Christians' attitudes and behavior in sexual matters have perplexed the people around them. The apostles were baffled when our Lord, speaking of divorce and remarriage, declared it to be adultery. If so, they thought, it would be better for a man not to marry. His whole audience was probably baffled when he said, "You have heard that it was said, 'You shall not commit adultery.' But I say to you that every one who looks at a woman lustfully has already committed adultery with her in his heart" (Mt 5:27–28). This is certainly tightening up the Law beyond all expectation. The leaders of his people were undoubtedly puzzled when he said, "For your hardness of heart Moses allowed you to divorce your wives, but from the beginning it was not so" (Mt 19:8). By these words and his immediate rejection of remarriage, he set up man's state in Eden before the Fall as a norm for our behavior. This teaching was shocking even to a people that Scripture itself says were well prepared for his coming.

Consequently, when this teaching moved out through the apostles and the early Christians into the pagan world, it was misunderstood, fought, and often very bitterly resented. The result, frequently, was martyrdom for those who insisted upon preserving their virginity or their chastity. So much was this the case that virginity or chastity was regarded by the pagans as a touchstone to identify Christians. Those who would not take part in the unchaste actions of their fellows or who preferred virginity to marriage were marked immediately as Christians and sent to the lions.

On the other hand, the martyrs never regarded chastity as that for which they died. Chastity, in itself, was a small thing in their eyes. It was their love for Christ, who wanted them to be chaste, that gave them their determination to be chaste. Their chastity was part of their witness to the Lord. Thus, when the bloody martyrdoms were over, many Christians withdrew to the desert to be witnesses again to Christ and to his love for us; and again, virginity or chaste celibacy was a part of that witness. We ourselves should not be wholly amazed if chastity might someday cost us our lives, even as it cost the early Christians theirs or, in our own time, Saint Maria Goretti hers.

From the earliest days till now, the Church has been firm on these matters. There has been many a difficulty within the Church, many a dispute and contention, and many a loss of members because of her firmness on points of sexual morality that the world, by and large, saw as unimportant, as matters of personal preference. So it is today also. The Church continues to insist that the entire area of sexual attitudes and behavior is of utmost importance.

It is most unlikely, then, that we can ever fit in with the world around us in matters of sex, if we really know what it is to be Christian—though too often we may have reason to be ashamed that we are not living as chastely as some pagans. If, then, we find that we are not at odds with the world, by and large, in our sexual behavior, we can be sure we are not living as good Christians. For Christ has given us both understanding and power concerning chastity that the world not only does not accept, but frequently cannot accept.

Though human sexuality, like that of brute animals, exists for the sake of procreation and the bondings biologically necessary for raising the young, it has social aspects far wider than anything found among beasts.

Perceptive Catholics today, who once might have thought of chastity as important only for individuals in their efforts to keep the commandments and practice virtue, have become keenly aware that recent weakenings of sexual restraint have given rise to grave social problems. The controversy stirred up in response to *Humanae Vitae*, for example, has shown that private sexual problems can have major public effects not only on the Church but on civil society and the whole culture.

The very nature of the Church was called into question as soon as sex was thought to be a private matter, to be dealt with solely by the consciences of individual couples. For, if sex is merely private, then, as we shall see, the relations between God and his Church are merely private. In such a case the Church, as anything more than a private gathering of like-minded individuals, would cease to exist.

As to civil society, had Catholics not been publicly divided on *Humanae Vitae* by the efforts of dissenting clergy and religious, one may well wonder whether the Supreme Court would have decided *Roe v. Wade* in favor of unrestricted abortion. But when Christians doubt, vacillate, and lack conviction as to what sex means or how to find that meaning in practice, those who have no doubts move in and make the decisions for society.

It seems no accident that our culture, which has long seen religion as essentially a private matter, whatever help it may gain from community support, should have come to its present notions of marriage also as essentially a private matter. Hence have come the shattering of families through divorce and remarriage, the abortions (legally justified by the Supreme Court, recall, on the grounds of "privacy"), the killings of "defective" infants and the incurably ill (increasingly tolerated on the same grounds of "privacy"), all of which result from making sexual action a private matter, outside the scope of the law to regulate. As a result, the "right to privacy" concedes to individuals powers over the lives of others that no state could ever legitimately exercise itself. "Privacy" has become the current euphemism for absolute and murderous individualism.

The great irony is that, as with other areas of individualism, government has now taken over from the jealous individualist, without his protest, what he would not allow to his family, friends, or the Church. Government ratification and enforcement of total privacy in sexual behavior has now made sex a public affair.

The federal government formerly had no function with regard to sexual matters; and even state governments were limited to police powers (for example, protecting from rape and maintaining public decency), to the regulating of marriage and familial relations, and to the support and the protection of children and of families. Now, both federal and state governments are deeply involved with sex.

Once ostensibly excluded from the bedroom in the name of privacy by the courts, governmental agencies now seek control in the bedroom not only over our actions but over our thoughts as well. As but one example, the Health Systems Agencies Act (HSAA), which was passed in order to regulate the spending of public money in the building of hospitals and the purchasing of expensive medical equipment, has been used also to determine, by means of HSAA-mandated state health plans, the ways in which children shall be educated in matters of health—including sex education in accord with Planned Parenthood norms.

Public approval of the private conduct of those who sadly call themselves "gay"—not so private, however, that they do not want public knowledge and acceptance of their activities—has become a basic issue between major political parties.

Our government has for long years been sending abroad contraceptives and techniques of sterilization to the rest of the world; and its officials are on record saying that they would like to see at least a quarter of the fertile women of the world sterilized. Drugs too dangerous for American women are being sent, in contempt for those poorer than we, to women in developing nations. And abortion has often been forced on reluctant foreign governments in return for U.S. aid.

Few Americans realize how much the intellectual life of this nation has been guided, for at least a century and a half, by convinced atheists along a road, worse than any paganism, leading back into that darkness at the beginnings of our race where man freely chose to worship himself rather than God. That was the proto-sin, the sin of Adam. This has now been updated in modern versions, secular humanism and Marxism, the two great currents of thought growing out of the philosophies of the late eighteenth and early nineteenth centuries and summed up in the slogan of Feuerbach (whose most famous pupil was Karl Marx), "The only God of man is man himself." If people are brought, however subtly, to worship themselves, whether as individuals, through secular humanism, or as a group, through Marxism, then, indeed, confusion, chaos, and meaninglessness will take over not only in other areas but also in their sexual lives, as we can see all around us now.

Speaking of such philosophies, G. K. Chesterton remarked more than sixty years ago,

> According to most philosophers, God in making the world enslaved it. According to Christianity, in making it, he set it free. God had written, not so much a poem, but rather a play; a play he had planned as perfect, but which had necessarily been left to human actors and stage-managers, who had since made a great mess of it.

Despite the "great mess" made of God's plan for human sexual activity, as for all else, he continues to direct his play and to lead it toward a successful conclusion. That we may share in his success, we need to learn what he is about, to understand what he has told us about our sexuality, so that we may indeed be free, free not with the sterile liberty of license and self-worship but with the freedom for which Christ has set us free, the freedom for which God created us—the freedom of his own children.

As Catholics, we are meant to be lights shining brightly in the darkness of surrounding sexual immorality. By the example of our chastity, by that puzzle and paradox that a chaste life represents in the eyes of those who do not believe, we are to bring people to Christ, who is the source of this chastity. Some of the things in our lives will be unique to Catholics, some will be simply the things that every man is called to by nature; in either case our witness can ring true only if we are indeed being chaste.

What We Are Looking For

To live chastely, however, it is necessary to understand what chastity means for Christians. Why be chaste? Why is God interested in sex anyway?

We, who live in a country still influenced by puritanism, even if only in reaction against it, have much need to be convinced of the true goodness of our bodies and especially of our sexuality.

At times what prevents this conviction is that we fear our sexuality because of its violence and the ease with which it can get out of control; we sense its connection with original sin and our own actual sins; and we dread God's just punishment for the sins it may easily lead us to. At other times, we despise our sexual powers because they seem gross or dirty or, more subtly, because we find pleasure in them but no sense of true meaning, significance, or human worth.

But we forget, when we are afraid of our sexuality, that the best protection from sin in this matter is to revere and to esteem our sexuality as God reveres and esteems it. We forget, when we despise it, that it is God who has made our bodies to function in these ways, that it is he who has made us sexual beings and has filled the entire world with sexual beings. Yet he intends for us to live in this world in a healthy, positive, holy, and Christian manner. Or we forget that the pleasure of sexual activity is intended by God only as an accompaniment to the achieving of its goals and true purposes, or we are ignorant of its true significance for man.

We shall need to work a bit to obtain a sacred conviction in these matters because sexuality is so degraded all around us. Talk about sex nowadays is open, constant, and unembarrassed. But unfortunately this talk is, all too commonly, coarse and cheap; and people's actions are correspondingly coarse, cheap, and degraded. Sex has become a mere pastime. The sexual organs are regarded by many as toys, simply for one's own pleasure. As a result, a great many people have no idea how good sex is. If you mention to them the sacredness of sex, they either take you to mean that sex is to be worshipped or else are puzzled and uncomprehending. No wonder they find no satisfaction in their sexual activities, no rest or peace, no matter how much they seek.

On the other hand, most of us have experienced the beauty of true chastity in people we have met. It is obvious in them, not merely in the fact that they are not fooling around all the time but in a certain quality of character that is well summed up by Saint Paul in his remarks to Timothy: "God did not give us a spirit of timidity but a spirit of power and love and self-control" (2 Tim 1:7). These three things—power, love, and self-control—are probably the three best characteristics for describing Christian chastity. Certainly they result from a chaste life.

Such chastity is our ideal. We are not interested in slipping into a state of repression, anxiety, fear, or constraints that cripple. Most of us have probably experienced some of these, too, at one time or another. It may even be said that they are necessary steps on the way to acquiring true chastity. Nonetheless, they are certainly not the goal.

As Christians, however, our goal is not chastity for its own sake. We are seeking, rather, to be like our Lord and our Lady. In the Bible, Mary is presented to us, when Gabriel speaks to her, as one who does not "know man", that is, sexually, carnally. She has no intention of so knowing even Joseph, though well aware that such knowledge is necessary for the procreation of children. Our Lord, when he speaks in the Gospels about sexual matters, adultery, fornication, and so forth, speaks in the same tone of voice, as far as we can judge, and with the same quiet seriousness that he does about any other moral matters. He does not make sex seem more important or more difficult or harder or scarier than anything else. Our question is: How do we come to his view of these things?

The Light of Christ

Putting on the mind of Christ requires that we proceed in the light of faith, thinking of what God has revealed to us about himself and about us. We wish to see what faith, our faith in Christ, implies for our behavior.

Some theologians have argued in recent times that, though the Church is able to define matters of faith, she cannot define moral matters. The reason they give is that morals are something other than faith and not deducible from it. Moral doctrine is in large measure culturally determined. It grows, these theologians argue, from the circumstances of time and place as well as from one's personal devotion to Christ. Therefore, it is not something that can be solemnly defined for all times and places.

Unfortunately, such an argument would ultimately make Christian behavior not much different—indeed, in principle no different—from that of the pagan. At most one might claim that the Christian has better and more solid motives for carrying out the moral duties of his state. As the Council of Trent long since pointed out, however, faith and morals are not two distinct items. The council stated its concern to be "with matters of faith and the morals that pertain to the upbuilding of the teaching of that faith". So, our concern here is with faith and the sexual behavior that flows from faith and in turn builds up the faith.

What, then, does faith teach about sexuality? Most obviously, that God created man male and female. But in that same passage there is something more pertinent and more fundamental: Man was created in the image and according to the likeness of God. Much later, Saint Paul, when writing to the Colossians, says of Jesus, "He is the image of the invisible God, the first-born of all creation; for in him all things were created, in heaven and on earth, visible and invisible. . . . All things were created through him and for him" (Col 1:15–16). Christ, then, is the image of God in which man was created. Jesus Christ, therefore, is the sole norm of what it is to be truly human, of what man is or is meant to be.

If, then, we wish to know the fullness of human good and not merely to inquire about those extreme moral evils that would destroy our nature, it is at Jesus and, in her measure, at Mary that we must look. He is the new Adam; she is the new Eve. In these two alone God's will for the human nature that he created can be seen whole and integral. If we look at human nature anywhere else, we are looking at a fallen nature. We can get a right picture of human sexuality—or anything else in our nature—only insofar as it is contained in Christ. In him alone will we find unfallen human nature in its absolute fullness, as it was intended by God from the beginning.

It follows, since integral human nature is understandable only in Christ, that integral human sexuality is a mystery of faith. It is not merely something that we have in common with the animals though we share certain physiological aspects of sex with them. The mystery of man's sexuality is the mystery of its likeness to Christ's.

The whole of the natural law is summed up in him. Rather, we should say, he *is* the natural law. His is our nature in its perfection. He is the norm for all that we do, think, or hope to be. It is Christ who sets all the questions and problems, contexts and answers; not we; not our sciences. The material universe was created through him and for him. He has come into it that he might bring it, in perfection and fulfillment, to the Father, even though, through sin, it had been delivered to slavery and death. For he loves all that he has made; and at the heart of the universe is the Heart of Christ.

If, then, we are to understand that part of the universe that is ourselves, and that aspect of ourselves that is our sexuality, we can do so only if we go to Christ, for any truly human sexual behavior is essentially an element, aspect, or component of Christian chastity.

First, however, we shall pause to understand a little more deeply the goodness of the material world, sex included, and see how God uses material things to communicate with us through symbols. Thereafter, we will turn to the Scriptures to see what he has said there on our subject.

2

GOD'S GOOD CREATION:
CHRISTIAN SYMBOLS

God and Matter

Unhealthy attitudes toward sexuality often spring from strong but hidden attitudes of disgust or dislike for our biological functions generally, our activity as material beings. Hence, before we begin to consider what God has revealed about sex, it may be helpful to look for a moment at God's attitude toward material things. The most obvious thing is that he likes them; he takes delight in them; he loves them.

Scripture recounts how God created the light, separating it from the darkness, created the sky and the sea, then the land and its plant life, created the luminaries of the sky, the fish and the birds, the creeping things and the animals, and finally, man. The material universe, all parts and aspects of it without exception, was created by God; he looked at each thing as it came to be and "saw that it was good" (Gen 1:10). All the while, the Bible adds, his Wisdom rejoiced, playing in this new-made world (see Wis 8:30). God's attitude toward material things, then, is that of a maker well pleased with what he has made.

The one exception occurs when he makes man. At the material level, man, too, is good; all his spiritual powers are good, but these are capable of being used or misused. So God waits before saying that man is either good or bad. Because he has given man the great gift of freedom, in likeness to himself, he waits to see what man will do with his freedom. God has left man unfinished so that he can become like God even in his act of creation, creating himself by the gift of God's grace, through his own free actions.

Christianity, therefore, differs greatly from the old nature religions of the Near East, of Babylonia, Egypt, and elsewhere. We know, as they did not, that there can be no evil in God. Since God is the sole source of all that is, nothing else exists for a creature to be modeled on or to be like except the infinite goodness of God. Hence, there is no evil in his creation except what his creatures bring about by abusing their freedom. Matter is good; it is not, as Hinduism and other major Oriental religions have thought, ambivalent or bad, a sort of cosmic illusion or force for evil embedded in the structure of the universe. Quite the contrary, the whole of creation is good; everything that exists is something that God wants to exist. As a wise man said in prayer to the Lord, "You love all things that are, and you loathe none of the things which you have made" (Wis 11:24).

Still more striking is the fact that God has taken up the material elements of this world into himself. By his enfleshment (the literal sense of the Latin term for "incarnation"), he took up a human body, as material as ours, with flesh and blood and all the biological structures and functions of our bodies. He made this human animality one with himself, so that we must say of this particular man, Jesus Christ, "This man, material though he is, is God." The eternal Word has become flesh forever. There is never a time this will cease to be true, now that it has once happened. We should let this sink into us because it is basic for everything that we will say.

Christians sometimes fail to realize the importance that Scripture gives to Christ's body, his own physical body, not just his mystical body. Firstly, we have been redeemed and have been sanctified through the offering of the body of Jesus Christ once and for all on the Cross. Only a material being can be scourged and crucified. Only in a body capable, like ours, of sensation and of pain could the infinitely spiritual God suffer, bleed, and die for our sins.

Furthermore, we were justified by the raising of his flesh and blood in glory from the tomb, by the new life of that body that had died for us on the Cross. His entrance into heaven was a bodily entrance. Christ's Resurrection and Ascension are, then, the ultimate proof of the goodness of material things, of man's body and of all the material creation that assists man.

This bodily glorification of Christ is the seed and root of our salvation and our glorification. We are called by Christ to do in our bodies as he did in his body: to suffer, to die, and to rise in glory in our own flesh, made glorious by the power of his Spirit.

This is the reason he gives us his body as nourishment when we receive him in Communion. It is the body of the Risen One that we receive. Though it looks and tastes like bread and wine, to us it has the same powers that it had right after Christ's Resurrection. The apostles were gathered together, the doors were shut, and Christ, body and whole being, was suddenly present. He willed to be there; there he was. So he does at Mass, in Communion, in the tabernacle—he is present because he has chosen to come there upon the altar when the priest consecrates. Though capable of multilocation and movement as fast as thought, Christ's body is still a human body; it is still flesh and blood, though glorified with powers that our bodies as yet do not know, but will someday have. His is also the body of the sacrifice that is offered; his is the body of the priest, for it is he who offers himself upon the altar to the Father.

Saint Paul, all through his epistles, never ceases to talk about the body of Christ, the flesh of Christ, the blood of Christ. He says very little, if anything, about the soul of Christ. Obviously, he speaks of the *living* body of Christ, alive by the life of his soul. But it is the *body* of Christ that is the center of his thought. All our hope centers on Christ's body, for example, when he returns at the end of time as Judge. Dominated by this mystery of the body of Christ as the source of salvation, Paul's preferred image of the Church is that of the Mystical Body of Christ, his material extension in space and in time.

The body of the one who is closest to Christ, Mary's body, completes the mystery. In 1950, Pope Pius XII defined solemnly the doctrine of the Assumption of our Lady, body and soul, into the glory of heaven. This doctrine emphasizes for us something that we might have forgotten in connection with Christ himself: that those who rise from the dead rise as male or female. Mary remains woman; she remains "she"; she remains female for all eternity, even as her Son is a man, "he", male forever.

Though flesh and blood, in the scriptural sense of human weakness, cannot inherit the kingdom of God, flesh and blood made glorious by their link with Christ's flesh and blood *do* inherit the kingdom. We will all be in heaven more truly male or female than ever on this earth, without marriage, but perfect in virility or femininity for all ages.

Christian Symbolism

Of course, Christ, Mary, and the rest of us, are not just material; we are spiritual as well. Our activities are at once bodily and intellectual, freely chosen and materially determined. Our thoughts, our emotions, our freedom, our passions, our digestion, and our sexuality are inseparably welded together in a single being. It is this strange sort of material-spiritual composite that God loves so much. Because he made us, he never forgets (though we often do) the sort of composite creatures we are; and he deals with us accordingly.

Thus, the greatest of his spiritual gifts he gives through largely material means. Our share in his divine life, exercised through faith, hope, and charity, is spiritual beyond any human notion of spirituality. Nonetheless, this is given to us in the sacraments through concrete material things such as water, bread, wine, olive oil, and balsam. Recall the catechism definition of a sacrament: an outward sign (in other words, a material thing) of an interior grace, established by Christ and conferring the grace that (as a material thing) it signifies, that is, some new mode or way of living the supernatural life of grace or some new growth in it. Materiality enters into the very notion of what a sacrament is. It is a means of grace, yes, but it gives this grace through matter, by showing forth to our senses some likeness and similarity to a mystery on the spiritual level. A sign of this type is called a symbol.

A symbol is, first, a type of material thing that, when perceived, leads us to a knowledge of something else. It is, therefore, a type of sign. Some signs are purely conventional: words, for example—whether spoken or written. When I say "fire", this means something in English; it would mean nothing at all in French. It is a sign that leads you to a knowledge of my meaning when I use the word in a sentence, but only if you already know what its conventional signification is. Further, the word itself will not help you to learn its meaning. The word "fire" designates a certain kind of physicochemical process but bears no resemblance to that process.

A sign, however, may resemble what it signifies. If, in this case, both sign and thing signified are material, the sign is called an image. Thus, a painting of blazing logs in a fireplace would offer us an image of fire.

But the material sign that we call a symbol has a sign value not only by some sort of convention or by material similarity but by the fact that its material form, structure, action, or appearance is similar to the immaterial or spiritual thing it signifies. Hence, once we know that something is a symbol, it can lead us by itself to knowledge of its significance and meaning.

For example, fire is widely used as a symbol of human love. Fire is bright and beautiful. It is mobile and active, spreading and growing as if alive. It warms us and gives heat. It is necessary for civilized life; without it we cannot cook our food, keep warm in winter, or melt metals out of rock. Yet, if fire gets out of control, it becomes something terrible, destructive, leaving only ashes. So it is with human love. Love brightens our lives and warms our hearts. It turns the indigestible events and tasteless dreariness of everyday life into true nourishment. Love draws joy and benevolence from hearts of stone. With little love, life is cold and painful; with none at all, life is impossible. Yet, if love gets out of control, it consumes, destroys all in its way, and leaves only ashen desolation. Fire in its different physical aspects, then, is like love in its immaterial aspects. Material fire leads us to a knowledge of love's "fire" by summing up and making manifest to the senses our own inner experience of love.

Many symbols flow from similarities almost universally observed and noticed, as in our example of fire and love. Many others are more strongly conditioned by the particular experiences of peoples or cultures. A man's aggressiveness, for example, chooses different types of symbolic action to express itself in different cultures. In our culture, it can show itself by bigness—owning the largest ranch, building the biggest factory, producing the most steel—or by excellence in sports. In other cultures, aggressiveness is manifested in the number of wives in a harem or by the number of children born, by heads or scalps collected, by grave risks taken or perils confronted, or in the various forms of male contest.

Human cultures, our own and others, are in large measure summed up by their symbols. One of the symbols of our own culture is the skyscraper. Recall people's reactions when a new building is put up that is taller than any other, for example, the Empire State Building in New York or the Sears Tower in Chicago. Such a building has a meaning and we know it, even if we find it hard to state explicitly what the meaning is exactly. The solid-gold Cadillac is a symbol with which we are all acquainted. So is the man in the gray flannel suit (and the blue-jeans generation) and the various status symbols. All these are purely material and external things—clothing, articles of manufacture —yet in the context of our culture, they sum up a whole range of social relationships by their physical similarity to the attitudes they signify.

At a deeper level, psychologists are coming to understand the psychological role of symbolism in man's life. They have discovered that, long before an infant is capable of speech, before he is capable of expressing anything, we would think, except by crying and wailing, he has begun to use symbols. As soon as he becomes aware of his bodily functions, he uses them for symbolic acts of love, rejection, and aggression. All man's sexual activity, as we shall see in detail, is symbolic activity. We have mentioned the range of aggressive symbols, some of which are subdued to social goods, but others not. Most of what we call culture—art, literature, and even science—is composed and built up of symbols. Politicians are well aware of the benign paternity expressed by kissing a baby or the fraternal goodwill embodied in a handshake and the use of the first name.

Finally, there are levels of symbolism of which ordinarily we are not conscious at all. Much of the work of Freud, Jung, and other depth psychiatrists has been to lay bare these hidden structures of symbolism that lie deep within us, of which we are not conscious, but which, nonetheless, work actively upon our motivation without our realizing their hidden biases.

These psychiatrists were interested because they had seen the enormous damage that can be done to a person if these deep symbolic structures are skewed or damaged or wrongly related to reality. In such a case, a man is at odds with himself or the world. What was created in him to symbolize one thing has been made to symbolize something else. The result can easily be psychosis.

Symbols, then, some of them conscious, others not, but all important, are continually at work within us. Many symbols, indeed, flow from man's very nature; and man cannot distort or change them without doing damage to himself. Symbolism belongs to the very essence of man, a necessary aspect of his being.

Returning to sacramental symbols, consider baptism. This involves immersing a person in a pool or tank of water, though this act is often reduced to pouring water over the person's head. But what does water symbolize? Universally, it is found to be a symbol of life, for every living thing needs water to continue its life. Without it we die in a terrible agony of thirst. With it, even in the deserts, plants germinate and cacti bloom.

At the same time it symbolizes death, because if our heads are held under water, we shortly lose consciousness and drown. Water in excess becomes the floodwaters that sweep away life from the surface of the land, yet render it fertile for new life to spring up. Water, then, kills; it also gives life. Immersion symbolizes death; coming up out of water, life. Thus, Christ chose to plunge us into water to symbolize our death with him on the Cross to our old selves and to the world, and to lift us out of water to symbolize our being raised to a new life in him through his Resurrection.

Not only are all the sacraments symbolic but the entire liturgy is saturated with symbols. In fact, the liturgy can be defined quite usefully as a series of symbolic actions through which man worships God and through which God's grace is given to man. The altar itself, the priest's gestures, the types of readings, the way we listen to the readings —sitting during the Old Testament reading and the New Testament letters but standing for the Gospel—the carrying of candles, the offering of incense, the bread and the wine themselves, the chalice, . . . an endless list of symbolic elements, all fitting to form the one sacrifice and the one banquet of Christ.

But the liturgy contains much more than rites and ceremonies. The liturgy reenacts symbolically the great mysteries of God's actions in history. For example, baptism represents God's freeing of his people from their slavery in Egypt by their passage through the Red Sea dryshod while their enemies drowned in the waters, prefiguring his liberating us from the power of Satan through the waters of baptism. So also, the Mass is a rich symbolic re-presentation of the whole history of the Jewish people and of God's relations with them and all mankind, from the first offering of the paschal lamb in Egypt to the sacrifice of the Lamb of God on the Cross to take away the sin of the world, the sacrifice that incorporates and transcends all other sacrifices. Sacrifice itself, of course, is a type of symbolic action reserved exclusively for man's worship of God.

The Paschal Liturgy carries this symbolism to its highest point. It should cause no surprise that the Church splurges on symbolism at this time of the year in her joy at Christ's bodily Resurrection, stressing in this way that the whole material creation is good and intended for the service and glory of the Father. There are not only the usual symbols to which we have grown accustomed—altar, candles, chalice, paten, music, incense, flowers—but there is a vast array of special ones. All the lights in the church are turned out, to remind us of the darkness of our sins. There is the entrance of the paschal candle; and the light coming from that candle, as the feeble flames are passed from one person to another, like the graces of faith and conversion. Palm branches, processions, breathings upon the water in the baptismal font, the consecrating and pouring of oils, the washing of feet, the consecrating of fire—these and many other symbols are crammed into one short week; most of them, into a single night.

It is right here, in its attitude toward symbols, that we find a tremendous difference between Catholicism and all the types of puritanism or so-called religion of the spirit that are such perpetual temptations to many people. The latter may, indeed, use many symbols; but they do so in a strangely minimalistic fashion, using symbols that are as abstract as possible, mere wraiths or ghosts of Catholic symbols; Catholicism is of the earth, earthly; as well as of heaven, heavenly. We see that material things are not only good but useful; not only for man's benefit and pleasure but for his service to God, even in the highest and most exalted moments of his religious life.

Thus, the whole life of the Church is symbolic, not only sacraments and worship but, as we shall now see, divine revelation and all morality. If, then, we do not understand symbolism, we will have but a small understanding of Christianity.

Symbols in Revelation

In the light of God's use of sacramental symbols to share with us his own life, it will be no surprise to find that his revelation of himself to us through the Scriptures also makes heavy use of symbols.

We ourselves, as material and spiritual composites, find it particularly easy and attractive to communicate with each other by means of symbols. It is true that the most characteristically human mode of communication takes place through words, which are nonsymbolic signs. But we have many symbolic ways of communicating also. Perhaps the commonest of these fall under the name "body language". Surely, a mother's caress of her infant or the studied casualness of a self-conscious young man at a party portray for us in flesh their inner attitudes and feelings. Often, too, when we do use words, we use them to represent a symbol we cannot present in actuality.

Since symbolic communication is part of our nature, especially at the deepest levels, God has used symbolism to communicate with us, to reveal himself to us, and to teach us more about ourselves. The mere fact that he has done so sharpens our awareness that man is a symbol-making animal, a creature that lives his life in the power of symbols. God, having created us this way, speaks to us in the language that is best suited to us—and this is often the language of symbols.

When we read in the Scriptures the history of our salvation, we find that both Testaments are so heavily crammed with symbolism that they often make extremely difficult reading. At times, the symbolism seems to get totally out of hand, as in Ezekiel or in Revelation, and we are tempted to say, "Well, we'll reserve that for another time." But even in the parts of Scripture given over, seemingly, to simple narrative, such as the Gospels, we find abundant symbolism. For example, Saint John's Gospel is constructed precisely to show the symbolic value that is present in the actual, historical deeds and words of Christ.

Why this profusion of symbolism? One reason is that God wished to save, to fulfill, and to bring to completion all the good that was already in man. Now, throughout history, religion had been, more than any other single aspect of man's life, the strongest focus of his symbolic activity. Thus, one reason God revealed himself to us was to rectify the skewed symbolic activity that constitutes so much of natural human religions. Even the highest of these, such as Hinduism and Buddhism, are in many ways profoundly in error; and these errors generate false attitudes toward the world and other men that are propagated through their religious symbols.

If, then, God was to redeem us fully, he had to set right our religious symbols. He could not obliterate symbolic action, for this would be to obliterate our nature. So he took the symbolisms that we are acquainted with, which he had built into us and our world. Even though they were badly damaged by sin, he took them, rectified them, and reoriented them. Through these restored symbolisms, he has enabled us to have a right understanding of the material universe and has revealed to us the true meaning of man.

A second reason is that God wishes to tell us things that lie beyond the range of comprehension of even the highest of our intellectual powers. He wishes to give us true knowledge of himself, of his own internal life as Trinity, of the Incarnation, and of all the other mysteries of the faith, far beyond human understanding. Great as is the human mind, it is still infinitely weaker than is necessary to get a proper grasp of God himself or of his mysteries.

On the other hand, a symbol, because of its concreteness, contains within itself tremendous potentialities that the mind cannot exhaust. This is especially true of natural symbols, because God himself created the material universe to show forth the spiritual; and, as we said above, there is nothing else, ultimately, for any material thing to be like other than God. Thus, sheep were created, among other reasons, that Christ might be the Lamb of God; lions, that he might be the Lion of the tribe of Judah.

Though these symbols, also, are not adequate to contain God's mysteries, yet by his creating them thus, they are better far than our limited concepts and thought patterns. This we see easily from the fact that theologians have been pondering the revealed symbolisms for centuries and have found ever new and true, though previously hidden, meanings there.

A final reason is that God wished his revelation to transcend all time, place, and culture because he wants to speak to every man so that he can be understood. Since a single symbol can pack a richness of meaning far exceeding the grasp of any one time, place, or culture, God can reveal things to us through symbols that lie beyond particular cultural conditionings. Since symbols touch the nature of man in the depths of his unconscious, they are able to speak to him universally, even when he is without education.

We may distrust symbols because we think of them chiefly as signs that are artful or contrived. "Symbol" is often used loosely and may refer to nothing more than some bit of "inspired prose" or, say, a movie's cheap way of manipulating emotions by paralleled images. Men easily find this sort of symbolism faintly embarrassing because, I think, it seems feminine to them. In fact, women seem generally to find the concreteness and emotional directness of symbols more satisfying than do men, who miss the abstract generality and rigorous clarity of conceptual thought. Men can forget, consequently, their own experience and the things psychology has shown us; they tend to hold back in the presence of symbolic activity, not to enter into it, to feel just a little silly if they do engage in it.

We distrust symbols also because they can be abused. A symbol has meaning; its meaning arises from the sort of thing it is. Like a word, it can be used by one person to express his meaning to another; it can be used as a part of a language. When it is so used, it should mean to the persons involved what it means in itself. But people can use a symbol falsely. While pretending to all the world that they mean what the symbol expresses, at the same time they are intending something quite different. In other words, they lie. Unfortunately, the symbols proper to every human relationship can be violated and used contrary to their meaning; such symbolism has then become a mere vehicle for hypocrisy.

Consequently, we can be either bored by symbols or sickened by them when they are abused. This is, however, only an argument for using them well, an argument for studying and understanding them more deeply. We will, therefore, be discussing in the rest of this book, Christian sexual symbolism: first, the natural symbolism of the body and of the marital act, then the further meanings of sexual actions that are made known to us in and through the Scriptures, then the meanings of corruptions of these symbolic acts, and finally the symbolism of continence and virginity.

3

SEXUAL INTERCOURSE:
THE NATURAL WORD OF LOVE

We have seen that God communicates with us through symbols, partly spiritual and partly material, in correspondence with our nature. Now we wish to consider the natural symbolism of sexual intercourse itself, that is, to learn those meanings that even people without revelation can come to know, meanings that God built into these physical acts through internal likeness and parallelism of structure. We will then be better able to understand the supernatural meanings God reveals to us when he uses symbols in Scripture.

Most obviously, sexual actions symbolize love. But the love so symbolized is not love in general. There are many types of love that are not sexual, in any popular sense of the term, and not related directly to sexual activity, for example, the love of a son for his father or of a daughter for her mother, the love of a brother for a brother, of one friend for another, and all types of civic love. None of these loves is sexual, in the sense of drawing to genital arousal and intimacy, whereas marital love is deeply sexual. Yet even marital love has many varieties and modes of expression other than sexual intimacies or intercourse.

Well, then, what kind of love *is* symbolized by sexual action? To answer, we must note that even the way our bodies are formed sexually has meaning that lies beyond the physical. Our bodies are not mere collections of functions, but express visibly part of the natural and intrinsic meaning of ourselves.

The Meaning of the Body

Consider a man's body. His genitals are external, hanging loosely from his body. On arousal, they point away from him and, at climax, expel his seed from him. He responds quickly to visual stimuli. The mere sight of a woman, especially if he senses that she is interested in him, can arouse him at once sexually. His sexual response is quick and strong; his whole body reacts rapidly. He can cease to act, cease even to be stimulated, with equal rapidity, especially if some other stimulus, say, an intrusion by a burglar, calls for immediate but different action.

Hence, a man has great freedom with regard to sexual activity. He can initiate it rapidly; he can stop it abruptly. Aftereffects are minimal or nonexistent. He can begin intercourse and carry it to completion even against the wishes of the woman. He can coerce a woman, rape her if he should so desire.

What all this signifies to him symbolically is not hard to fathom. As his genitals and his actions through them are largely external and outwardly directed, so at the psychic level he is directed outward and focuses his interest spontaneously on things outside himself. Even as his arousal and orgasm tend to be quick and soon over, so on the psychological level he tends to action rather than simple contemplation of what attracts him. As his sexual activity is aggressive, so he is interested in display and in manifestation of his sexuality, if not directly, then in contest against other men. And the whole of his life manifests his inner need to take initiative.

Because of this highly external and other-directed genitality, a man's family remains in large measure psychologically external to him. His sexual independence and freedom of action signify a corresponding psychic independence and freedom with regard to his family. He may father more than one family; he may sire offspring whose existence is of small concern to him. The family is part of his life, but not the totality of it. The family extends him in space and time, in range of influence and power, and is able to give him a type of support and assistance that the rest of society cannot provide but often makes necessary.

Correspondingly, he will establish very strong relationships with the world beyond himself and his family. Always he senses a duty to act in the world at large, to make full and proper use of his powers in whatever field of activity he lives and operates. He is one who builds in the world.

A man's interiority, consequently, is something that comes from the mind. It is through the mind that he grasps the external world, grasps even his own feelings and his own sexuality, for that matter. For, once he has reached adulthood, however pleasant his feelings or emotions, he is not satisfied until his mind has understood them and traced them. And through this interiority of the mind, he is then able to build, to construct, to make the world a suitable place for himself and his family. Thus, a man is largely verbal and conceptual, using his mind to obtain understanding and so to affect the world.

On the other hand, he is also expendable. His body is made both for dangerous actions and for quick reaction in response to danger. He can fertilize many women, one after another, so that if one man is left with a thousand women, he is capable of generating children of all of them. Society does not need an individual man, then, the way it needs each individual woman. It can afford to send men into battle to protect, even at the cost of their lives, the women and children at home.

A woman's body is very different. Her genitals are interior, hidden. Her response is largely tactile. Mere seeing does little to arouse her; touch does a great deal. A woman's response is much slower than a man's. She is slower not only to be aroused but also in subsiding; and many a marital problem comes from the fact that the husband, having subsided quickly from his sexual excitement, turns away and pays no further attention to his wife though she is still fully aroused.

This prolongation of the effects of intercourse within her body signifies an even greater prolongation in her mind and emotions. And if she conceives, for long months she will be heavy with child, thus beginning a relation with that child that the father can never have.

In order that a child may grow within her body, there is an empty space within her that only another person can fill. Yet she will not know him until he is born. Because of this inner space, open for the mystery of new persons, a woman's interiority is not primarily of the mind, brilliant though her mind may be, but is rooted in her womb and its openness for the seed of her husband and for a child.

Sensing the child as the desired filling of that central emptiness that must otherwise remain part of her, a woman is led to find that missing center in a family, and her fulfillment in the raising of children who will be worthy of her love. Thus, she is not greatly concerned with the abstract class of beings that constitute the not-yet-materialized needs, hazards, and threats that the man must deal with if he is to preserve his family in a world that is not easily made subservient to their welfare.

Rather, her attention is focused on the concrete being within her and on her other children, already born, around her.

This explains something of a woman's special power of nonverbal communication. She must be able to understand her newborn infant and respond appropriately to his needs. She must reassure, encourage, and assist this helpless creature who cannot speak, who for a year or more will not be able to communicate with her by words.

Even when she is not pregnant, a woman does not ordinarily have the bodily strength to resist a man successfully if he is determined to rape her or to kill her children. Her efforts to repel him, however savage or frantic, are concentrated on protection and defense; she lacks the man's aggressive strength. Though willing to give her life, if need be, to save her children from attack, frequently she has not the power to do so. She needs someone who can protect both her and the family her life centers on.

This bodily weakness with regard to conflict and assault grounds a woman's greater fearfulness or sensitivity to danger and signifies her psychic need for security. Without the latter, even her physical fertility, by nature intermittent, is further reduced. But when secure, the woman nourishes her child with the milk from her own breasts; and a nursing mother is that which a man must protect above all else.

Nor is it strange that the protection a culture offers to its women and to their children, gathered about them or still within the womb, is the sign of its vitality. The preservation and transmission of culture seem to be universally symbolized by the infant at his mother's breast, by the children at her knee. For she is called by her nature to nourish them spiritually as well as physically. As her body needs more and better food when nursing, so children turn her mind to draw in all of the more stable and contemplative aspects of the culture, to digest them and transmit them in forms suitable to her children.

Thus, all that the past has brought forth, as from a womb—language (one's "mother tongue"), stories (the concrete historical memory), arts and literature, and domestic skills—she takes in and, through her ability as first teacher of her children, serves as the cultural memory of the entire people. The father, on the other hand, more naturally teaches the culture's abstract understanding of its own sociopolitical nature and of the world as a whole, along with those active skills more useful outside, even if for, the family. He is more at ease in training young adults to labor at generating the future, to lay bare by intellectual analysis the possibilities of the world, and to risk the dangers involved in bringing them to be.

At the highest level, then, a woman's bodily unsuitability for combat symbolizes her basic drive for commitment, a desire and a need for love and, in a certain way, for guidance by the man she loves and trusts. Men, outwardly directed, see their responsibilities to their families as met in large measure by their efforts to attain certain societal goals they have set for themselves. Made to take initiative in the world, yet in such a way as to promote the good of their family, they know a basic need to have and exercise authority, in the world perhaps, but especially over their family, so as to hold the inner and outer portions of their life in unity. But, spurred by ambition and concentrating on personal achievement as measured by their goals, men have a natural tendency to avoid marital commitment as not always helpful to these goals, if not an actual entanglement or impediment to them.

Thus, it is clear how fully in accord with our nature are Saint Paul's commands, "Husbands, love your wives" (see Eph 5:25, 28, 33; Col 3:19); and "Wives, be subject to your husbands" (see Eph 5:22, 24, 33; Col 3:18). The man who truly loves his wife satisfies her greatest need as a woman, her need for the security of steadfast love and faithful protection. The wife who obeys her husband confirms the need he has for authority so that he can accept his full responsibility toward his family. She thus helps him to hold fast to a commitment he might otherwise be tempted to reject; whereas a wife who disregards her husband's authority robs him of his function and undermines his ability to give her what she most needs and desires, his abiding love. So, too, the husband who is not concerned to make manifest in body, mind, and heart his love for his wife makes it far harder for her to submit to his authority, no longer seen as being exercised for her good but arbitrarily or merely for others. He thus weakens her ability to give him that support, in his wrestling with the world, that he needs from her.

There are many other things our bodies symbolize antecedently to the dynamic of the marital union. Let us glance at one, less obvious, symbolism that Pope John Paul II has analyzed at great length: the symbolism of the physical nakedness of husband and wife in each other's presence.

We find this first in the Garden of Eden, where man and wife, as first created, were both naked; yet they were not ashamed. Physical nakedness seems at first easy to define. It is the lack of all clothing, all covering, all protection, all that is not the person himself. Thus, when two are present to each other, it is the exposure of one's whole body to another's gaze, scrutiny, and judgment, without anything that can enhance, screen, or protect.

Nakedness before another is more than mere nudity, however, for it symbolizes that each is meant to be uncovered to the other spiritually. This does not mean confessing prior infidelities or other sins to one another—for this tends, generally, to be an obstacle to transparency. It means rather that each stands in the present moment without psychological covering or pretense, in the presence of the other. Neither spiritually, mentally, emotionally, nor physically is one covering or concealing any of one's interior self. And each accepts the other, seen thus naked, whatever defects are thus exposed.

In a state of original innocence, one could stand so, in front of one's husband or wife, without any trace of shame. As Christians in a fallen world, we are constantly being recalled by our Lord and his Church to that state.

But in our fallen state, nakedness before another calls, especially in a woman, for no small trust and humility. Will her husband accept her for herself, as she is in herself, regardless of any imperfection, fault, or flaw, whether physical or spiritual?

In turn, the husband must be able to give himself to her as he is in his masculinity, without pretending to be less or more than he is. Only through her can he discover what it is to be a man, to be truly male. Each of them stands as a personal gift from God before the other. Hence, each is not only to revere and appreciate the other but to worship God through the other, because it is he who has given the gift.

The Meaning of Intercourse

In sexual intercourse itself, the man takes the initiative, but in response to the physical presence and attraction of the woman. She responds to his arousal by her own. As he penetrates, she opens and yields herself to him, permitting him to take possession of her. Letting him act, she also acts to draw his seed from him. He labors and thrusts upon and in her, in order to pour into her his semen.

The fullness of intrinsic symbolic meaning in intercourse is seen from the fact that any such description of the physical act can be read, with scarcely a change, as a description of the couple's psychic activity. The man's initiative and the woman's opening are not merely physical but also psychological. The man's dominance in penetrating and taking possession is an attitude of mind and heart, not mere bodily power. The woman's gift of herself to the man, his gift of himself to her, are spiritual and psychological as well as physical. His aggressive giving of his substance to her, her yielding of her substance, hidden deep within, to him, describe spiritual realities no less than biological ones.

The woman shows submission and responsiveness, an unfolding, a centering of her attention upon him. She seeks, as an abiding psychological attitude, to draw forth what is best in him, not just from his body but from all levels of his being. Likewise, when the man penetrates her, he focuses all of his activity, all of his substance, all of his responsibility, all of his manhood upon her. He is fascinated with her; he desires to protect her. In his case, also, these are meant to be abiding attitudes.

The most obvious aspect of sexual union is the pleasure it gives. But even this physical delight, though so strongly and intensely felt in the flesh, symbolizes something beyond itself. For the pleasure one receives, as also the pleasure that one gives, is a pleasure that comes from, through, and by another person.

The fact that intercourse is with another person gives rise, of course, to the greatest pleasures in marriage. One is filled with joy as a newly-wed, for example, at being received by the person one most loves and respects precisely in and through one's sexual organs and powers. What was before, if not shameful, at least ambiguous, is now validated and made in the strongest sense acceptable. One's sexual desires and activity are now known as good, not merely in an intellectual way but through one's own experience of the beloved's pleasure produced by one's own sexual initiative or response. One's pleasure, then, is not an isolated pleasure centered on one's own body, validating nothing and generating shame. It is a pleasure of mind and heart in which the pleasure of another becomes one's own.

Yet, given our weakness, this interpersonal aspect imposes what we

sense as limitations or constraints upon us. There are times we would
desire to do things that, at least under the circumstances, should not
be done. There are things that, little as we feel like it at the moment,
we ought to do. This person is not simply an object that one is dealing
with—an object being by definition something one can take total possession of and use as he wishes, whatever the effects on the object. The
beloved is another person, of equal rights and stature, of equal dignity
before God. Hence, one is not free to use the other for one's pleasure
—or other purposes—nor even as one upon whom pleasure may be
imposed. Any attempt, obviously, to force the other person sexually
contradicts the signification of this built-in "limitation" on intercourse
that is constituted by the other person.

But there is another aspect of interpersonal limitation on intercourse.
No man is capable of giving all of himself to his wife. Even if he could,
he may not do so; he belongs to God. Similarly, no woman may give all
of herself to her husband. Neither spouse owns himself. Both spouses
love each other, are bound to each other; but only God truly possesses
either or can claim the total love of either. Total union with one who
is not God is impossible. And were it possible, it would be idolatry,
giving the creature the status of the divine. And on the other hand,
only God can own and take total possession of any person without
destroying or degrading that person.

Two human creatures, then, can never be so united that they are
only one, something that appears symbolically from the very fact that
the two bodies cannot melt into one another as they imagine at times
they desire to do. Any attempt to go beyond this limit produces only
pain and agony.

This physical separateness in union acts as a symbol of what occurs
at the psychic level. In the very act of intercourse there arises the realization that each is alone even when most intimately united with the
other. The love one seeks to express is known, in the very expressing
of it, to be inadequate. No love of a creature can take the place of the
love of God. This aloneness, then, is itself a symbol of an openness to
God—not merely as the agent who may create on this occasion another human being but as the only one who can truly satisfy one's love.
Through the other person, one is invited to love God more deeply and
more perfectly.

It is not that one should love the other person less in order to love

God more; rather, just because one loves God more, he loves more all those he loves. Indeed, the richness of God's infinite love makes up for and compensates for our own lack of goodness. One's partner is always a limited human being, who may not be able or willing to give the pleasures one desires to have or even to receive the pleasures one desires to give. And honesty compels the same admission of oneself. But knowing that God alone can satisfy all our desires, we can more easily bear with these limitations that serve to remind us of the Center of all love.

This physical act of union, however, remains always the symbolic expression of the desire for an ever deeper emotional and spiritual oneness with each other. Now, biologically, intercourse can, and frequently does, result in the fusion of the male principle with the female. When the act has thus its total consequences, a new human person comes into being. This fusion of the two principles is a further intensification of the union of the two partners in one flesh, the flesh of their child. At the same moment, as a union that they make possible but do not control, it signifies their subordination of themselves as parents to the growth and development of the child.

The child's symbolizing his parents' union has yet another aspect, one of anticipation and the desire to make one's partner a parent. Though intense in many cultures, including that of biblical Israel, this desire is much muted in our culture. Rarely strong, it is often not only absent but repudiated—with immeasurable loss for society as well as for individuals. Yet the symbolism remains, no less than the reality: the mystery of parenthood, which offers new strength and maturity to the personality of each and without which neither can realize all his natural potential. The fullness of bodily union continues to signify that fullness of mutual love that seeks the other's sexual perfecting through parenthood.

A wife desires, at least on the symbolic level, to give her husband the fullness of manhood, the gravity, the dignity, the sense of responsibility and sobriety that characterize a father. The husband, in turn, desires, as Abraham did for Sarah, to give his wife that particular richness, warmth, and fierce tenderness that are characteristic of a mother.

This union of man and woman, though so private in act, is manifested and made public through their children. A child is not merely conceived, he is to be nurtured and educated to take his place in the world. The parents' surrender and self-giving in sexual union, then, as ordered toward maturation and perfecting through children, both symbolizes and effects the whole communal structure of human society, built up through familial relationships into ever higher-level communities. Precisely as generative, moreover, sexual intercourse manifests the community of the successive generations of mankind, the common bonds that unite the children of Adam throughout all ages.

It is not surprising, then, that in no societies, save those decaying in the last stages of individualism, has marriage been considered a private affair. Everywhere it has been subject to social regulation and control. The private will of two people has never been adequate, by itself, to validate their union, whatever their love for one another.

In this context too, the limitations of the physical act are symbolic. Sexual intercourse is not in itself an act creative of a child; it is only procreative. Each parent contributes, from his own biological substance, to that unique and single gift that God may use for the creation of a new human person. But since the parents are not the creators of their child, they do not own the child, just as they do not own each other.

Thus, a sort of adoption must take place, a fact that is the ultimate basis for adoption in its ordinary sense. The adopted child, it is true, has genetic materials not found in his adoptive parents, and thus has a material substrate more different from theirs and from their natural children's than they do from one another. But, as a human person, the adopted child is no further from these adoptive parents than their natural offspring are.

Natural Marriage

All these things, and many others, are said simply by the act of intercourse itself. Only a rare person, however, who is going to understand, realize, and appreciate all these things, especially when he is as young as most people are when they marry. The meaning of marital union, of which we have glimpsed only a bit, is too rich for a young person just entering marriage to understand fully.

Nonetheless, he can know that some such richness of meaning is present. He can begin to see something of it, enough to desire it and to strive to turn this objective symbol that is his sexual union with his wife, or hers with her husband, into a word of love. Intercourse is meant to become a type of language by which husband and wife are able to express to each other all that they wish to say in the way of love and spiritual union.

To make this meaning fully one's own, one has to learn what that meaning is. The desire to do so, so as to be able to speak well this word of love, grounds the institution of marriage. Marriage, then, is the institution by which those who do not yet know how to say totally by their act of sexual intercourse all that sexual intercourse means bind themselves to live in such a way as to achieve that knowledge and understanding and to grow through practice into expressing in each marital act what are, at that moment, the most appropriate aspects, if not the totality, of that meaning.

Human beings are imperfect. Such an ideal will never be fully realized in this life. Nonetheless, the direction is clear and, through meeting and talking with older people who have been married for long years, one sees that the ideal can be well approximated. Because of just this imperfection, natural marriage is, with some qualifications, indissoluble. It cannot be broken up or dissolved, because there is no defect of love that can invalidate a solemn contract to overcome all of one's defects of love and to assist one's spouse in all ways possible to do the same. The ground for entering into this union is precisely the knowledge that both are defective in love's perfection, and that neither person is as yet able to intend fully what his body is already saying by the act of intercourse.

Whatever the other person's faults, then, they are always to be dealt with in love, tender or stern as the situation requires. But it is precisely to this love that one commits oneself by marriage.

Saying all this, of course, is much easier than doing it; and marriage requires great self-sacrifice. This is not to deny that intercourse is a healing balm emotionally for the inevitable minor irritations of early marriage while two people are attempting the difficult task of oneness in spirit, mind, and heart. Coming together in body presupposes and invites forgiveness of the small offenses that are the residue of the self-sufficiency that has ruled prior to marriage.

But not all is that simple. One is forced to grow, as each finds the defects in the other and, perhaps more painfully, in oneself. Marriage is meant to make it easier, however, because of one's love, to surmount such defects—to surmount them, since remedy may not be possible.

70 · The Meaning of Sexuality

Many defects in any person are permanent as long as this life lasts. It is, perhaps, especially hard for a husband to learn to rejoice in the woman whom God has given him, not as meeting some abstract ideal of his own but as she is in herself, something far greater than any adolescent dream: a real human person destined for eternal life with God.

The symbolism of sexual intercourse also shows us why marriage is essentially monogamous, meant to link only one man to only one woman. That a woman should have but one husband seems symbolically clear. No matter how many men, one after another, she might choose to open herself to, if she conceives at all, unlikely enough in those circumstances, it is the sperm cell from but one of those many partners that is joined with the ovum of her body to initiate a new human life. She cannot multiply the gift of her substance according to the number of men who lie with her. Psychologically also, a woman, even if promiscuous, tends to dream of one man to whom she might eventually give herself.

It is different for the man. As we have mentioned, a man can have fertile intercourse with many women. He can beget a child with each of them. So, polygamy—one man as husband for several wives—does not have the wrongness of polyandry—one woman as wife for several husbands. In much of human history and in many societies, polygamy has been well established, God permitting it for a long while even in Israel.

Hence one might think that the full symbolism would be present in each case; yet this is not quite true. For although the husband can multiply his activity and the giving of his substance, the gift of himself to one woman means deprivation for another. There is division, not unity. Polygamy is, then, a highly defective kind of marriage. For, ideally, at least, in a man's relations to one wife, their children, their neighbors, and God, none of the things he gives to one need be taken from another. The reason is that these loves can all be well ordered, one with respect to another. But the love that a man would have for several wives cannot be so ordered. He cannot give himself rightly to one without depriving another of the love she reasonably desires. Thus, monogamy is the proper form of even natural marriage, in the sense that it is the fullest and richest and that which most perfectly respects the symbolism of sexual union.

Natural marriage, then, is constituted by a reciprocal vow or promise

—at least to each other, perhaps to God—to do all things with love, not merely the act of intercourse itself but everything signified by this act, that is, the totality of their life together. Consequently, it also involves the right to receive everything in love.

When we look at our lives, we see that much of what we do, whether with respect to God or to other people, comes not from love but from selfishness. Hence, marriage is a commitment to grow in selflessness. It is a commitment to a sort of asceticism, and often to penitence and reparation for the evil things we sometimes do to one another. So we are enabled to grow and progressively to bring our selfishness under control by learning to give ourselves in selfless love to each other; through each other, to our children; and so to all men, all from an ever growing love for God.

Consequently, the act of intercourse is a symbol not merely of marriage in a static sense but of marriage as progress and as growth. For we can utter its full meaning only when we have learned, through asceticism and through penance, the self-control that is needed to get beyond our selfishness. Only then can we truly mean and fully intend in mind and heart what our act of intercourse actually says in and through a symbolism that, strong as it is naturally, has been charged by God with even greater meaning through his revelation.

4

SEXUAL SYMBOLISM
IN THE SCRIPTURES

Sexuality in Scripture

Since we wish to gain from Scripture an understanding of the meaning of our sexuality, especially in its relation to Christ, we should note first that Scripture speaks of sex in several ways.

There are many scriptural accounts of human sexual behavior, sometimes with comment, sometimes without. The Bible is forthright about such matters; and, although it does not emphasize sex, it does not hesitate to say what it means. We are told, for example, that David desired Bathsheba, had her brought to him, lay with her, made her pregnant, and had her husband murdered to prevent his discovering David's action. Such straightforward narratives about sexual activity, especially when, as in David's case, they are accompanied with God's judgment as to its wrongness or rightness, make clear to us some facts of a moral nature about sexual behavior. But they rarely do more than suggest the significance of sexual activity apart from those particular circumstances.

We learn much about God through knowledge of his Law, seeing what he has thought important to command or forbid us to do. From the commandment, "You shall not commit adultery", for example, we learn something of his concern for human fidelity in marriage. But, again, the reasons for the prohibition, its intrinsic meaning and reasonableness are left in the dark. There are many very detailed regulations concerning sexual matters in the books of the Law. In the New Testament, Saint Paul tosses off a whole series of injunctions for Christian sexual behavior, refining the Old Testament ones, omitting some, and adding others. But just such alterations raise serious questions as to whether or how far even his injunctions might be mutable as times change.

Yet the Bible has vastly more to say about sex than is contained in its narratives or laws. Chiefly by use of sexual symbolism, it tells us of the meaning of sex and offers grounds for understanding sexual morality. No symbol contains, however, the fullness of the reality it points to. It is never possible to find in the symbol all that is, in fact, true of the mystery that is symbolized. Hence, we are not trying here to construct a *proof* from the symbolism. Rather, accepting the Church's Tradition, we seek to see how her teaching is consistent with and enlightened by this symbolism. This latter cannot be treated as an independent source whence one could force a position on the Church. The Scriptures are to be understood, as Catholics have always sought to understand them, in the way the Church that wrote and collected them, identified and transmitted them, has understood them. If someone says, then, that our use of symbolism here is not coercive as an argument, we must agree; it is not meant to be.

First of all, we need to distinguish two kinds of sexual symbols that are easily confused. The more common "sexual symbols" are those, so much studied today in psychological and psychiatric circles, that are symbols *of* sexuality. That is, something that is not sexual is used as a symbol of something that is.

For example, the rose, which is not sexual as people ordinarily perceive it, is taken as a symbol of a woman's sexuality. The snake, for equally obvious reasons, is in many cultures taken as a symbol for a man's sexuality. Evidently, one may use such sexual symbols to avoid explicit or even conscious reference to sexual matters. And conversely, a psychiatrist may learn a patient's unconscious attitudes toward repressed sexual events through observation of his use of such symbols.

There are many such symbols in the Bible, the rose and the snake among them. But our interest here is not primarily with these. While they may illustrate more deeply the nature of sexual activity itself and not merely, as some wrongly assume, rehearse surreptitiously its physical description, yet they cannot go beyond that to the meaning and significance of that activity.

But there is another meaning of sexual symbols, that is, those that symbolize *by* or *through* sexuality. As seen in chapter 3, sex organs, sexual emotions and psychic reactions, the marital act itself, and even an entire marriage are symbols of things other than themselves and beyond themselves, of spiritual things that are not sexual at all.

This is the sort of sexual symbolism that Scripture is richest in. God uses the natural symbolism of our sexual activity and relationships to tell us much about himself and our relations with him. How this is done is best seen by turning to the Scripture and discovering how God has in fact revealed to us the supernatural meaning of sex.

Christ and His Bride

To begin at the beginning, we find in the second chapter of Genesis the story of the creation of Eve. In the Garden of Eden, God has just created man and is showing him the animals. "The man gave names to all cattle, and to the birds of the air, and to every beast of the field; but for the man there was not found a helper fit for him." (Gen 2:20).

In the ancient Semitic world, a name indicated a being's innermost nature or destiny. To give something a name, then, or to change its name meant to be able to know its inner nature, to govern it accordingly, and to determine its destiny. Here, then, man is being set over the animals; God is giving him the power to govern and even change them, and to share the divine dominion over them. But none was found that could be a helpmate for man and be his companion. Man is master of creation, but he is alone, for nothing in creation is his equal. Then

> the LORD God caused a deep sleep to fall upon the man, and while he slept took one of his ribs and closed up its place with flesh; and the rib which the LORD God had taken from the man he made into a woman and brought her to the man. (Gen 2:21–22)

God makes the woman from the man. Her being is drawn from his. Of the same species, they are equals. Though different, they are to be made one.

> Then the man said, "This at last is bone of my bones and flesh of my flesh; she shall be called Woman, because she was taken out of Man." Therefore a man leaves his father and his mother and clings to his wife, and they become one flesh. And the man and his wife were both naked, and were not ashamed. (Gen 2:23–25)

This is the first mention in the Scriptures of a symbolic theme that will be often repeated till their very end: that the sexual union of man and woman makes them two in one flesh. Here, the obvious sense of this theme is that the bodily union of man and woman in intercourse represents in some way and symbolizes the fullness of their psychological union as a couple and as parents, united not only in their own sexual union but in the flesh of their children.

In the time between this passage from Genesis and the great prophets who arose during the last years of the Divided Kingdom, the biblical teaching on the right use of one's sexual powers is set forth in great detail but always in purely secular terms.

For example, the sexual union of Abraham and Sarah, through which Isaac was conceived, is the first fulfillment of the promise that initiates the history of salvation. But their marriage, though approved and blessed by God, is not sacred except insofar as God protects it from infringement by the king of Egypt. Nor is their intercourse seen as a religious rite. Later, in the Law, there are many detailed prescriptions with regard to sexual behavior, prohibitions as well as things to be done. But there is no hint that there is anything sacred in any positive sense about what is sexual. On the other hand, even in marital union, any flow of seed seems to have made both partners ritually unclean.

The reason for this is that God himself has no sexuality. God is not male, though he is infinitely masculine. In his own nature he is spirit, without sexuality, which as such belongs only to creatures and, so, lies wholly outside the domain of religion and the sacred. This awareness was one of the major gifts of divine revelation to man's religious life upon earth. Divine sexuality was always to be a sign of paganism and idolatry.

It must have come, then, as a great surprise to the Israelites when suddenly the prophet Hosea was inspired to speak of Israel's relation to God in terms of human sexual union.

Hosea is the first to develop, bluntly and straightforwardly, another theme that continues through the rest of Scripture. This is the theme of the people of Israel as the unfaithful bride of the Lord, the God of Israel. Hosea begins abruptly by saying, "The LORD said to Hosea, 'Go, take to yourself a wife of harlotry and have children of harlotry, for the land commits great harlotry by forsaking the LORD'" (Hos 1:2). What he is talking about is their worship of idols, of the gods of the peoples around them, and their seeking to live in accord with the standards of their more powerful and cultured neighbors.

God continues:

Plead with your mother, plead—for she is not my wife, and I am not her husband—that she put away her harlotry from her face, and her adultery from between her breasts; lest I strip her naked and make her as in the day she was born. (Hos 2:2–3)

Then he threatens to take away from her everything he has given her. Notice the strong sexual symbolism he is using here, of a wife engaging in prostitution, opening herself to every comer. This symbol itself is sexual, but it is chosen to illustrate something spiritual, to represent in human terms the horror of unfaithfulness to God. Sexual misconduct is included among the sins for which Israel is being rebuked, but only as one item among many. The great crime is that they have gone after idols; if they are unjust to the poor, are liars, thieves, adulterers, all this is just one or another way of denying the Lord's sovereignty by rejecting his commandments in the service of alien gods.

He continues:

She shall pursue her lovers, but not overtake them; and she shall seek them, but shall not find them. Then she shall say, "I will go and return to my first husband, for it was better with me then than now." (Hos 2:7)

This, of course, was forbidden by the Law. If a wife, divorced by her husband, married another, she could never return to the former husband. If he took her back, both became unclean. But the Lord is above his Law.

Therefore, behold, I will allure her, and bring her into the wilderness, and speak tenderly to her. . . . And there she shall answer as in the days of her youth, as at the time when she came out of the land of Egypt. [And now speaking to Israel directly,] And in that day . . . you will call me "My husband". . . . And I will espouse you for ever; I will espouse you in righteousness and in justice, in steadfast love, and in mercy. I will espouse you to me in faithfulness; and you shall know the LORD. (Hos 2:14–20)

Clearly, the symbolism has gone well beyond that of an adulterous wife, God is taking back his unfaithful people to himself, as a husband might take back a wife he loves in spite of her unfaithfulness. Infidelity to the Lord is to be understood only through this symbol of adultery, this rending of the most intimate of human bonds; and God's for-giveness, only through the outrageous violation of the Law by a love-smitten husband taking back the adulteress. God uses marital union and sexual infidelity to symbolize relations that completely transcend the sexual, his love and permanent fidelity toward his people, in spite even of their idolatry.

This theme is developed at length through the rest of the Old Testament and also the New. Ezekiel, to give but one example, tells us more about the original wedding, tells us how Israel had been begotten by a wandering Aramean of a Hittite mother, how (referring to Israel's being led out of Egypt and the long journey through the desert) the Lord had picked her up, washed her of her blood, let her grow up, and then said:

> And you grew up and became tall and arrived at full maidenhood; your breasts were formed, and your hair had grown; yet you were naked and bare.
>
> When I passed by you again and looked upon you, behold, you were at the age for love; and I spread my skirt over you, and covered your nakedness: yes, I pledged myself to you and entered into a covenant with you, says the Lord GOD, and you became mine. Then I bathed you with water and washed off your blood from you, and anointed you with oil. I clothed you also with embroidered cloth and shod you with leather, I wrapped you in fine linen and covered you with silk. And I decked you with ornaments, and put bracelets on your arms, and a chain on your neck. And I put a ring on your nose, and earrings in your ears, and a beautiful crown upon your head. (Ezek 16:7–12.)

Thus, the Lord recalls his wedding with Israel, his dearly beloved, his bride, although she had since proven so often adulterous and had fornicated so often with idols and alien gods.

The final, and, in some ways, the strongest Old Testament presentation of this attitude of God toward his people is found in the *Song of Solomon*, a book that sometimes gives offense to Christians. It is filled with glowing, incandescent love poetry, sensuous and rich, strongly sexual in its imagery. There is no mistaking its natural meaning.

Yet, in another sense, there has been a great mistake as to its meaning. Many people see nothing in it beyond its sensuality. But Jewish and Christian traditions have agreed in seeing that this love poetry, whatever its original sources, was interpreted by the author as God's love song for his people and theirs for him, as his rejoicing in his bride and her rejoicing in him. It is the bright reflection in the present of a future in which God and Israel will be made perfectly one with each other—Israel no longer unfaithful, seeking only the Lord even when he seems to have vanished and she cannot find him, not turning aside after anyone else.

The impact of all this on Israel was very deep. The fidelity of the Lord to his one bride despite her faults and infidelities began to make clear to his people the ideal of human marriage, that this too could only be monogamous, one husband with one wife. The perfection of monogamy, which would also ban remarriage after divorce, was to come only with the Messiah, our Lord Jesus, who alone could give to his Church the fullness of grace that this ideal would require. Yet ordinary polygamy did wither away in the Judaism of the last centuries before Christ as God's people began to understand more fully this symbol of God's love.

Some people may say, "Well, that's fine for the Old Testament. The Jews were a carnal people." One difficulty with this reaction is that one finds as much sexual symbolism in the New Testament, though the image is changed slightly. Instead of Israel's being described as the bride of the Lord, it is the Church, the New Israel, that is presented as the bride of Christ.

In the Gospels, our Lord makes frequent use of the traditional sexual imagery of the Old Testament. Thus, he often speaks of "an adulterous generation", a phrase that has become so commonplace that we hardly advert to its meaning any longer. What he means by it is precisely what the prophets meant, that his generation of Jews were in fact committing adultery, though this time not with idols. Their refusal to accept Christ, their refusal to see in him at least a prophet sent by God, showed that Israel's heart was fixed elsewhere and, consequently, was adulterous. She was once again faithless.

Further, Jesus uses nuptial imagery often in speaking of the kingdom of heaven. "The kingdom of heaven may be compared to a king who gave a marriage feast for his son" (Mt 22:2), where of course the king is God the Father and his Son is our Lord. Or, again, the kingdom is like ten virgins waiting for the bridegroom to return from the wedding feast to take his bride into his house (see Mt 25:1).

Even John the Baptist, that rugged ascetic out in the desert, subsisting on grasshoppers and wild honey, clothed in rough camel's hair, refers to Christ in just such terms. When John's disciples indignantly asked how it was that Jesus also was baptizing and drawing people away from John, he replied,

> You yourselves bear me witness, that I said, I am not the Christ, but I have been sent before him. He who has the bride is the bridegroom; the friend of the bridegroom, who stands and hears him, rejoices greatly at the bridegroom's voice; therefore this joy of mine is now full. He must increase, but I must decrease. (Jn 3:28–30)

He is referring to Christ our Lord as the bridegroom of Israel and of all his Church.

Saint Paul takes up the same theme in several places. Most important for our purposes is the passage in Ephesians, where he instructs us that husbands are to love their wives

> as Christ loved the Church and gave himself up for her, that he might sanctify her, having cleansed her by the washing of water with the word [referring to baptism on the one hand and to the Jewish prenuptial bath on the other] that he might present the Church to himself in splendor, without spot or wrinkle or any such thing, that she might be holy and without blemish. Even so, husbands should love their wives as their own bodies. He who loves his wife loves himself. For no man ever hates his own flesh, but nourishes and cherishes it, as Christ does the Church, because we are members of his body. [Now, referring back to Genesis] "For this reason a man shall leave his father and mother and be joined to his wife, and the two shall become one flesh." This is a great mystery, and I mean in reference to Christ and the Church. (Eph 5:25–32)

Notice here he has mixed two metaphors, two images of the Church. The Church is the Bride of Christ; as members of the Church, therefore, we are made members of his body because he is one flesh with her.

Saint Paul uses this same theme in exhorting his Corinthians against fornication.

> Do you not know that he who joins himself to a prostitute becomes one body with her? For, as it is written, "The two shall become one." But he who is united to the Lord becomes one spirit with him (1 Cor 6:16–17).

The union of Christ with his Church, then, affects each of us individually. Since a man's sexual union with a woman, even in fornication, makes the two of them one flesh, the Christian may not fornicate, because to do so would be to join Christ's body, whose member he is, to the body of a whore. So strongly does Saint Paul see the one union to be the symbol of the other!

This imagery is brought to its fullness when we come to Revelation, where we find that our final union with God in heaven is described in the same way.

> "Hallelujah! For the Lord our God the Almighty reigns. Let us rejoice and exult and give him the glory, for the marriage of the Lamb [that is, the Lamb of God, the Lamb standing as slain forever] has come and his Bride has made herself ready; it was granted her to be clothed with fine linen, bright and pure"—for the fine linen is the righteous deeds of the saints. . . . "Blessed are those who are invited to the marriage supper of the Lamb." (Rev 17:6–9)

And in describing the consummation of all things, he says:

> Then I saw a new heaven and a new earth; for the first heaven and the first earth had passed away, and the sea was no more. And I saw the holy city, new Jerusalem, coming down out of heaven from God, prepared as a bride adorned for her husband. (Rev 21:1–2)

Heaven, to which all of us look forward, the consummation of the world, is shown to us as the wedding, the marriage feast of Christ to and with his Church, the consummation of that union in eternity.

Father, Mother, and Children

If we look carefully at the scriptural passages that deal with the spousal relations between God and his people or between Christ and his Church, we find that most of them say nothing at all about children, even when, as in Ephesians 5:22–33, for example, children are talked about in the verses immediately following. Further, where children *are* mentioned, they are not begotten of that spousal relationship.

This strange omission of children from the sexual symbolism we have seen in the Bible so far is balanced, however, by two other scriptural symbolisms: maternity and adoptive paternity.

From at least the time of the prophet Hosea, the Old Testament speaks of God as Father, as the One who has brought Israel to be. A few examples will suffice.

Hosea writes: "When Israel was a child, I [the Lord] loved him, and out of Egypt I called my son. . . . It was I who taught Ephraim to walk", (11:1–3). In Isaiah we find, "The LORD has spoken: 'Sons have I reared and brought up. . . .' Ah, sinful nation, a people laden with iniquity, offspring of evildoers, sons who deal corruptly!" (1:2, 4). Note how, within three verses God speaks of the people of Judah as sons he has reared and yet as the sinful offspring of evildoers. Already, we can see that God's children are his by adoption. Their natural birth as human individuals is attributed to their human parents; God is not called their Father because of creation.

In Deuteronomy, Moses says of Israel,

> They are no longer his children because of their blemish. . . . Is not he your father, who created you, who made you and established you? . . . Ask your father, and he will show you. . . . [Again, God's fatherhood is not that of their natural fathers. Though the creation of each person in the womb may be a factor in his fatherhood, this is more likely a reference to his creating them as his own people.] You were unmindful of the Rock that begot you, and you forgot the God who gave you birth. The LORD saw it and spurned them, because of the provocation of his sons and daughters. And he said, "I will hide my face from them . . . for they are . . . children in whom is no faithfulness." (32:5, 6, 7, 18–20)

Much later, Isaiah prays to the Lord, "For You are our Father, though Abraham does not know us. . . . You, O LORD, are our Father" (Is 63:16; cf. 64:8).

Only in Ezekiel does one find a link between the symbolism of fatherhood and that of husband and wife. Even this is indirect, by way of the symbolism of the motherhood of Jerusalem. Thus, the Lord says, "You took your sons and your daughters, whom you had borne to me, and these you sacrificed to them [idols] to be devoured. . . . You slaughtered my children" (Ezek 16:20–21). There is a similar language again in Ezekiel 23:4, 37.

The notion that his people bears children for God, then, though visible in the Old Testament, is much muted. There is, however, even in these passages of Ezekiel, no direct begetting by God of the children of his spouse. The basic relationship, though the word is not used, is that of adoption. Born naturally of human parents, they are made his when he espouses Jerusalem, their mother. She has borne them for him, but not by him.

With the coming of our Lord, there is a sudden clarity of focus. The same sexual symbolisms recur. But now the relationships become much more complex, for God is revealed to be not only Father but Son and Holy Spirit, only one Being yet three distinct Persons.

There is only one Father, from whom not only every family and lineage but every fatherhood and all those called father take their name (Mt 23:9; Eph 3:14–15). There is only one natural begetting by him, the eternal generation of his eternal Son and Word, Jesus Christ (for example, Jn 1:1–5, 18).

We are made children of the Father by being made the brothers of Jesus, not as if the Father begot sons other than Jesus, but by being given a share in the life of Jesus (Gal 3:26–27). Thus, with the sole exception of Jesus, his Only Begotten, all the children of God are *adopted* (for example, Gal 4:5; Rom 8:23, 29–30).

This adoption, however, unlike all human adoption, gives a new principle of life, the Holy Spirit. (Hence, in his first letter especially, Saint John speaks of our adoption as our being born or begotten of God, a phrase he never applies to our Lord.) The Holy Spirit is the Spirit of the Father, who has given him to Jesus triumphant—for he is also the Spirit of the Son—to give to us. The Spirit, then, as the Spirit of Jesus, cries out, "Abba! Father!" within our hearts as he did in Christ's heart (Rom 8:13–17). It is the Spirit who makes us sons of God, by making us one with Christ, the only Son (see Jn 3:3–8). The reality here lies painfully far beyond and above all symbols; but they can still give us endless light if we use them as the Church would have us do.

But there is another symbolism needed here, for to God's adoptive fatherhood the Bible adds the corresponding motherhood of the Church. As in the Old Testament, our adoption takes place in principle when God takes his people as his bride. This was done, once for all, when Christ died for her on the Cross (Eph 5:25–27).

But Christ is nowhere said to beget children of his Church: He is the Son, not the Father of anyone. He enters into no sexual union with his Bride. (This, it is important to understand, does no damage to the spousal symbolism. The sexual union between husband and wife is, indeed, the best symbol we have for the quality of love between Christ and his Church. Yet Christ's love for the Church is not sexual, though a man's love for his wife, which is sexual, can be more like Christ's love for the Church than any other natural love a man may have.)

The question then is: How do we become her children if the Son does not generate children of the Church for the Father? For she is without spot or wrinkle, and we are born into this world outside of her and in sin. Natural birth does not suffice, as it did among the Israelites, to make us members of his people.

As just seen, Christ's union with her leaves her still a virgin. The ancient tradition of the Church has, therefore, compared her to Mary. She brings forth virginally, as Mary did, the members of Christ's Body. Just as the Holy Spirit was the agent of the Father's begetting of the human nature of the Son of the virginal Mary, so he is the agent of the Father's regenerating us of the virginal Church into the life of Christ. Thus, we can be truly said to be born of the Spirit (Jn 3:9).

In sum, we find, from the first page of the Scriptures to the last, the varied aspects of man's sexual life being used to symbolize the relationships between God and his people. Man's vocation and dignity, his sins, his redemption, and final glorification are presented to us under the imagery of birth, marriage, infidelity, penitence, a renewal of vows, and a final reunion, which becomes perfect union in eternity. This symbolism all of us must understand, for it shows us what God thinks of our sexuality: something so good that it can be used to express the deepest and the highest truths about the relations between God and man.

5

THE CHURCH: BRIDE OF CHRIST
AND MOTHER OF THE LIVING

We have seen how natural marriage is the institutional expression of the natural meaning of sexual intercourse. In the sacrament of matrimony, Christ takes up this natural marriage to symbolize something far beyond it. Even as intercourse symbolizes marriage, as bodily union signifies an entire life together, so God has made natural marriage to symbolize something that lies entirely beyond the sexual: the relations between Christ and his Church, and the Father's adopting us as his children through Christ's gift of the Spirit to his bride. God has made marriage to symbolize relationships more intimate than its own sexual relationship, stronger, more tender, more open, more demanding. This sacramental symbolism involves all that is present in the marital relationship but gives it a further meaning at a level of communion in which there is no possibility of sexual activity.

Christ's Unmerited Love for His Church

Christ's love was not given to the Church for any merit on her own part. The Father freely chose this people as his Son's Bride; and Christ loves her because she is the Father's choice for him. He had to win her for himself by his battle with Satan upon the Cross. He espoused her there when his side was pierced, his Heart was opened, and water flowed forth, the sign of the bridal bath of baptism. He had not found her worthy of himself; only his death made her to be a Bride without spot or wrinkle or any such thing. Her beauty was his gift alone.

As a husband with his wife, Christ is the initiator of union with his Church. As God is masculine with respect to the whole of his creation and with respect to the whole of humanity, Christ is masculine with regard to his Church. The Church has no initiative in relation to Christ except that which Christ has already given to her. Without his grace, she can do nothing.

Christ takes pleasure in his Church as a husband takes pleasure in his Bride. Finding his delight in her, he seeks to share with her all his gifts. Since he experiences the Church's happiness as his own, he gives to her everything that he has to offer to mankind. Only through her, though often in ways that are not visible to us, do his gifts reach the world of men. Those who have somewhat scornfully pinned the tag "triumphalism" on her claim that Christ has loved her this much show merely that they do not share very strongly his love for her.

Chief of his gifts is the Holy Spirit. Through the Spirit, he guards the Church from harm and keeps her faithful to himself. By the power of his Spirit, he maintains her in purity of doctrine and worship. By the Spirit's action, the Church conceives and bears children for the Father. Since through the Spirit we live with Christ's own life, we are nurtured and brought to spiritual maturity under her guidance and love.

The Church, on the other hand, must be receptive of grace and has to respond to the love Christ has shown her. She may not be simply passive. If one needs any argument against a woman's being passive in marriage, one would find it right here, for that which she symbolizes through her part in the marital act is the Church's response to Christ. Passivity as her "response" would destroy this symbolism. (The one exception would occur when, by her husband's engaging in something evil, the act has already been so changed in what it symbolizes that any active response by her would signify cooperation in evil.)

The Church responds to Christ to give him pleasure, having her sole pleasure in him and in the fact that he takes pleasure in her response. From this, we can see that the Church's interest in seeking new members is not simply fear that those who are not visibly hers will be lost.

Not only Christians today, after Vatican II, but the Old Testament and the Church Fathers knew that God had revealed himself beyond the limits of Israel, as he did, for example, to the pharaohs known by Abraham and by Joseph, to Balaam, and to the Babylonian kings in the book of *Daniel*. They knew that God gives to every man the grace to be saved, even though he has not heard of Christ from other men.

Neither, however, does the Church so disesteem her Lord's fidelity as to think that all have access to him and to salvation if not, somehow, through her. Her apostolate has an urgency that implies much more than bringing to others mere academic knowledge of Christ, or theological theories about him.

If the Church is so concerned to bring ever more people to the knowledge of Christ, it is so that she may bring forth for the Father through his Spirit all those whom Christ desires as his brothers. There is no race, there are no cultures, there are no tribes or languages that are naturally alien to her. All are meant to be within her; all are meant to be her children. As the Fathers of the Church said repeatedly, "He alone has God as Father who first has the Church as mother."

Christ's Fidelity to His Church

As seen in chapter 3, sexual intercourse symbolizes the fidelity that is institutionalized in natural marriage. In the sacrament of matrimony, this natural fidelity is made to symbolize the fidelity of God himself. Christ's union with his Church is wholly incapable of dissolution. There is no way it can be undone in time or in eternity, for Christ cannot be faithless. He is always faithful even when we are unfaithful. He cannot go back on his covenant with his Church, no matter how faithless the Church may seem to be in the eyes of the world because of the sins of her children. He knew that we would not be fully faithful, and he died to deliver us from the evils of our unfaithful hearts.

At this point one might object and argue that divorce with remarriage is indeed possible, for the Lord has changed wives himself. He was first wedded to Israel but has now abandoned her. Because she was unfaithful and rejected him, he has divorced her and married the Church of the Gentiles.

But he has not abandoned Israel. Saint Paul tells us that Israel is an olive tree from which the branches have been broken off through their own fault. We, the branches of wild olive trees, were incapable of bearing any fruit except what is bitter and hard, of no use at all. But through our being made one with Christ, we have been grafted into the still-standing trunk of Israel, the trunk of the patriarchs, prophets, and kings. Thus, we have been enabled to bear fruit that is sweet and good.

By being incorporated into Christ, we are the new Israel, but only in the sense that we are made one with the old, being new growth from the same roots and trunk. The branches that have been broken off are no longer drawing life from the trunk of Israel, though still calling themselves by that name. But God in his fidelity wishes to bring them back and graft them in again, for, just as a branch broken off a tree can still live with what remains in it of the life of the tree and even after a time can still be saved if it is grafted back in, so, Saint Paul tells us, God will graft back these branches.

There remains, then, only the one true people of God. The Church is not a new bride. We now see that she has indeed to be described less statically than she herself once thought, when her only children had but one lineage. The changes brought by her growth and maturation have been more surprising and disconcerting than those changes a girl undergoes at puberty. But they are the same sort of changes: those she has needed to become ready to bear children. So the Church is Israel grown up, become mature, and bearing children for the Father from among the Gentiles.

And when Israel according to the flesh reaches her supernatural maturity, when those who are Jews by carnal generation finally recognize their Lord and come to him, then all the promises to Israel will be fulfilled. This will also be the fulfillment of all that he has given to the Gentiles. It will be, Saint Paul says, "life from the dead" (Rom 11:15), the consummation and perfection of the Church, when his Bride will be radiant in the beauty of all her children as well as in herself.

The fundamental limitations on bodily union in sexual relations symbolize, we have seen, reverence and awe for one's partner, who has been created for God and is owned by him alone. Such reverence signifies in its turn Christ's reverence and respect for the freedom of his Church. He permits the Church to go her own way—here we are speaking of the local churches, for the Church Universal, like Mary, is indefectible by God's special favor, though always free. The local church will suffer for her sins. She will go into exile from those regions where she is unfaithful. Always, however, there is the promise that, as with ancient Israel, if she returns, he will forgive. The words of the prophets remain true for the new Israel as well as for the old.

Our Sexuality in the Light of Christ's Mysteries

All these things apply to each of us individually as members of the Church. As we come to understand these mysteries somewhat, we will find that they teach us much more than we have yet understood about our own sexuality. The supernatural perfection that is symbolized by marital union will reflect its splendor back upon our own sexual activity and make us see things not visible except to those who know by faith its ultimate meaning.

Only in this context does Christ's teaching against divorce with remarriage make sense. Sacramental marriage is not just the union of man and woman, still weak in love, seeking to sustain and help one another. Nor is it, as often thought, a mere contract between the two parties. Christian marriage is part of a solemn covenant, not so much with each other as with Christ.

For Christ's espousal of his Bride upon the Cross was the sealing of the New Covenant in his blood. The children of this covenant enter into it, then, and ratify it in their own persons by their marriage, as they image forth and symbolically represent Christ's marriage to his Church. This is the ultimate reason why husband and wife are called to sacrifice themselves, as far as death, if need be, for the true good of one another. For our Lord commanded us, "Love one another as I have loved you" (Jn 15:12); and the way he loved us was to sacrifice himself for the unfaithful upon the Cross. As each Mass renews this sacrifice and as each Communion strengthens Christ's union with his Bride, so Christian marriage is the sacramental representation of the covenant of eternal love Christ has entered into with his Church.

Thus, Christ's own fidelity is engaged to enable husband and wife always to be faithful. If they will genuinely rely on this covenant that God has made with them through his Son, lean on his promise, trust the fidelity that is eternal and immutable, no matter what the circumstances, then their fidelity is assured as they transcend their own weaknesses in him. His Spirit, whom Saint Paul calls the "down payment", the "deposit", the "pledge", is given already as the bond of their espousal (see 1 Cor 1:22).

Corresponding to the giving of one person to the other through the gift of a man's substance to his wife, we have God's gift of himself to us through his Holy Spirit, who pours out the love of the Father in our hearts and who makes us sharers in the life of Christ by grace. We give ourselves to the Father, in turn, through the same Spirit, by responding to his grace actively even as a woman opens herself to her husband in love.

So, all of us, whatever our walk of life, when we seek to find the will of Christ for us, it is to give him the pleasure of our serving him as we should, of doing the things for him that will give him pleasure; and we find joy in that. "In his will is our peace."[1]

As Christ has the sole initiative in relation to his Church, so there is nothing that we can do to initiate any process with regard to God or to our Lord. It is Catholic doctrine, solemnly defined as far back as the sixth century, that we cannot desire any grace unless God has already given us his grace to desire it, that we cannot in any way long to repent or seek sorrow for our sins unless God has already given us the grace to do so. He alone can take the initiative; only he can convert us.

In fact, he need not wait upon our willingness. If he does not take the initiative, we will be unwilling and firmly set against any conversion. But his grace can still reach us and open us up and make it possible for us to be converted. Sooner or later, he does require our response, our cooperation; but the initiative is solely and exclusively his.

This doctrine gives us further proof of his love. By it we are taught that all our longings for his joy and peace and all our desires to know and love him better and to serve him more faithfully are signs of his love already at work. The mere presence of holy desires indicates an initiative that he has already taken. And yet Christ's love is like the love of a husband for his wife in this also, that it is a free love. The husband's love, unless it is no more than passion, results from a decision. He need not have offered it in the first place, though he has obligated himself now to love, in spite of all, because he freely promised to do so. So Christ has done for us.

Knowing that they only procreate their children, good parents do not act as if they own them. They respect their freedom, according to their age and education, despite the pain that this respect for their freedom may cause them when the time comes for them to leave their parents' home to found their own. This parental respect symbolizes in

---

[1] Dante, *Paradiso*, canto 3, line 85.

its turn God's respect for our freedom and for us as persons. Although he could, God does not coerce the human will. At the moment of our death he will say to each of us, "Now, let your will be done!" And if our will then is to refuse him our love and service and to insist upon our own ways rather than his, those will be the most terrible words a human heart can hear. Though he died in torment to prevent it, he will let us have our choice.

The symbolism of Christian marriage reaches even as far as the Beatific Vision—that absolute and perfect union of man with God that constitutes our utter happiness—that Scripture describes as the wedding feast of the Lamb and the final consummation of his marriage with his Church. The Church will then be united with her Spouse in a spiritual ecstasy far beyond all marital ecstasy as she enters the joy of her Lord. As Saint Paul says, "God may be everything to every one" (1 Cor 15:28). God, on his part, will rejoice totally in his creatures now made perfect, now fully his, now at last what he intended them to be from the beginning, in every way in his image, Jesus our Lord, and according to the likeness that is his Spirit.

But far beyond all created things, there is the life of the Trinity, the eternal giving of the three Persons to one another. The Father gives the totality of the divine nature to the Son, giving him everything that he, the Father, has except simply his being Father. The Father, through the Son, gives the totality of the nature that they possess in common to the Holy Spirit, who receives actively their gift so as to be one being with them, except for that which constitutes them Father or Son. It is this life of total gift and of total response that is the ultimate thing symbolized by the act of sexual intercourse. This is its tremendous sacredness, its tremendous intrinsic holiness.

With this background, we can now understand the basic principle of Christian sexual morality: We ought so to engage in the natural sexual activity of body, mind, and heart that its basic symbolic structure is always preserved and honored, so that this structure may serve rightly to symbolize in turn the relations, in the Spirit of the Father, between Christ and his Church. If God has created marital union to signify these great mysteries of the faith, how great a responsibility, then, lies on married couples (and, in their own way, on all the unmarried) so to act that this meaning and significance is fully preserved in their action and is meant and intended by them!

This principle contains within itself, I think, the full range of all Catholic sexual morality. It explains, too, why the Church has held the positions she has held in all those varying domains where people had thought her inconsistent, holding one thing as to one type of human sexual behavior and something else as to another. No, if understood from this point of view, all her teaching falls in place as simple and consistent. Christ is the norm. His relations to his Father and to his Bride, the Church, form the norms for union among Christians in their marriages and families. Indeed, as possibly suggested already by the examples we have considered, those relations are norms for all sexual behavior whatever.

6

CHRIST ON THE CROSS:
SEXUAL LIES AND COUNTERFEITS

We have spoken of the symbolism of sexual intercourse, of both its natural meaning and the meaning it has in the order of grace and redemption. We have seen that intercourse expresses its full meaning only in marriage and that marriage is the institution that crystallizes the intent, the purpose, and the resolve of the two parties to discover together and to express fully to each other the integral meaning of this act.

But more than marriage is explained by the symbolism of sexual activity. The entire range of moral problems that all people confront in this domain can receive here a unified and straightforward explanation. We will consider first what makes certain sexual actions wrong even at the natural level; then we will look at each again from the point of view of God's revelation.

Natural Symbolism of Misuse of Sex

On the natural level, what God asks of us is that we truly "do what comes naturally". This is not a matter of mere spontaneous liking and desire, but of what is in accordance with the nature he has given us. For our nature is a share in his, even apart from the life of grace, since our nature and entire being is made according to the Image of God, which is Christ.

At this level, we can restate the principle mentioned at the end of the preceding chapter: We may never use sexual activity, the living and naturally symbolic language of marital love, to tell a lie; nor may we ever corrupt it by using our sexual powers and organs for actions that are only seemingly sexual, but whose meaning has been radically altered.

Lies

The first type of abuse of the sexual powers, then, is falsehood. The "word" one says is integral; the symbol is undamaged. One's sexual activity is in full conformity on the physical level with the way such actions should be done. One says, "I love you" with his body, but his mind is saying something else. The genuine "word" of love is used to tell a lie.

Consider adultery, for example. The man and the woman committing the adultery are having intercourse, usually lovingly and in such a way that no one could tell from watching them that they are not married. But though they are saying in the symbolic language of the body, "I am wholly yours, yours alone, forever", at least one of them knows that this is not true. At least one cannot give himself to the other since he already belongs to someone else. At least one is wrenching apart his bond of commitment to his spouse and attempting to confer the gift of self upon this other party. It is a lie, and a great lie, a falsehood that is able on the natural level to undercut a marriage and destroy it.

Usually less grave, but an all-too-common sin of falsehood within marriage itself, is the act of intercourse done without charity. This is most obvious when a husband forces sex upon his wife against her will. So doing, he makes the symbol of love serve for coercion, whereas true love reveres freedom; for personal satisfaction only, whereas love is for another; or for contempt or even hatred, the antitheses of love.

But a man can fail in charity also if he is inattentive to his wife's needs and pleasure during intercourse. Perhaps a minute after obtaining his own satisfaction, without regard to hers, he is snoring. On the other hand, a wife who deliberately chooses to be cold, even frigid, toward her husband or who, without grave reason, refuses to cooperate with him sins against charity. In such cases there is a withholding of the love that is symbolized by their actions; there is a rejection, in one way or another, of the personal element in the symbol; one is taking for oneself rather than giving to the other. What they mean by their act of intercourse is not what that intercourse means of itself.

Today, there is a widespread abuse grounded on the state's claim to grant a true divorce, that is, to dissolve a genuine and valid marriage so completely that the former spouses are free henceforth to enter into new and valid marriages with new partners. But, in fact, whatever power the state may have over the marriages of the unbaptized, it has no power whatever to dissolve a Christian marriage. What really happens in most cases is that those who have pledged themselves permanently to each other to overcome all their defects of love reject this pledge and seek to break the covenant because of these very defects that they have solemnly undertaken to overcome together. Hence, their pledge to their new partners is a lie, since its sole basis is their refusal to honor such pledges. Their act of intercourse has become an adultery.

A different falsehood enters into the sin of fornication, that is, when two people, as yet unmarried even though perhaps engaged, have intercourse with each other. They sin because they are saying by their act, "I am yours totally, irrevocably, forever", and yet in fact they know that, though they love each other, their gift is transient, that it is not complete. They know that they do not mean by this word of love what it means in itself. If they did mean it, they would be married, right on the spot, by common-law marriage; and they know that such is not their intention—or, if their intention, not within their power.

There is, of course, fornication that falls many moral levels below that, between two people who love one another, even if not as much as they think they do. Promiscuity, bedding down with one "lover" after another, picking up somebody at a party or on the street, prostitution, and so forth are far removed from truly human relationships. Indicating, at root, one's own selfishness and a contempt for other persons, such barefaced lies exclude from the sexual act almost everything God intended to be there except, at best, mere physical pleasure.

These actions spring from a sort of adolescent insecurity in the person that makes him seek out whatever prop he can find with which to bolster himself against this insecurity and to substitute for the adult person he feels lacking within himself. Having no sense of true personal identity, lacking "faces" in their own perception, such people engage in what might be called a faceless intercourse, often literally such. They are not interested enough in others as persons to want to see their faces; they themselves dread being seen as persons by others. Hence flow all the means used by profligates to keep their intercourse from becoming too personal.

The Substitute Symbol

On the other hand, there are abuses of the sexual powers that so alter the basic structures of sexual activity that the resultant actions have

new and quite different meanings. The very nature of the act of intercourse is changed. Some fraud, some forgery, some shoddy substitute
is passed off in place of the splendor of the integral act.

These altered acts are not necessarily lies; that is, the person who
performs such an act need not mean something different from what
that action means in itself. What is said by the altered symbol may be
in fact a true statement made by the person using it; his mind and heart
may be in accord with what he does sexually, though this need not
be the case. But what he is saying is, itself, whether so intended or
not, corrupt and evil because he has perverted and undone the nature
of the sexual act. If the perfection of human nature is genuine and
unflawed love, then acts that corrupt the bodily signs of such love are
evil. Whether or not they are also used for telling lies, they symbolize
some corruption of love or some refusal of love.

Consider the evil of masturbation. Though not a symbol of love at
all, it is a symbol nonetheless: of withdrawal from reality, of self-pitying
loneliness, of the sterility of the self loved in itself. What was meant
for fertility, children, and family, the root and source of life and human
community, is turned into a mechanism for pleasure, relief of tension,
or material to use in a laboratory analysis or a sperm bank. Hence,
masturbation is a symbol of fear and anxiety—of fear to love, of anxiety with regard to other people, withdrawing from them and seeking
to live without them. Evidently, it symbolizes frustration. For there is
no person to receive the power that is in the man's wasted seed; the
woman's stimulation and orgasm result in nothing beyond themselves.
Masturbation binds the person doing it to no one, but states symbolically personal ineffectiveness. One desires to avoid the risk of love and
the responsibility of fruitfulness; he wishes to be by himself or, more
tragically, passionately desires to love and to be loved yet chooses to
be alone.

It is obvious, therefore, why masturbation can quickly become a
habit. The person who performs such an act knows at least subcon-
sciously what it symbolizes. He feels as a result deep shame, degrada-
tion, or inadequacy. These feelings increase his isolation and frustration
and generate still stronger pressure to state in action his desperation,
even without pleasure. One sin begets another.

Masturbation, then, poisons human happiness. It is almost impossible for anyone enslaved to such a habit to enter into marriage posi-

tively and fruitfully because masturbation chops away, at their roots, the love, the outgoingness, the generosity, and the openness to life and to responsibility that the true sexual act is meant to have.

To cure a habit of this sort requires a real effort, under the competent direction, encouragement, and skillful advice of one's confessor, for the problem is usually not principally a question of chastity or sexual purity. Masturbation is linked to everything in a person, to the entire personality and emotions; all aspects of one's life are in some way tied in to that act. The whole person is somehow frustrated, anxious, unwilling to love. But the rewards for making the effort to cure this habit are great. As this slavery is overcome, one becomes master of himself and can grow at last to adulthood.

The symbolic structure of homosexual activity is similarly corrupt. What is ostensibly a symbol of love between two men or two women contains nothing that can truly be received, personally and as abiding gift, by the other person. It is a shallow symbol: of sentimentality, of perpetual juvenility and adolescent ambiguity, of not really knowing which sex one is, and of a sense of sexual inadequacy. Hence, those who so act will typically try to get closer to those of their own sex in order to discover and find themselves in these others rather than in their own selves. Or a man will seek weakly to draw or extract from others what he senses he lacks, rather than to acknowledge his responsibility for accepting its presence, already within him at least in germ, and so to grow to his own proper maturity.

Far more profoundly, there is no gift of one's substance for fruitfulness, no openness to the creation of human life. Each remains essentially alone. There is no true entry into the other as person, no lasting gift of oneself to the other, no genuine receptivity. All remains on the surface; each is the same after the act as before. In homosexual activity there cannot be true face-to-face communication, so true intercourse, one with the other, is precluded. How far all this is from the total gift of one person to another in marriage is evident.

Homosexual activity involves, if not a radical contempt for one's own sex, for all sex, in fact, then at least a fear of sexuality as such, for sexuality implies another whose appeal is in that otherness, in being very different from oneself in body and temper of mind. But the person who is homosexually active fears the very nature of sexuality as something open to such difference. Often this fear is accompanied by a certain hatred of the opposite sex. What is other is not needed, is declared not desirable; only what is like oneself fascinates and is sought in the other.

The solution to a problem of this sort, as is the case for any type of perversion, requires the effort of the whole person, because the whole person is sick, not just his sexual appetite. In fact, the primary illness is not one of sexual desire at all. No matter what one's sexual attractions may be, whatever one's temptations are, if he is still capable of free choice, he is capable of chastity if he is humble enough to want and seek God's grace. The great illness here is self-pity and the consequent refusal to accept one's psychic condition as a call to at least temporary and total continence. But homosexual attractions, as such, need not make life intolerable. With God's help, they can be sanctifying, if only one sets about quietly to follow the commandments God has written into our nature.

One can now understand why the Church has always been so strongly opposed to contraception. Whatever its mode or variety, it substitutes something alien for the symbol of love. Contraceptives are either physical barriers or chemical withholdings of the conditions for fertility.

They enable what appears to be the marital act to be so performed that it now embodies an exclusion, a withholding, a negation of the most basic effect of sexual power. In the case of the woman, she refuses the power of the man over her body. In the case of the man, he refuses to let her fruitfulness present him with another like himself, whom he does not want.

In either case, what the barrier to sexual power or its withholding symbolically expresses is sterilization of one's partner or oneself. It is not, then, by accident that many who have accepted contraception sense no difference save in efficacy or convenience between condoms or diaphragms and the pill or the IUD, or that many have now gone so far as to have themselves or their spouses permanently sterilized. The true symbol of love, mutual gift and reception, is excluded by any form of contraception. Intercourse becomes the symbol of feminine dominance instead of masculine, of masculine impotence instead of strength.

Though it is possible that a couple intend what the contraceptive act says, I think that most, especially these days when even priests teach in contradiction to the Church, do not. There may well be true love between them, and no desire to set up barriers to love. Yet the psychological and moral power of this barricaded and obstructed union works gradually, slowly, imperceptibly, because of its intrinsic meaning and symbolic significance, on their subconscious and eventually on their conscious minds to generate that cold and self-centered hostility to new life known as the "contraceptive mentality".

More generally, the fact that one lies against the symbol of love or perverts it need not mean that there is no love present for the other party involved. There may well be deep love, but it is a love that is somehow disjointed. Hence come the terrible weight upon the conscience and the dull aching of heart that are the spiritual results of twisting the body's actions out of joint from their true meaning.

In sum, then, sexual symbols must be used only in truth. If one cannot use them to express the truth, they should not be used at all. Further, no sexual symbol should be set aside to have something else substituted for it. If it is sometimes difficult to wait until one can use sexual action properly, the difficulty can always be overcome by steady reflection and prayer upon the true meaning and depth of love that God has intended it to convey.

Natural family planning (NFP), we might mention in passing, is symbolically quite different. The couple knows, indeed, that they are not fertile as a couple, that he will not beget, she will not conceive. Yet the act itself is not altered. The couple remains essentially open to life; if not, there are easier means at hand they could be using.

It is perfectly true that the use of NFP can be selfish. A couple using NFP can mutually lock themselves in against children as effectively as they can with contraception. Yet this need not be the case; and the method itself helps against such misuse. For since one is not always free to have intercourse when using NFP, he is thereby invited to offer a greater gift, sacrificial in character, and to transcend his desires. Further, to use NFP effectively, the couple must come to greater trust in each other about their sexuality and to take all its aspects into account, thinking as a couple whose fertility is the property of the couple, not of either individual alone.

Dating

The same general principle applies to other sexual problems. For example, it helps to answer some of the questions that arise for young people when they begin to date and eventually seek to discover the person with whom they wish to spend the rest of their lives.

To gain some clarity in the difficult matter of necking and petting, recall that these actions, also, are symbolic. They signify in various ways the desire to give oneself to another and they manifest externally the feelings of the heart. Obviously, these actions lack the fullness of meaning found in intercourse. Many of them are far from being universal expressions of sexual love; the meaning of something like a kiss is largely a matter of convention, though there do seem to be natural gestures as well, such as fondling, embracing, and exposure.

But whether conventional or natural, what is most important about these activities is that they are all in some sense incomplete. They tend to arouse and stimulate but not to satisfy. Their thrill is quickly dulled by repetition. The couple then tends to go further, not because their love has grown that much—it often has not—but to find actions that renew the original sense of mutual affection, and also because these symbols are themselves exciting and tend to draw one toward still more stimulating action. Yet the unmarried are usually not able to say these things in truth to one another, for caresses and embraces are the natural preludes to intercourse, intended by God as only partial symbols of love, by means of which the couple suitably prepare themselves physically, emotionally, and spiritually for consummation in intercourse.

If the couple is married, the place of these things is obvious. But if they are not married, there is a problem. They are not permitted to use these actions as a married couple does. They cannot say by these means that they belong to each other, that they want the other to be ready to receive the total gift of love. But that is just what these actions generally signify, which is why they are so stimulating even to those who, quite seriously, want no such stimulation. Clearly, too, a couple may not use these symbols of love primarily for their own gratification and pleasure; that would be a still greater lie, using these signs of self-giving simply in order to get for themselves. So it is evident that the unmarried may not embrace or caress each other for the sake of sexual arousal or pleasure. They may not consent to such stimulation, even if it should accidentally occur. To act otherwise would be a sort of fornication or masturbation in emotion and desire, even if not in act.

Well, then, let us suppose the common case of two people who like each other very much, who are genuinely interested in each other though not yet engaged, and who wish by their caresses to do nothing more than show something of their genuine affection for each other. They really respect each other and have drawn a line beyond which they never go. They see clearly enough how terrible a thing it would be to use these symbols of love as instruments to destroy the soul of a person they like—poor friendship, indeed!—or their own, and they want none of that. What then?

A problem still remains. If such actions are continued or repeated week after week, whether with the same person or with others, even though the couple never step across the line they have drawn, there is, in this constant use of a language intended to be only preliminary, in the repeated and unfulfilled use of these symbols of love, a wearing down of their meaning, a loss of sensitivity and expressiveness. When someday they wish to use these symbols to express the depths of the unique love to which they are then resolved to consecrate their whole lives, they find they do not know how. As with flags on the Fourth of July or at a political convention, as with the "Star-Spangled Banner" at ball games and graduations, it is hard to recapture the fullness of meaning.

For those not yet engaged, then, kissing, embracing, and caressing, at least if prolonged or intimate, seem out of place. The pleasure of emotional warmth and the expression of mutual sexual acceptability are not sufficient reasons under the circumstances to permit the degree of harm done to the couple's ability to manifest true love, even if there should be no danger of impurity.

Those who are engaged, since they are committed to each other, even though not yet fully, have sufficient reason to manifest their love, even by prolonged kissing and embracing, Their love has led them to an initial gift of themselves, even if still partial, and may be quite rightly shown by these natural symbols, provided, of course, that this leads neither of them into sin, provided they do not get themselves violently overwrought, and provided the engagement does not go on forever.

For, once a couple foresees that their engagement has to be prolonged, then intimate kissing and embracing and other warm signs of affection should be accordingly widely spaced out and rare, precisely to avoid the dulling and growing stale of the signs of love.

The Religious Significance of Misuse of Sex

As Christians, however, what we have said is still insufficient. Thus far, we have restricted ourselves to the level of natural symbolism. But divine revelation has elevated this natural symbolism by putting it to use to tell us not merely about our own psyche but about God and his love for us. Thus, the moral quality of various types of sexual activity should be clearer when we look at the things symbolized by these activities in the light of revelation. The Christian sees all sexual activity and judges of its rightness and wrongness by comparing what it signifies in itself with the truth he has from faith: his knowledge of the Father, who has regenerated us as his children in Christ, and his understanding of the union between Christ and his Church.

Christian Understanding of Sexual Lies

First consider the use of sexual activity to say what one does not truly mean in one's heart.

Speaking most generally, though we cannot see any need for God to have revealed himself to us, yet, once he has done so, it is unthinkable that he should have lied to his people. Neither could God's Word lie to his Bride. Of his very nature, he cannot, for his own purposes or pleasure, swear to her a permanence, a totality, an exclusivity of love that he does not have.

In particular, fornication, that is, the sexual union of two unmarried people, symbolizes at the supernatural level the old paganisms. A man who fornicates could never represent the God who married Israel, who knew in advance her weaknesses and infidelities, yet who committed himself to her alone forever. Nor could he represent Christ in his union with the Church, for whose purification from infidelity he willingly suffered torture and death. Rather, he would resemble one of the old pagan deities, who conferred their favors on their people as they themselves capriciously chose at the moment.

A woman who fornicates can symbolize only those ancient peoples who worshipped such deities. This worship was always conditioned. If their gods failed them in battle or in harvest, the people would either abandon them for the more powerful gods of their conquerors or add them as minor figures to an empirically more powerful pantheon. Of unconditional devotion, the pagans' religions knew nothing. Obviously, the fornicator could not represent the Church, to whom Christ has given his Holy Spirit to keep her forever faithful to himself.

Adultery, on the other hand, denies the uniqueness of Christ or of his Church. A wife's adultery says in sign that there is some spouse suitable for the Church other than the Lord. Her adultery thus symbolizes the sin of idolatry when committed by believers, even as Israel before the Exile, while worshipping the Lord (Yahweh), still went after and worshipped foreign gods.

Conversely, a husband's adultery signifies in symbol that Christ could turn away at times from his only Bride, the Church, and give himself to some other, ignoring his marriage covenant with her for whom he died.

If there has been in Judaism and in Christianity a sense that adultery by the wife is somehow even worse than adultery by the husband, one can see why: for to deny the only true God and Jesus, whom he sent, is a greater sin than to deny the unique position of any creature, even the Church.

We can see also why adultery is not punishable by death under the New Law, though it was under the Old: for Christ chose to take our sins upon himself and to die for his sinful and adulterous people, so that his Bride might be thenceforth without spot or wrinkle or any such thing. If, then, a wife's adultery is the graver sin, and yet the Husband suffered death in her stead, we cannot demand more than he; the servant is not greater than his Master.

Dissolution of a consummated, sacramental marriage is ruled out on the same grounds. Civil divorce there can be: separation from bed and board if a sufficiently grave crime has been committed by one spouse or the other. This would correspond to the Exile, to God's driving his people away into pagan lands, leaving them isolated and despised among those whose prosperity they had envied enough to worship their gods. Incapable of joining the pagans without total loss of identity, they yearned for the Lord but could not find him until he had brought them to true repentance. But he could never simply abandon his people and, as seen in chapter 5, could not, no matter what their iniquity, ever cast them finally aside to marry another; so also, Christian marriage cannot ever be dissolved.

This is an area where Catholics are indeed fortunate, for despite the cultural decay produced by the social acceptance of state power to dissolve a marriage, they know that God has made the sacramental marriage bond incapable of dissolution. It still remains possible for them to enter marriage in full love for one another, to give themselves without any restrictions, without any holding back. If their marriage fails tragically in human terms, the permanence of that bond is their strength. Unable to give up or surrender, they must labor and pray all the more vigorously to help each other to the perfection of love, even at the cost of great sacrifice. For they know, by the joining of their agony to Christ's, that sacrifice is the strongest language of love, beside which the act of intercourse itself is very little.

Similarly, insensitivity or frigidity, to the extent that it is willed and chosen, is utterly alien to the Christian. How could Christ be indifferent to or unconcerned with those who love him, he who died for them? On the other hand, we children of the Church can, indeed, be cold to Christ, refuse him support in his labors on behalf of all our race, pay him no attention, not wish to hear him speak. This is the sad state of tepidity, where Christians do little more than go through the external motions of their faith, content to be inert and uninterested in Christ. Yet the Spirit keeps the Church from such coolness to her Lord; and to act sexually so as to imply the contrary is evil.

Christian Understanding of Sexual Perversion

If we turn to the fraud, the counterfeit, the use of the sexual powers in ways other than God intends, we see, in general, that God cannot be thought to separate his love for us from his sharing his life with us by making us his sons in Christ. Neither could Christ delight himself with his Church without granting her fruitfulness by the gift of his Spirit, nor could the Church receive and enjoy the gifts of the

Holy Spirit while refusing to be fruitful, refusing to give that life to others.

As to masturbation: Christ did not come to please himself, as the Scriptures phrase it (Rom 15:3); he came to seek a Bride. He did not stay by himself. He came and sought out his people, at the risk of rejection—and indeed he was rejected. Yet, to his own great cost, he espoused her on the Cross and made her fruitful by giving her his Spirit, that she might become the mother of all the living. Nor might the Church ever delight in the gifts of the Spirit in isolation, not seeking to share them with those who do not yet know Christ. Such a refusal of missionary endeavor could bring only decay and decline to the local church that so turned in upon itself.

To learn what male homosexual activity would symbolize in terms of Christ and the Church, we first must ask what masculine figure other than the Lord is shown us in revelation. Who besides the Lord takes the initiative? Who else is other than and radically different from the feminine creation? The Old Testament sets before us in this guise the lovers of Israel: foreign gods and the foreign states they rule. Many things are bound together here in the Bible—the gods, the nations who worshipped them, the technology that these nations had but Israel did not: chariots, horses, elephants, and weapons of war. These are all the things that were summed up, in Roman times when our Lord walked the earth, in the one word "Caesar".

Male homosexual activity, then, symbolizes at the supernatural level man as in love with one like himself, enamored of the strength of the state, seeking from it the strength to be savior of himself. It is a refusal of the femininity of the Church, her weakness in human terms. It signifies secular humanism, for which Feuerbach's insistence that the only God of man is man himself captures the essence of the tendency to refuse to accept the true otherness of God. The state, its technology, its power for war, its attempt to solve all problems independently of God or his Church, its taking all initiative to itself—this is indeed a male principle. But we know that Christ has not wedded himself to the state, to technology, to secular "progress", or to war—however good these things may be in themselves when not loved but only rightly used. Christ is wedded only to his Church.

The only other masculine principle in Scripture is Satan, who sets himself up as God, who takes the initiative in tempting and deceiving the whole world, who apes God's majesty and his power to judge and condemn the sinner, but without understanding the love that God is. It is, then, no great surprise to find the frequent links in history between male homosexual activity and devil worship.

As to lesbianism, the question must be asked in a similar fashion. What feminine figure or principle is given us in Scripture other than the Church? Who or what other also bears, brings forth, entices, responds to, and draws forth the male principle? The answer, clearly enough, is this: God's good creation, the whole created order. Lesbianism, then, signifies a Church who would turn away from the Lord to embrace what is like herself: created, dependent for fruitfulness on union with Another who is *not* like herself, lovely with a beauty given by that Other, incapable of initiative with regard to God. What lesbianism symbolizes is not a Church at all but nature worship, a worship of Isis or the Earth Mother rather than Christ.

A seemingly similar feminine principle—though I know no scriptural warrant for saying so—is the psychologism of our day. This is a fascination with the psychic interior of others, where the interest centers in the same sort of interior that the would-be knower has. He is not drawn by a true psychology or psychiatry, that is, by a desire to know another *in his otherness* in order to help him to help himself to psychic health. Rather, the "pop psychologist" seems to be looking for insight into what he senses to be askew within himself or trying to gain support and validation for himself in virtue of others' experiencing similar things. This essentially feminine-feminine relationship would again symbolize a Church turned away from God to the created world, but this time to the interior creation of the human heart.

Symbolically, contraceptive intercourse implies that God might give his grace and pour out his Holy Spirit without permitting them to have their fruit, without granting the Church to bear him new children. Conversely, contraception signifies that God would not mind if his people were to enjoy the pleasures of his light and consolation and yet refuse to bear the fruits of grace: pure faith, strong hope, the vigorous activity of charity toward God and all his people, through lives of virtue after the example of our Lord.

Contraception has, however, another aspect. As a barrier to the effective power of one's love for one's partner, it symbolizes what happens when a person goes to confession, drawn out of sentiment, say, for Christmas or Easter, and deliberately withholds mention of some serious sin. This obstruction of the truth renders completely void the absolution received and adds to his prior sins the sin of sacrilege.

Contraception also resembles the act of those who go to Communion in a state of known mortal sin. Here also there is a withholding; a barrier is placed to the gift of all of oneself. Although one goes through the motions of love and even though there may be a genuine urging and prompting by love, yet by the imposition of this barrier of attachment to sin or of shame to accept forgiveness, whatever love may be present is rendered fruitless and inefficacious. For in Communion God not only gives us all but asks all from us. So also, the contracepting partner withholds the procreative power of love, and thus knowingly refuses the total gift of himself. Barring the creaturely conditions for God's creating new life, even as the impenitent communicant bars the creaturely conditions for God's re-creating the supernatural life, he symbolizes a violation of what is holy and commits something akin to sacrilege.

Life, Death, and Love

One can summarize by pointing out that, at both the natural and the supernatural levels of symbolism, the perversions divert that which exists for the generation of new life into a refusal to let the generation of new life take place. At the least, this indicates a certain lack of hope, a discouragement as to the future. Instead of transmitting life to those who will live after us, whom we will see only beginning their lives, we find that the raising of children is too hard, too painful. We feel that it is too difficult to share life so intimately with another person where the other is so very different in body and heart—and, too often, also in mind—and so we back away into what is familiar and engage in some type of fraudulent relationship instead.

But more, there is a relation between sexual sin and death that human beings have known for long generations. As we can see as far back as the epic poetry of Ugarit 4,000 years ago, in the plays of Euripides 2,400 years ago, in the gladiatorial shows of ancient Rome 1,800 years ago, and in countless other cases, deviated sexual lust becomes bloodlust; frustration of the life instincts begets the death instinct. Separating the power to give life from those actions intended for the giving of life is a sort of killing, and ultimately symbolizes a putting to death.

The tragic linkage of male homosexual activity to suicide is well known. While exact numbers are hard to come by, the rate of suicide among the homosexually active seems to be twenty or more times higher than in the general population. While not as dramatic, something similar can be said of masturbation, though this seems more often a symbolic prelude, a sort of little suicide in advance, than its cause.

Academic ethicians usually see no relationship between contraception and abortion. They regard these two acts as wholly different from each other. One is merely a withholding of life; the other, the killing of an innocent person. Yet, as those in the pro-life movement have increasingly been discovering, a woman who repudiates contraceptively her partner's power over her body gradually slides psychologically to a point where she becomes willing to repudiate the fruit of that power if in fact it has begotten a child within her. A man most typically will resort to contraceptives out of subconscious self-hatred or fear of responsibility, not wanting to bring into the world another like himself or not daring to. It is all too easy for him, then, if a child has, in fact, been begotten, to choose, out of that same self-hatred or fear, not to allow this new one like himself and so frighteningly dependent on him to come to birth.

A bond between death and the misuse of sex is found not only in counterfeit sexuality but, somewhat differently, when natural intercourse is lyingly done. The lie is told because of a decision to follow one's desires regardless of cost. And, like a jinni from a magic lamp, what results from those brief moments of self-satisfying falsehood comes forth unforeseeably. Support from one's parents, spouse, or other relatives is often lacking or deficient under such circumstances; and selfishness, panicked and alone, can easily turn to savagery or to despair.

We know of David's adultery with Bathsheba and his murder of her husband. Murderous jealousy easily brings men to kill women they think have betrayed them. Adolescent fornication has often led, in cultures less permissive than our own, to tragedy through the hopelessness of an adolescent sentimentality that has found no bounds, no limits, and has not discovered the courage or the strength to intend what those young people are saying to one another by their sexual activity. In our culture, an undesired pregnancy is more commonly met by killing the child inside his mother through abortion than by the young parents' mutual murder or suicide pacts.

There is a deep connection between suffering and death, however, and genuine love. This is visible not merely negatively, in the sad consequences of the misuse of sex, but positively. True lovers have always sensed how much pain their choice steadfastly to love any human creature exposes them to. The Christian discovers the full depth of this connection in the Cross of Christ. There we see what Love suffers for the sake of those who are loved. It is on the Cross that Christ died for love of those who tormented him, willing indeed to suffer, to be rejected, to be killed by the people he loved, since his death would bring their salvation. Anyone, then, who loves with the love of charity, that is, by the power of God's love, will suffer, and suffer deeply.

It is just this link between true love and suffering that is rejected by sexual sin. One refuses to risk the grief and pain that can be inflicted by a spouse or by children. One is drawn by desire or driven by passion. One insists on pleasure or, at least, a release of tension. In any case, one rejects the cross that is formed when sexual desire lies athwart the love of God, and refuses to suffer the pain of frustration.

The answer to all sexual problems, then, is to take up this cross, to return in repentance to Christ on His Cross, to accept the suffering that charity will bring to our lives. There is no reason to despond or to yield if we are tempted to self-hatred because of our sexual sins, or to self-pity because of the harshness of the battle to be fought against them. In truth and in love we go to the Lord. He loves us. If we doubt it, let us look long in faith at the crucifix. There we will see what true love is. We will see that which united Christ with his Church. We will learn what it costs, indeed, to be husband or wife; but at the same time we will gain from him the power and strength to pay what is needed.

There will be life-giving pleasure, too, according to our state of life, if we do not seek that pleasure at the expense of the cross. We will then also find rejoicing in our life and a foretaste of the delights of heaven, as we come to realize more deeply what it means that Christ died for love of us and to sense that we are beginning to love in some degree as he does.

7

CHRIST, FATHER OF THE WORLD TO COME: VIRGINITY AND CONTINENCE

We have looked at what sexual activity, as the language of true love, means by its very nature and also at the fullness of supernatural meaning given to it by Christ. We have also seen how the prescriptions of the Law as to sexual behavior have been given their fullest weight and meaning by the teaching of the New Testament.

It is true that much of what the Law prescribed or forbade in this area, since restricted by time, place, and culture, has not been taken over, at least literally, by the Church. But far from being abrogated as mere culturally conditioned and obsolete regulations, as some mistakenly hold today, those commands of the Law have been reasserted through the symbolic and therefore universal language of the New Testament in a purer and, from a merely natural viewpoint, much stricter form. Just recall the Lord's words: "Every one who looks at a woman lustfully has already committed adultery with her in his heart" (Mt 5:28). Yet even this degree of virtue has been made possible for our weakness by the grace of Jesus' love. All the prescriptions of Christian sexual morality arise from the symbolism we have been considering and are dependent on it. All of them, consequently, flow immediately and directly from what God has revealed about the nature of his love.

But an understanding of the supernatural glory of Christian marriage and sexual union and an understanding of why certain types of sexual activity are seriously wrong is not enough. God has told us much more about what our sexuality symbolizes and shows forth as we bear witness to him in the world. Let us turn, then, to a very different sexual symbolism from the one we have just been looking at, that which the Scriptures employ to help us understand virginity and continence.

Symbolism of Premarital Chastity

The attitude of the Old Testament can be summed up quite briefly, in a few lines from the Song of Solomon, where the spouse, who is God, speaks of his beloved Israel: "A garden locked is my sister, my bride, a garden locked, a fountain sealed" (4:12).

Physically the maidenhead is an enclosure, a bodily sealing off of a virgin. Symbolically, the world has always seen it as a sign of her reservation of herself, of her being sealed off against indiscriminate loves in order, ultimately, to be the sacred receptacle, the vessel within which God will bring about the mystery of a new life through the action of her husband. Consequently, throughout the Old Testament, although one finds no trace of a *state* of virginity, that is, of a mode of life in which a woman chose, for the love of God, to remain a virgin throughout her entire earthly existence, yet there is a great esteem for virginity, precisely as a preparation for marriage.

The virginity of a young man is not as obviously symbolic, because his body, unlike that of a woman, is the same after his first intercourse as before it. All the same, his virginity is heavily charged with symbolic meaning, for to maintain his virginity, he must establish from early on a rational control over all the tremendous upbuilding drive and vigor of his sexual powers and appetites. Often enough, he will have to struggle vigorously. Erections, wet dreams, and other spontaneous sexual movements or desires may well be more frequent for him than if he were to find a sexual outlet with a young woman or yield to masturbation. Nonetheless, a young man is able, by the grace of Christ, to achieve and maintain an ever more mature control and mastery of his sexuality.

By establishing this control over that which is, so to speak, the preeminent element of opposition in the subrational world to the action of reason, he shows symbolically that he is capable and competent to subject the world to the good of his family-to-be, that he can provide for them by his labor in the world and can protect them from the forces of nature and from enemies. The symbolic meaning of a man's virginity, then, is a dominion over the subhuman world for the good of his prospective family that images God's dominion over the entire universe for the good of his family, the whole people of God.

Further, this mastery of his sexual desires symbolizes a man's freedom to procreate or not, as his truest love may move him. The importance of this freedom within marriage is obvious today in a culture that gives so great a value to regulation of family size. But for the Christian, whom God may call to a celibate life as priest or religious as well as to marriage, this freedom is a basic aspect of the maturity he needs if he is to discern whither God is calling him. In this aspect, also, a man's virginity is a likeness in his very flesh to God, whose power to create, naturally or supernaturally, is infinitely free. Hence, too, a husband has in his family or in a familial context a headship that his wife does not. This symbolism of premarital chastity also explains something that is otherwise very difficult—especially for young people—to understand: how it is, in God's providence, that young men and women often have strong sexual desires, appetites, and emotions long years before they are morally free to use these powers and satisfy these appetites in marriage. It takes even longer for them to develop the intellectual and emotional maturity to enter marriage prudently. Yet they are physically capable and desirous of the act of intercourse; they are even physically capable of having children. Why should they be put under so much strain when they are not ripe for the satisfaction of those desires? What is the reason for this seeming dislocation in the course of nature?

The answer would seem to be this: A young person has to learn complete continence and to gain mastery of his sexual drives and desires before he is ready to give himself totally in marriage. Sexual intercourse is a symbol of the loving self-gift of one spouse to the other. But a person who does not already possess himself cannot give himself. If a husband is not capable of perfect self-control, he is incapable of giving himself perfectly to his wife. So, also, a wife must be mistress of her emotions and feelings if she is to yield herself in true freedom as a gift to her husband.

Many a time, moreover, husband and wife are obliged to self-control, continence, abstinence in the strictest sense—for example, if one's spouse is ill; immediately before and after childbirth; when they are separated from each other by business or war. Certainly their love can be no less then; yet love must show itself at these times precisely in total abstinence from sexual activity.

But there is still another aspect of premarital chastity that we ought not neglect. In practically all cultures—even in our own, although with our cultural deterioration it is no longer obvious among us—there are initiation rites that usher the boy at puberty into manhood. Only after these is he allowed to join the men in hunting or war or the other manly activities of the tribe or people. Only then is he one of the adults. In our country he enters into his majority, comes of age; he may vote, make contracts, and dispose of property, and he is subject to military service. Among Jews, he has his bar mitzvah, being made for the first time subject to the Law. In any case, some rite, ceremony, or symbolic gesture takes the boy into publicly recognized manhood with its duties and its privileges.

Given the nature of this transition, these rites are strongly related to the boy's sexual maturation, to his physical ability to beget a child. In those peoples where a girl also has a rite of passage, it is connected with her first menstruation, her ability to conceive.

The point of interest to us here is that these rituals are usually closely tied to the boy's ability to bear pain and to endure hardship in the context of hunting, fighting, and other modes of male activity. The rites are symbolic answers to the question: "Can he endure the suffering that naturally accompanies a man's contests with nature and with other men courageously enough to have sufficient chance to win out?" If a girl undergoes a rite of passage, it is generally more closely related to bearing the pains of childbirth or, occasionally, to other pains that a woman must endure among her people.

Consequently, some of these rites, especially in more primitive societies, have been exceedingly painful and bloody. Circumcision is one of the more common ones, practiced not on the infant, as among the Jews, but on the adolescent. There are many other rites of passage, both more painful and more dangerous.

All these rites seem to indicate that there is a need, deeply rooted in the human psyche, that the instinct that makes a man physically capable of procreation be somehow tied in with pain or suffering, with contest, and with victory, whether over other men in battle, or over animals killed in defense or hunted down for food.

The essential meaning of these rites can be seen when we look at Christian chastity. This is the Christian "rite of passage". There is no need for circumcision, for any other bloody and symbolic rite. Christian chastity is itself the symbol of both the suffering and the contest—the effort to control one's sexual drives is painful and difficult; dominance over them is the conquest and victory. Perfect chastity alone proves that a boy has become a man; that a girl has become a woman. Each person must be subjected to the inner conflict: to the deep, obscure, but powerful emotions of the girl; to the very obvious physical passion of the boy. Only by chastity can they give proof of themselves as men and women who are adults, who have matured enough to accept full responsibility for their sexual powers, not treating them as means for amusement or experimentation.

All too often, a boy tries to prove his manhood by imitating, in some kind of sin against purity, those whom he judges to be men, but who are not yet such. He runs with the crowd. They claim to have intercourse with their girlfriends or with prostitutes. He thinks he must do the same to show himself a man. Or a girl seeks to prove her womanhood. She feels that she has been left out if she does not have intercourse; her companions are doing it; she cannot think herself a knowledgeable adult unless she has done so too. Yet fornication proves only that the young people are physically capable of engaging in intercourse and, cruelly, that they are not yet capable of acting as Christian adults.

The basic insight, then, found in the rites of passage of so many different cultures and expressed in so many barbarous ways, shows itself most perfectly and finds its fulfillment in Christian chastity. The boy, through manly effort and self-sacrifice, claims his manhood by control and mastery of his sexual passion, becoming a man like Christ, the sole example of perfect manhood. The girl moves into womanhood through her control of her emotions and her still merely instinctive desires for a love whose true nature she does not yet understand, subjecting these emotions and desires to the demands of a freely chosen love for Christ in chastity.

From all aspects of its symbolism, then, the total continence of unflawed virginity is not only the sole form of chastity for the unmarried but the most perfect possible preparation of both man and woman for marriage.

Virginity and Fruitfulness

A woman's virginity seems to have been universally recognized, even by the pagans, as relating her to God directly and not only as preparing her for his creating a child in her womb through the action of her husband. As far back as records of human religion go, we find that some women were consecrated as virgins in order to carry out religious functions, to be servants of the gods, or even to act as priestesses. The reason was simply that a virgin is sealed. Being closed off to man, she is symbolically consecrated to the divine.

So, also, throughout Christian history, women have chosen to consecrate their virginity to Christ. They seek, as virgins sealed to all power but his Holy Spirit and as images of his Bride, the Church, to give him in her name that exclusive love that is symbolized by marriage. Those we designate as nuns today were solemnly consecrated in early times under the hands of the bishop, showing the importance to the Church of those who manifest directly her pure love for her Lord. For the Church is the unique Bride of Christ; as Saint Paul says to the Corinthians, she is a chaste virgin espoused to the one Lord (2 Cor 11:2). Spoken both to individuals and to the whole church in Corinth, this remark applies to the Church Universal and to each of us within it.

A man, too, can be directly related to God through perpetual virginity. A man's consecration to God, however, is not one of union so much as of oneness, of likeness, of identification, especially in action. Recall the passage in Genesis where the man names the animals before he receives the woman. Many commentators on Scripture take this as a statement, in ancient Near-Eastern symbolism, of man's power over creation; and they find in this the most obvious explanation of the phrase that man was made in the image and according to the likeness of God, that is, man shares God's rule over the world. By his virginal dominion over his own sexual appetites, then, he gains a further way to image God, symbolically, with respect to his governance of the material world, for it is a man's task to subdue the world not only for the good of his family but, ultimately, to make it subserve the glory of God by grace. A man labors that the whole temporal order be formed into an instrument for God's service and praise; he must, then, refuse to be enslaved to it as he finds it in his own flesh.

It has, of course, been seen by Christians from very early days that man's creation according to the image and likeness of God is also manifested through his spiritual powers of intellect and choice of the free will, which reflect the perfect spirituality of God. We have mentioned the virginal man's freedom with regard to marriage and the likeness to God he has thereby. But he has also a greater clarity or transparency of mind and heart for contemplation. The writings of the saints bear witness to this heightened contemplative power; the most persuasive witness, perhaps, is that of those married saints who came eventually to lives of total continence, such as Saint Jane de Chantal, Saint Thomas More, and Saint Gregory of Nyssa.

A fairly clear parallelism exists between these relations to God and those we noted earlier as preparatory to raising a family. But the parallel can be carried further still, to spiritual fruitfulness and the raising of children for God directly. Thus, Saint Joseph, a husband given wholly to his wife in love, remained always a virgin. He kept himself such initially, perhaps, because of his love for Mary, but permanently and principally in consecration to God. Yet Joseph is the man Saint Luke refers to as the father of Jesus (Lk 2:27, 33, 41, 48). He is one who, without procreation, nonetheless took the place of a human father to our Lord and was more perfectly father to him than any of us will ever be to our children according to the flesh.

This power of the consecrated virgin to be a parent, preeminently and spiritually, can be seen in greater detail in Mary, the mother of our Lord and, thus, of his Body, the Church. Perfect virgin and perfect mother, she shows even more fully all aspects of the symbolism of virginity summed up entirely in one person. As a virgin, she was enclosed, reserved for God alone, having within her no rival love. And because she was perfectly reserved for God, without ever any flaw or withdrawal of her love, God chose her and came to her to work within her directly the same mystery of creation that he works indirectly in other women. But he came himself, so that the Child formed of her was God, not merely man.

Thus, the virgin is one reserved for God alone, to whom he then comes in order, through the virgin, to give himself to others. This explains something that has often bothered people about the sexual symbolism of the Scriptures: a seemingly strange union of the notions of virginity and fruitfulness. If one understands virginity properly, however, there is no contradiction. Christ is virginal, yet he is "Eternal Father" or the "Father of the world to come" (cf. Is 9:6). Saint Paul, while speaking of virginity, tells us that he wishes that all men were as he is, that is, virginal or at least perfect in celibate chastity; yet he says to his Corinthians: "Though you have countless guides in Christ, you do not have many fathers. For I became your father in Christ Jesus through the gospel" (1 Cor 4:14–15).

This is the basis of the religious life within the Church and is meant to be true, as well, of all who are celibate. They are to be fathers or mothers of great numbers of people, not just of one family begotten of their own flesh. Parents of all those whom Christ leads toward holiness through them, they find abundant fulfillment even in this life. Their joy is to nurture the divine life of those entrusted to them and to govern and discipline them for their more abundant growth.

Likewise, bishops, since called by their office to be totally devoted to their local church, have either not been married (whether in East or West) or, if married, have had to remain totally continent. Yet they are spoken of, after the example of Saint Paul, not only as the shepherds but as the fathers of their people. The priests of the Latin Rite, celibate like bishops because married in Christ to the Church, are also called "Father", as are monks in the East. So, also, in religious institutes, we speak of the founder of the order or of the one who drew up the institute—hence, of one who serves as model of that form of religious life, living perfectly the life of celibate chastity—as "mother in Christ", or as "father in Christ". The fullness of virginity, then, requires the fruitfulness of a spiritual parenthood that has graver obligations than natural parents have.

Eunuchs for the Kingdom

But what we have said is not yet quite the fullness of the symbolism of virginity in the Bible. Our Lord himself uses still another sexual symbol when speaking of virginity, one that is strange enough to require some comment. Speaking of marriage, he described its original character and, on that basis, prohibited divorce with remarriage. The apostles took alarm at this, since the Law permitted divorce, and said to him, "If such is the case of a man with his wife,"—that is, if he is not able to divorce her—"it is not expedient to marry" (Mt 19:3–10). A little cynical, perhaps, but it was their reaction. Our Lord replied: "Not all men can receive this precept, but only those to whom it is given. For there are eunuchs who have been so from birth, and there are eunuchs who have been made eunuchs by men, and there are eunuchs who have made themselves eunuchs for the sake of the kingdom of heaven. He who is able to receive this, let him receive it" (Mt 19:11–12).

This is a cryptic statement. But "those to whom it is given" have always understood it. He is inviting men to a state of perfect celibacy, asking men—those who can receive it, as he put it—to live celibate lives. Those who can truly understand it are called never to marry.

But, and here is the strange thing, he uses as a symbol of this a eunuch, a man who has been castrated, a man who, in consequence, is impotent and has no capacity for sexual intercourse. Christ says that there are some who are born this way and there are some who are made so by men—this refers to the eunuchs of the Oriental harems, an institution that was ancient even in his time—and then he says that those who remain celibate for the sake of the Kingdom of God are like these. Now, of course, one can say that what he means by this is that, just as the true physical eunuch is incapable of sexual intercourse, so those who are to be celibate for the Kingdom of God should be just as completely removed as the eunuch from all sexual activity, not through castration but through the fervor of their chastity.

True enough; but such exegesis does not exhaust the symbol that Christ is using here. Castration is a brutal and grave deprivation. Through it, a man loses much of what belongs to him as a man, something so important to him that many would declare it essential to his psychic stability and healthy self-image. Yet this loss, apparently, is something we should see in virginity itself.

The meaning would seem to be that virginity and celibacy are always relative goods. They are undertaken only for the sake of something else; they are not complete in themselves. They always represent a true deprivation of some present good for the sake of something that is still to come. They manifest, in one way or another, a love directed toward God or toward man that has not yet achieved its fulfillment and that deprives us of any possibility of fulfillment in this life. We are searching for Someone whom we desire to love far more than ourselves, who is present, who sometimes lets us feel his presence but will not, in this life, let us see his face.

For this reason, Saint Thomas Aquinas speaks of virginity as something that would have had but a trivial place in the Garden of Eden had Adam and Eve not fallen into sin. For had man not sinned, there would have been no need of special preparation for marriage. Man would have had the necessary control without effort. There would have been no need for waiting, for this expectation and readying oneself for something still to come—whether union with another person in marriage or with our Lord in heaven, outside this world and its conditions altogether, which is the hope of consecrated celibates and virgins, those who have made themselves eunuchs for the kingdom of God.

Our redemption, as wrought for us by our Lord and as shown us in his own Person, though it has its initiation and its beginning right now, looks forward to the *eschaton*: to the last age, to the end of the world, to the final judgment, to the new heaven and the new earth. Thus, only in Christ, who came into a fallen world to suffer and die and, only then, to enter into glory for its re-creation, is it possible to live in a *state* of virginity or celibate chastity. It is the state of those who are consecrated directly to God, who are willing to be sacrificed with Christ on the Cross, but who also hope and expect his direct action to raise them to new life even now, the life of mystical union with him, yet know that the fulfillment of his action will come only at the end of time, not in this life.

Thus, those who are religious must indeed experience serious deprivation, a sense of loss, a sense of nonfulfillment in their human nature and being. But it is a loss, a nonfulfillment for the sake of a vastly greater fulfillment.

Therefore, if religious fail to give themselves to charity, actively and vigorously according to the special nature of their vocation and call, or if they seek to live more or less as other people do, apart from their celibate consecration, or if they repine or hold resentment for the concrete ways in which they have been forced to share Christ's Cross as a result of others' malice or ineptitude, then they can easily fall away, as many a recent example shows.

If there is not an intense and consuming love for Christ, looking forward to his coming and regarding him as above everything else desirable, if he is not one's motive in serving the poor, in preaching the faith to those who have not yet heard the great good news of him, in helping people to be just and charitable to one another, then indeed the purpose and the preparatory value of one's celibacy or virginity has been lost. Then, not only does the religious feel castrated; he feels nothing to compensate for the pain of this loss. He gains no sense of charity and divine life growing actively and vigorously within, no sense of development and being led toward final fulfillment. Then by necessity the things of this world will take over, fulfillment will be sought through earthly means, and he will refuse to live longer in the state of a eunuch for the sake of the kingdom.

But it is not religious only who are invited to make themselves eunuchs for the sake of the kingdom. A validly married Catholic whose spouse has gone off with another, a man of strongly homosexual orientation, a woman of deep maternal affection whom no one chooses to marry, and many another unwilling celibate are all invited by Christ to accept this "castration" for his sake and for a fulfillment beyond this world. His language shows that he knows the pain of what he is proposing to them; his grace will grant them success if they seek it from him.

Further Reflections

Always there are these two aspects to virginity or chaste celibacy: on the one hand, it is a preparation and a readying of oneself for sharing in God's creative activity, whether by the generating and raising of children or by making the world a suitable place for the human family or by bringing to the Church those meant to be her spiritual children and helping them grow in Christ. On the other hand, it is not merely a waiting and a longing but a deprivation and a suffering, albeit for the sake of a greater good to come. But in both aspects, its ultimate meaning is perfect love, a consecration of oneself to Christ, loved above all else, a love centered on the Lord directly and without intermediary as well as through all those he loves.

The same two aspects are visible even in natural human love. Sometimes we read in literature or learn in actual fact of a man who has fallen deeply in love with a woman but who must wait for years because he is off at war or because she has not returned his love while he labors to win her affection. But he waits and keeps himself chaste for her sake indefinitely, year after year, in order that he may win her and be worthy of her. How many more women, through a fidelity that seems part of a woman's nature, have done as much for a man they love!

We can see, too, that it is impossible for a philosopher working simply as a philosopher, that is, in the light of reason alone, to understand why the Church has defined that the state of virginity, for those who are called to it, is better and happier than the married state. As a philosopher, the most he can see is what man is by his very nature. What the philosopher sees is, so to speak, man unfallen, since man's nature is the same after the Fall as before. Faith tells us, however, that man has fallen and that this state of virginity, precisely because of man's sinfulness, is a state that, *if* God calls him to it and *if he* lives it in its fullness, will more effectively ready him for close union with God than will marriage.

It is evident, then, how much nonsense has been written about the harm done by continence and virginity. There is no harm in perfect love; and since virginity has meaning only as a preparation for perfect love, there is no question of harm coming from it, whether it be directed toward the perfect love of husband or wife in marriage or toward the perfect love of God, which consecrated virgins seek throughout their entire existence here on earth.

Psychological harm does come as the natural result of frustrated stimulation to people whose "chastity" is mere refraining from sexual intercourse without being grounded in charity. Refraining from physical action, they give free rein to their thoughts and desires. Interiorly at least, they are not pure or chaste. On the other hand, harm can come to those who fear sex, who see sin in every stirring of desire or passion, who do not learn as adolescents to distinguish between arousal or orgasm that is freely chosen and that which comes unbidden and unwilled. As a result, they refuse or are unable to live at ease and in peace with the sexual body that God has given them.

It is, then, of considerable importance to see that the state of virginity or the quasi state of premarital chastity is always intended by God to aid us to grow in love of him and of our fellow men.

8

INTEGRITY: THE VICTORY
OF THE RISEN CHRIST

The Nature of Integrity

Virginity and every kind of chastity, whether before marriage, in marriage, or apart from marriage in some form of celibate life, are to be seen primarily as anticipations and expressions of love. Such chastity is love preparing to give itself, love still in expectation of total fulfillment, whether through the mutual self-giving of human marriage or through that direct gift of oneself to Christ that is the spiritual analogue to marriage. In either case, one is given to him through his espousal to the Church, awaiting the wedding feast and the final union with him that we all will have, please God, in heaven.

All too often chastity has been considered as simply the avoidance of unchastity, as a successful guarding against sexual sin. But if chastity is not mere avoidance of evil but is rather a mode or aspect of love, then since love can grow indefinitely, so can chastity. Indeed, chastity is the splendor of love, the radiance that shines forth from charity in those who have made this love of God and man the absolutely primary thing in their life. Their love is then capable of directing their sexual desires in full accord with faith. As charity grows, its splendor too will grow. Neither has any limits save our own failures.

If chastity is the splendor and the glory of charity, then we should see it in connection with that which is the origin and source of charity in us, namely, Christ's Resurrection. By his rising we were justified and given newness of life in him. He arose physically, bodily, in glory, still human, still male—his resurrection was a victory of human nature over sin, death, the devil, and all that is opposed to God. His Ascension was his triumph. Through his enthronement at the Father's right hand, Jesus is able to make all his chosen ones partakers of his victory. As risen and glorified Lord, he shares with us what he won by his suffering and death.

Christ's victory, then, is our victory because individually and personally we are united with him by the action of his Spirit as members of his Body. He has made a perfect atonement; now that we are one with him, we are meant to share in its fruits. By the power of his grace working in the weakness of our flesh, we too can triumph over the world and the devil.

These things the early Christians were very much aware of; but we tend to forget them and are a little surprised when we read in Scripture about the tremendous joy of the first Christians at their release from sin. Christ's triumph was the source of their happiness and joy, even in suffering and in persecution. Underlying all else in the different parts of the New Testament is this joy at the good news: Christ has set us free from sin. The same tone is present in Ignatius of Antioch and Clement of Rome and, a hundred years later in Irenaeus—the tremendous joy of those for whom Christ had totally broken the chains of sin.

But today, all too often, we feel ourselves oppressed, dragged down by our weakness, and enchained by sin. Concupiscence, desire, and the heat of our passions seem to have made slaves of us again. If we do not actually fall, at least we are constantly battling; and we find this battling so tormenting that it deadens our joy in Christ. If we are honest, we have to admit at times that we are not really all that happy and glad about our Lord's victory. We do not spontaneously sing to him, preach him, talk to others easily and gladly about him. We do not feel that we really do share in his victory. We look forward to sharing in it eventually, but not now.

One can give many reasons for this state of affairs: our need for desolation and temptation to purify us of our hidden pride; the necessity for aridity to strengthen our prayer and selflessness of service; our own careless forgetting of his victory. But there is another question to consider here: What are we looking for, and how we are meant to go about finding it?

As seen in the last chapter, Adam before the fall was free of any need to fight to control his passions. It was not that he could not feel sexual desire, anger, fear, or sadness. He could; but he felt them only in a well ordered, suitable manner, when it was appropriate and right to feel them, when his mind, enlightened by faith, made evident the circumstances that called for them. Eve shared this gift, traditionally called "integrity" by theologians.

Thus, though Adam and Eve could have had intercourse when still unfallen—and, according to Saint Thomas Aquinas, with far greater pleasure and delight than any couple could have since the Fall—yet, until they desired it by a free and deliberate choice under God's grace, there would have been no stirring of passion or desire moving them to such action beforetimes, running ahead of their own free choice.

This gift of integrity belonged to Adam and Eve before the Fall but not after. Afterward, they were naked before each other and were ashamed. The mere sight of nakedness left them feeling no longer innocent. The new Adam and the new Eve, Christ our Lord and his Mother, were gifted with this same integrity. Remaining wholly free from sin, they always possessed this perfect freedom from concupiscence, from any disordered drives of the flesh.

Unfortunately, we often tend to think of integrity as rather like castration, as if people who were integral had no passions: no fear, no sexual desire, no anger. Or else we think of integrity as somewhat like a bolt of lightning from God, by which he would move in on the instant to stop any inappropriate stirrings. It is, in any event, something we think he has given to certain rare individuals but not to others, as if that were the end of it. Christ did not obtain it for *us*, apparently; we are all too painfully aware of our own battles with passion and of the unruly strength of our desires.

But integrity was, very probably, quite different from such notions. Rather than being a sort of passivity, a lack of nonrational stirrings, a change of nature, as if one had no sexuality at all, it seems to have been a gift from God of perfect attention to the meaning of any sexual action envisaged, in full awareness of one's situation and concrete circumstances, along with an immediate perception of how that meaning fit or failed to fit those circumstances and situation. Thus, one was able to choose whatever activity was appropriate at that time, sexual or otherwise, to express one's love for God and one's fellow men.

Consider, for example, a man and a woman who are just beginning sexual intercourse, who are fully aroused, but who have not yet come to orgasm. If there comes a flash of light, a sudden whiff of smoke, and a cry of "Fire!", they go no further. Immediately both deflate and are quickly set free of each other; they can rush for the children and take to safety. The mind's power of attention, then, is sufficiently strong, even at the most natural level of our lives, to have complete control over passion at its hottest, wildest, and strongest if the focus of attention is sharp and clear enough.

If we are right, then, as to the meaning of integrity, it is something to which man, even in his fallen state, might again approximate by the power and the grace of Christ. If one is truly close to Christ, if one's union with him in prayer has become habitual, then it is indeed possible to see the beauty of a woman or of a man with immediate, even subconscious, understanding of its relation to God, to appreciate fully the greatness of God's gift to this person, yet to be repelled at once by the evil involved in any suggestion of unchaste action or desire.

Perhaps an example will illustrate this. There is a rather amusing story—apocryphal, I fear—told of a very holy bishop, a saint whose name I have forgotten, at an early council of the Church held at Antioch. One morning this bishop was standing with a number of other bishops in front of the church. As they talked, a famous and beautiful courtesan, a prostitute who enjoyed the favors of the imperial court, came sauntering by, displaying her wares. All of the bishops modestly dropped their eyes until she passed by, except this one. He watched her as she came; he watched her as she passed by; and he watched her as she went down the street. The other bishops looked up, saw him still gazing after her and immediately reprimanded him for letting his flesh dominate his spirit. He paid no attention, still watching her. Finally, he turned back and with a very deep sigh commented: "How terrible a thing it is that a woman gifted by God with so great a share of his own beauty should use it for the destruction of the souls of men." He turned and left the other bishops, went down the street after her, and converted her. History or parable, this shows, I think, the sort of integrity that can be achieved even in man's fallen state.

To regain such integrity in our present life requires effort. It is not achieved overnight. Yet any priest who has been around a while knows well enough that there are young men and women who, from the very beginning of their adolescence, have learned how to do this. They have had struggles, sometimes very difficult ones; and yet, as they have grown and matured, they have managed to remain chaste. Those who do not so manage, who fall into one or another sort of sexual sin, will have further struggles, for like so many of God's gifts, integrity will not be given save to the victor in battle, since the victory itself is his gift. Still, for all, there is but the one basic pattern of effort and growth, in cooperation with the grace of God won for us by Christ.

Integrity, then, is within our reach, even if not totally or permanently; for it is never our possession as it was Adam's. But Christ's grace is waiting, and the effort is one worth making; the results can be achieved, some of them in fairly short order.

It often requires a painful struggle to reach the first level (the basic conquest of chastity of which we have spoken). It requires less to maintain chastity and to advance in it thereafter, except on those occasions when, for better knowledge of ourselves and for our humility, God permits violent temptation to attack us. But for the most part, once gained, chastity enables us to live in great peace. As it grows—for, being a form of love, it can always grow—it suffuses us with a tranquil attentiveness that is a reasonable approximation to the integrity that Adam had before the fall or, better said, to the integrity of Christ our Lord, in which it is a sharing.

This fullness of chastity, then, is something that *can* be had and that gives great joy when possessed. It is something that every one of us can demand of our Lord in virtue of his Resurrection and Ascension. It is something he has promised us, if we will only cooperate with the grace that he has won for us.

The Road to Integrity

The Scripture has given us some indication of what this kind of effort requires. When the people of Israel came out of Egypt and were journeying toward the Promised Land, they had to wander through waterless deserts till God would hear their prayers and let refreshment flow from the flinty rock. They had to battle enemies, the wandering tribes of the desert, and, still worse, the peoples who were already established at the borders of the land they hoped for: Amalekites, Ammonites, Moabites. There were constant confusions and bewilderments as they found themselves in situations they did not understand. They learned day by day what God wished of them; yet they disobeyed, rebelled, and often yearned to go back to the familiar things of Egypt —and to slavery.

So it is with ourselves as we seek to become chaste, to remain chaste, or to gain a chaste integrity. The effort thrusts us quickly into a desert; battles soon follow. We find enemies we had not expected, within ourselves, in unforeseen situations, among our friends. There is a lot of confusion and bewilderment at the unfamiliar psychological terrain that opens unconsolingly in front of us. This is particularly true in these days when, within the Church, especially in the matter of sexuality, there is revolt and rebellion even among priests and bishops, like the revolts of Korah, Dathan and Abiram, and the others who rose up against Moses (see Num 16).

Nonetheless, there is no reason for discouragement. Those who are faithful now in their efforts, even despite their falls, will, like those who were faithful then, succeed. As the great crime then, which blocked them out from the land of promise for thirty-eight years, was refusal to believe that God would give them the territory he had promised them, so for us, the one obstacle that can turn our lives to misery is the refusal to believe that God will give us the victory of perfect chastity. But things are better for us than for them, for we have the grace of Christ; and even if we have despaired, he will take us back if we are willing to turn and come.

There is, however, an error that priests, religious, and others who seek to help people in sexual matters need to guard against: the seemingly charitable thought that, since the road that one has followed himself in gaining some degree of chastity has been extremely difficult, he should seek to avoid having anyone else follow it. He would spare others the pain of traveling so rough a road, not by accompanying and encouraging them as they traverse it but by directing them along some different path.

Scripture indicates, however, that there is no possibility of avoiding an arduous journey to the land of promise, especially if one has already seriously mistrusted the Lord's promise. Given our fallen nature, we can be sure that no other road is better, and that most other roads will lead simply further into a wilderness where neither chastity nor integrity can ever be found but only arid desolation and fiery serpents.

To achieve the chastity and integrity we desire, what is most needed is union in heart and in mind with our Lord. We too often simply forget his victory. We fail to stay close to him in our thoughts, though we can share in his victory only by being one with him. Such conscious union is gained, first of all, through prayer.

Saint Joseph—he who married the Virgin to protect her and to safe-guard her virginity—offers us a marvelous example. There can be no doubt about his manliness; he was the man God chose to teach Jesus what it is to be a man. Yet to live worthily for so long in close union with Mary, with no smallest defect of unchaste desire, Joseph could not have had an integrity much less than hers and Jesus'. However strong it was when he and Mary were espoused, it was by continuous converse with her and, far more, with Jesus that it grew with the vigor needed.

Since prayer is our chief mode of conversation with Christ and his mother, our enjoyment of their words and presence, it is easy to understand how Saint Joseph, the patron of chastity for men, should be at the same time the patron of prayer for all. Thus, Saint Teresa of Avila sends us to him as the person from whom we can best learn how to pray on the mysteries of Christ. If we come to live with Jesus and Mary as Saint Joseph did, chastity will quickly grow within us.

Spiritual reading is also a great help. It not only gives us much to pray over but is an important way to learn Christ's mind and attitudes in a day when one reads and hears so many things—and not only in movies, on TV, and in other media—that are diametrically opposed and hostile to what Christianity requires of us in sexual matters. Self-control, mortification, and some suitable bodily penance are also needed.

But all these things are powerless and empty, even deceptive, without charity. If chastity is truly the splendor of charity, then, if there is no charity, if there is nothing to radiate, if there is nothing present to be splendid, one cannot be chaste, no matter what penance, no matter what prayer, no matter what reading, no matter what other activities one engages in.

Young people will sometimes go to Communion daily, or at least once a week, because they have a problem with chastity. They mastur-bate, fall when they are with their girlfriends, or whatever; and they have heard that the Eucharist is the sacrament that gives chastity. This is true, but they have misunderstood it. What they are thinking of is something that will magically quiet their passions or remove their temptations or at least give them, without further ado, the strength regularly to overcome the temptations.

They have not understood that the Eucharist is principally the sacra-ment of charity. No one has shown them that if the Eucharist makes us share still more in the life of Christ and offers us a greater intensity of that love by which he died for the salvation of all, then their whole life must be reoriented outward toward other people. Such a young person needs to be taught the connection between chastity and charity and how the Eucharist will give him greater grace to turn away from himself and outward toward others, so that he can live as the servant and the slave of all, as did Christ, who came not to be served but to serve.

We must, then, receive the sacraments—penance and the Eucharist —as often as we reasonably can, for they are the essential substance that feeds the life of Christ within us. But it is not good to eat heavily and never exercise. Without giving ourselves seriously to the practice of fraternal charity, we will slowly grow flabby spiritually and eventually fall ill and die.

So, the goal, the purpose, the focus of our reception of the sacraments must always be to let our Lord join us to himself in his life of perfect charity. Charity is not just any love for others, but the love that grows from faith and gains its strength from hope. By it, we love God above every creature, because we know by faith that he alone is worthy of all praise, love, worship, and service. Since we believe that God created all men because he loves them all and desires the salvation of each, we therefore also love them—for God's sake, not because of their own good qualities. Whether we like them or not, we know that Christ loves them. His love is sufficient for us; and loving them, we know his love more fully in return. It is this love that makes us truly chaste; for, as already seen, any failure in chastity is somehow a turning away from this love.

The secret lies in love, just as the secret of all genuine sexual relationships is love: giving oneself or preparing to give oneself to the person beloved by the integral symbol of love. It is a matter of leaving childhood, where a person is solely a recipient of his parents' love, and entering adulthood, where he is fit to be a parent—of his own children or God's—where he is capable of giving love even if he receives little or no love in return, giving his own love constantly and firmly, even as God gives. Since God gave his Only Begotten Son to suffer and die for all men, so we must be willing to suffer and to die out of love: to suffer and die for spouses and children, our own or others'—all of this for the sake of that perfect union with God that is our marriage with the Lamb of God in heaven forever.

II

THE MEANING OF
FERTILITY AWARENESS

9

TOWARD A THEOLOGY OF
NATURAL FAMILY PLANNING

In recent years we have seen increased attention given to natural family planning (NFP) within Catholic programs of marriage preparation. There have been tremendous advances in the understanding of human fertility and human procreation. But there have also been many questions of morality that have been raised. The purpose of this volume is to offer a theology of natural family planning.

As Catholics, we have to look at some length at the foundations of our understanding of sexuality. It is impossible to comprehend sexuality correctly by looking at it all by itself. All that we are able to know about human life from psychology, sociology, history, philosophy, physiology, physics, and so on is pertinent insofar as these approaches are rightly subordinated to faith, since each of them shows us aspects of this complex image of the Creator that we are. We must see it in the context of all that the human being is. We must see it, further, in the context of the entirety of our faith. It is only when we have looked somewhat slowly, somewhat leisurely, in the context and the framework of faith and its understanding of human beings, that we will be able to understand our sexuality.

If today's Catholics have weakened in the degree to which their understanding of sexuality is distinctively Christian, it is not only by reason of their unconscious assimilation of secular viewpoints but also for historical reasons. For most of the last 350 years moral theology has been making an attempt to find ways to explain and support the various positions that the Church takes on various questions that could be used easily in confessional practice. It has often been a search for formulations that would sum up the Church's moral teachings in a matter of moments for penitents.

These carefully crafted formulations have generally been used to good purpose, but without any special moral sensitivity or perceptiveness. Doing so has certainly had its value in pastoral practice. But by overly stressing such summary formulations, we have tended to separate moral action from the actual understanding of these matters in faith. We have risked isolating them from other things that God had revealed to us about ourselves and our actions. It became too easy to know what we ought to do or not do, without understanding why such action agreed with or contradicted our faith. More recently, of course, false teaching has entered the Church from the surrounding culture. Without denying or downgrading explanations that are stated in terms of the natural moral law, I do not think that Christians grow well on such arid soil, for they need the rain of grace and faith that descend on the grass (see Ps 72:6).

Even when using the natural moral law to consider these matters, however, it has been possible to improve our understanding of sexuality by putting these questions in the light of faith. For instance, speaking of *the* purpose of intercourse (as if there were but a single purpose) has long been brought into question, for various reasons. It is certainly better to talk about the *purposes* of intercourse, and yet even this phrasing suffers from a related problem, namely, the risk of confounding the conscious goals that sexually active persons may have with the intrinsic finality that God has built into such actions. The very fact of such controversy in this area of thought brings out the need for far deeper consideration of what faith shows us about God's plan for man and for the sexuality with which he endowed him.

The fullness of God's plan for us is not exhausted by reference to such true but narrow categories as the natural ends of "procreation" and "mutual love". God's creative action demands a yet greater reverence from us if we would speak of it at all. For our purposes here we will take this up by reflecting on the fact that all sexual activity is symbolic, and, indeed, at all three levels of symbolism: the conventional symbolism of particular human cultures, the natural symbolism found in the way in which we are made, and the supernatural symbolism revealed to us in the Scriptures.

In many cultures, for instance, a kiss is a symbol of love, and in a specific context the type of kiss says much about the type of love that is intended. At another level, fire is often seen as a symbol of love, precisely by being warm and fascinating, but also dangerous. And love itself (including sexual love and sexual activity) is symbolic of things other than itself. This level of symbolism will be very important for what we wish to look at here. In particular, human love is used in revelation in ways that are symbolic of the relationship between Christ and his Church, as we will see. Sexual activity, of course, is also unconsciously symbolic, for it has a meaning built into it by its very nature and structure as something that is always present and always active, even if we ourselves are not consciously aware of its presence, or are utterly incapable of grasping that meaning, and even if we mean something quite different in our activity.

Now, there is often a certain discomfort with symbolism that is not simply coincidental. It is something that has bothered Christians all through the centuries. We know from the iconoclast controversy, a great heresy back in the eighth century, that some people simply would not tolerate for use in Christian worship any images or their veneration, whether it be the crucifix or paintings or any other type of image. There is a strong iconoclastic movement within Protestantism even today, especially in the Calvinist tradition. Their churches are very bare. Images, crucifixes, and all sorts of external things of this kind (the musical, the visible, the sensible)—all these things are set aside. Today we often find the same spirit again afoot in some Catholic churches, for once again there is a strong desire to simplify and strip away the sensible, the sensual, the carnal, and the corporeal.

At one level, the reason for this tendency, I think, is that we are proud of our minds, that we take great joy in being able to think, to choose. We sense ourselves as superior to all animal creation in virtue of our minds and our ability to think and choose. We might, perhaps be able to do theology without reference to the body; but we cannot have liturgy or a church without one. We cannot have Christianity except in our bodies and with our bodies and through our bodies. We have to put aside the pride of our minds and allow our minds to operate in the way that they truly exist in us, namely, as the spiritual and intellectual principles or "forms" of our bodies We are not two beings. We are not a mind or a soul *in* a body. Each of us is a single, flesh-and-blood being who can also think and freely choose.

Theology is always conditioned by time and place. It is developed in a language that ties the individual theologian to his particular society and linguistic group. His culture, the contingent social interests of his day, and his personal experiences are obvious in all that he does theologically. The sacraments and the liturgy (but not the theology of these things) transcend all such limitations because the primary symbols of life and death, of the varieties of love, and of spiritual nourishment and intoxication transcend all cultures.

Speaking somewhat generally, there are important differences in the way in which men and women tend to view their bodies. Typically a man considers his own body (or another's) in terms of its powers and skills. In sexual as in other matters, his language centers on bodily action and on physical feelings of pleasure or pain. He evaluates a body more on the basis of what it can do and accomplish than on its appearance. He sees even the beauty of a woman's body more in terms of what sexual activity she might be interested in or of the ease with which she might bear a child than simply, say, in terms of its harmony. A woman, originally brought to the man as a gift from God, as his helpmate, is one who is named by him. This is a kind of sign of his authority over her. Yet she is his equal in nature, drawn from his side, and brought to him by God. She is naked, and the man accepts her. When sexual intercourse is about to take place, it is the man who normally takes the initiative: he is usually the first to get aroused, often in anticipation merely by thought or by sight, as they wait for one another to undress or as they undress each other. Although the woman depends on his arousal to initiate her own, she is not passive but, rather, responsive to him. She indeed invites him, draws him; she may even seduce him.

A woman regards her body much less in terms of power and ability than does a man. She sees her body in terms of unity, grace, beauty. It is psychologically part of her in a way that a man's body does not seem to be part of him. Her body enables her to interiorize things that are not herself—her clothing, for example, becomes part of her, whereas a man's clothing does not become part of him. Her thoughts and words about sexual matters center far less on actions and physical response than on emotional relations and on the inner feelings of the heart.

We could profitably consider the goodness of Christ's body, of our own bodies, and of all material things. In the course of this study we will see how the Church keeps the goodness of the material world before us by her use of symbols. For our purposes here, a symbol is a material thing that, by its own likeness to something spiritual, leads us to a fuller knowledge of that spiritual thing. Our own human nature is pervasively symbolic; not merely because we are partly material, partly spiritual (a condition that is the root of symbolism), but because we have been made in the image and according to the likeness of God. By our very being, we reflect God. Not surprisingly, then, God's communications with us have been in large measure through symbols. He has spoken to us not only in the symbolism of the liturgy and of the sacraments but through the manifold symbols of the Bible.

It is this context, an understanding of the Christian meaning of human sexuality, that is crucial for resolving the questions that have arisen about natural family planning. It is my hope that these pages will be of help to Christian spouses as they try to live in and for Christ.

10

THE NATURAL MEANING OF
TEMPORAL PATTERNS OF FERTILITY

Fertility is the capacity to generate new living beings of the same species, the capacity for reproduction. In its full or integral sense, human fertility belongs only to a couple, to a man and a woman together, and not to either one individually. In this respect, it is quite unlike the fertility of self-fertilizing plants or of those lower animal organisms that can reproduce asexually or that are parthenogenetic.[1] Secondarily, of course, "fertility" indicates the physical capacity of a person (whether a man or a woman) to contribute all the bodily elements that need to be provided by a person of that gender for a child to be conceived.

Fertility (in either sense of the term) is absent in childhood. Neither a boy nor a girl is fertile. She cannot conceive; he cannot fertilize. The highly specialized gametes that are needed for the generation of offspring, with their half-complement of chromosomes, cannot yet be formed in the body of a child. The process leading from repeated mitosis to the necessary meiosis in the gonads requires a long, slow maturation of the entire body. Puberty is the name for the onset of fertility in each sex.

Fertility begins in the adolescent male as he enters his final spurt of bodily growth. At this time his muscles take their adult form; his senses, especially sight, gain new sharpness and sensitivity; his passions

---

[1] The existence of a whole species of animals of just a single sex, where the sole method of reproduction is parthenogenesis, seems only recently to have been confirmed. There is now evidence for this phenomenon in some twenty species of fish and some twenty-five species of lizards, and at least one species of snake. See Charles J. Cole, "Unisex Lizards", *Scientific American* 250, no. 1 (1984): 94–100 and the appended bibliography; see also Demian D. Chapman et al., "Virgin Birth in a Hammerhead Shark", *Biology Letters* 3, no. 4 (August 22, 2007): 425–27, doi: 10.1098/rsbl.2007.0189.

(especially physical courage, anger, and sexual desire) become strong and virile; and his own socialization as an adult takes place. All these things and more are needed if he is to be biologically successful as a husband and a father. Analogous changes take place during the latter part of the adolescent girl's growth spurt, which generally comes just before menarche.[2]

A young man's fertility is continuous from puberty onward. Although his desire may fluctuate, and even psychic impotence may occur, his seed remains steadily powerful. Usually, of course, he can contribute it at will. Ordinarily he remains fertile throughout his life and undergoes no equivalent to menopause; during his fifties, however, spontaneous arousals generally decline sharply in frequency.

A young woman's fertility is cyclic during the years when she possesses it. Only once in a lunar month or thereabouts does her body release an ovum that can be fertilized. Simply from a consideration of the relative lengths of time, infertility is the rule. In addition to the limitations on fertility that are set by the woman's monthly cycle, a long period of infertility is induced by pregnancy. This infertility continues for some three or four weeks after childbirth, and much longer if she breastfeeds her child regularly and often.[3] Finally, with menopause, a woman ceases to ovulate and becomes sterile for the rest of her life.

---

[2] There are usually two growth spurts in males: one in early adolescence (prior to the beginning of nocturnal emissions) and one in middle adolescence, but only one such growth spurt in females (prior to menarche). In the first two years after menarche, ovulation is not yet regular, occurring in 45 to 55 percent of cycles. See F. R. Vollman, *Major Problems in Obstetrics and Gynecology: The Menstrual Cycle* (Philadelphia: Saunders, 1977). Psychic changes in the female are almost the inverse of those in the male. Males experience an increase of self-esteem when they enter middle adolescence (after their first nocturnal emission), but girls often experience an initial loss of self-esteem after menarche. The rapid increase in estrogen after menarche closes the growing ends of the long bones, so that on average a girl grows only about one and a half inches in height after menarche. See H. Klaus and J. L. Martin, "Recognition of Ovulatory/Anovulatory Cycle Pattern in Adolescents by Mucus Self-Detection", *Journal of Adolescent Health Care* 10 (1989): 93–96.

[3] Breastfeeding alone, with no other action to decrease fertility, is sufficient to space children at intervals of up to four or five years, although such large intervals are rare because they depend on a pattern of very frequent feeding. See Peter W. Howie, "Synopsis of Research on Breastfeeding and Fertility", *Breastfeeding and Natural Family Planning*, ed. M. Shivanandan (Bethesda, Md.: KM Associates, 1986), pp. 7–22; also R.V. Short, "Breast Feeding" in *Scientific American* 250, no. 4 (April 1984): 35.

The generation of children is contingent on the woman's menstrual cycle in a manner whose temporal patterns show the influence of both male and female patterns of fertility. The length of the fertile times, that is, those during which their sexual intercourse can result in conception, is not determined simply by the length of life of the ovum, for sperm may still be active within a woman after an act of intercourse that occurred several days before ovulation. Nor is the fertile time determined solely by the normal survival period of the sperm, for the ovum may have been released nearly a day before impregnation.[4]

In sum, the fertility of a couple begins only when both individuals are sexually mature. It ceases definitively when the woman reaches menopause. Within these limits it is cyclic. There are thus two basic types of temporal process that must occur together for there to be fertility: (1) the maturing and the aging processes in each individual and (2) the cycles of alternating fertility and infertility in an adult couple, modulated by the interruptions due to the conception, the birth, and the suckling of a child.

Meaning

What is the meaning and the symbolism of these seasons and periods of fertility? Here, as in other aspects of sexuality, the primary level of meaning can be discerned for the most part from a careful description of the facts at the level of the human perception and understanding of these facts. We must also acknowledge that certain aspects of human fertility generally escape our notice. Their meaning will also need to be considered in due course.

Most obvious, yet most important, is the fact that the potential for becoming a parent is present separately in each partner, even though human fertility in its full or integral sense belongs only to a couple and is realized only through their union. The natural meaning of intercourse is sexual union, that is, the union of the couple in a sexual way. Intercourse bespeaks the sort of union of souls as well as of bodies that can be properly found only in marital love (see chapter 3). Inasmuch

---

[4] H. Klaus and M. U. Fagan, "Natural Family Planning: An Analysis of Change of Procreative Intention", *Journal of American Medical Women's Association* 37, no. 9 (September 1982): 232.

as it is sexual, it symbolizes a total openness to the other person as well as to the children who could come from intercourse, even if neither individual consciously desires children.

In fact, this natural meaning of sexual intercourse remains the case even when one or both of the individuals consciously intends not to have children and takes some sort of contraceptive action to prevent the generation of children. As the very term "contraception" suggests, the opposition to conception that is chosen in contraception may well mean that the deliberate choice to stifle fertility contradicts the natural meaning of sexual intercourse. The fact that fertility properly belongs to the couple, and not to either individual alone, symbolizes that as the result of their sexual union the child ought to come into the world from the hidden depths of mutual love, originating in human love and delight (see Wis 7:1–2). Human reproduction calls for a pairing between a man and a woman who act in virtue of their full humanity, united not only in body but in heart and mind, and dedicated to the generation and upbringing of children who come about from the proper use of their fertility.

Although children can feel some degree of genital pleasure, they are not fertile. Even if some sort of sexual intercourse were to be forced upon a child, the child would be incapable of fertility or of conjugal love, for the child is not yet ready at the bodily level for the generation of children, and at the level of human maturation they are not yet ready for the demands of spousal love. Only gradually do they become fertile, and only gradually do they become ready. Provided that their surroundings do not prematurely stimulate them, their interest in sexual relations will be stirred seriously only at a later time. When a child is not yet physically mature enough to appreciate the relationship, any genital relationship whatsoever is abusive. It is likely to frighten the child, and it may cause an arrest of psychosexual development such as is encountered in homosexuality. By many, homosexuality is considered to be an arrest of psychosexual development at the level of same-sex attraction.[5] In short, the infertility of the child (compared with the fertility that goes with adulthood) indicates that procreation is for adults. The slow process of a child's maturation points to the abiding need for

---

[5] See Erik Erikson, *Childhood and Society*, 8th ed. (New York: W. W. Norton, 1993 [1963]), p. 274.

adult care within a family, where love and trust can allow the child to grow in security until he is really ready for intercourse in marriage.

Now, the growth curve of humans is unique among mammals in its shape and slowness. The young of other species are able to care for themselves in substantial measure long before a human infant can do so. The length of human childhood—some twelve to fourteen years —points directly to the need for the family. Bringing children to full physical adulthood and to normal socialization takes still longer.

Becoming a good parent is not a matter of merely random events. It calls for each partner to dedicate attentive effort over a large portion of a lifetime. A mother not only gives birth to and suckles her children but must nurse their cultural development. The father must provide for and protect his wife and children, especially during her pregnancies. The stable presence of both parents is of major importance for the proper sexual orientation and socialization of the children, so that they can learn how to love properly by gaining the experience of giving and receiving love within the family. In brief, the integral meaning of sexual union is the family: the stable, monogamous, and fruitful union of the spouses.

It is, then, no surprise that the pattern of healthy psychic maturation is strictly coordinated, as psychologist Erik Erikson has well argued, with the acquisition of those habits of mind and heart that gradually render one fit to be a parent. Only when one has reached the stage that Erikson aptly calls "generativity", that is, a stage when one can love unselfishly and steadily, even without being so loved in return, is one ready to raise children, and only then can one be truly considered an adult. All this indicates that the generation of children is the business of adults, the proper task of the mature. The power, both physical and psychic, to generate and to rear children is the defining property of adulthood, the pivot of adult life and action.[6]

Fertility normally comes to an end well before the end of adult life. Menopause sets in about the time when the alertness and unflagging energy that is needed to care for small children begin to fade. Thereafter, being unable to produce further ova, a woman is sterile; and

---

[6] See Sigmund Freud, *A General Introduction to Psychoanalysis*, trans. Joan Riviere (Garden City, N.Y.: Garden City Publishers, 1935), p. 277. Note too that even the most chaste celibate must become father or mother, not carnally but psychically and spiritually, in order to live well in Christ. On this point see pp. 117–18.

everything in her body that made the conception, carrying, or nursing of a child possible shuts down and gradually withers away. Her uterus becomes involuted; her ovaries become smaller; her breasts and milk ducts change.

Sterility has in common with infertility an inability to conceive. But the difference between these conditions is great. In a woman, sterility is either the inability to produce a viable ovum or some condition that prevents its union with the sperm of her husband, whereas infertility implies only the temporary absence of a mature ovum. When it works, the pill sterilizes a woman temporarily by suppressing ovulation; it also reduces the motility of the fallopian tube and changes the structure of the endometrium and of the cervical mucus.

The structural meaning of sterility is reflected in the Church's canon law for marriage, which considers the matter under the heading of "impotence". Genuine "antecedent and perpetual impotence"[7] invalidates an attempted marriage, for intercourse is the natural symbol of marital love as well as of openness to children, but intercourse is impossible for the impotent. Without any possibility of sexual intercourse, no other relations between man and woman suffice to constitute marriage.

On the other hand, canon law recognizes that sterile marriages can be valid[8] even when a couple knows before their wedding that one or both of them is sterile. The fact of sterility does not nullify a marriage so long as there is no refusal to have children, should it eventually prove possible (for example, a man who has genuinely repented of a vasectomy may enter into marriage). What would invalidate an attempted marriage would be a sufficiently clear intention against having children, not the mere inability to have them. The fact of sterility might mask this intention, and so couples in this situation should examine their motivations carefully.

What should we make of the case of a putative marriage in which the act of consent was conditioned by the resolve totally to exclude children? If this resolve implies no refusal in principle of either party's right to intercourse (in fertile as well as infertile periods), then it would seem to allow for a valid marriage, even if the couple are agreed that

---

[7] This term designates impotence that is prior to the exchange of consent and that would require extraordinary means to repair, for the situation will not resolve itself over the course of time simply by natural processes.

[8] *Code of Canon Law*, can. 1084.3.

neither will use this right. But should their resolve totally to exclude having children condition that right itself, as would seem almost certainly the case in practice, or should it imply that they will always practice contraceptive intercourse, it constitutes clearly a putative marriage that is actually null and void.[9]

It is crucial to see that the times of infertility are not times of temporary sterility but actually a stage in the cyclic process that makes procreation possible and thus a preparatory stage for burgeoning life and growth. Infertility is the natural condition of all individuals during childhood and of adult women during the larger portion of their menstrual cycle. The early infertile portion of the menstrual cycle is but the quiet period of growth prior to the healthy ripening of a new ovum, and thus quite unlike sterility. It is followed by the later infertile phase, the interval before the next cycle (days 8 to 13) in which the corpus luteum is still alive. Beginning with day 14, the corpus luteum tends to die off if there has been no conception and the preparatory stage for the next cycle begins. Infertility is natural in the strongest sense of the word and, indeed, is required if fertility itself is to be of full value to the species.

This inner vitality of the infertile periods can well be compared with the cycle of the seasons of the year.[10] The seasons also show certain times of manifest fertility and other times that are infertile but not sterile, for they are equally necessary for the life-giving process taken in its cyclical structure. The continuous and rhythmic (but seldom completely regular) alternation between fertility and infertility would seem to symbolize, at the minimum, human oneness with the natural world and the way in which we share within ourselves the natural world's cyclic rhythms. But the time of infertility also symbolizes that the wintry and least promising seasons of our lives still give good grounds for hope in the hidden growth of a fertility that leads to new life. The various nature religions witness to this understanding, with their myths and mysteries that are centered on the death and resurrection of their fertility deities.

---

[9] See *Code of Canon Law*, cann. 1101.2 and 1055.

[10] As but one example, see John and Nancy Ball, *Joy in Human Sexuality* (Collegeville, Minn.: Liturgical Press, 1975), pp. 52ff.

A woman's old age, however, is no longer a time of preparation for renewed fertility and possible conception. The source of new life within her has dried up. Her womb is as good as dead, although she is not. Since sterility represents the loss of the ability to contribute new members to the race, some connection with death is symbolized here, but not the death of the individual woman. Her sterility does indicate a sort of preparation for death and even a partial dying—the dying out of the power to give new life. Her role in fending off death from the race and giving it a continuing future by bringing new members to life is finished. Interestingly, it is only in this century that significant life expectancy beyond menopause has become common.[11]

Yet precisely here we see that a woman is much more than one who bears children and that adult life (for men as well as for women) is meant to contain much more than the raising of children. The sterility of old age indicates also a laying down of the burdens connected with pregnancy and childbirth. Just as a man's continued fertility symbolizes his never finished task of caring for his family through his activity in the world outside the family, by working for the good of all families, so a woman's task, even though brought to an end so far as contributing to the common good through new members of her own family, is only augmented and increased, for it is now extended to the larger community.

Even within her own family, the greater portion of a woman's effort as a mother is to act as the conserver of the past and the transmitter of the culture to her children. But once her children are grown, she is enabled so to act for the common good of society, not just for her own children. Thus, the sterility of age, which is just as natural as the infertility of childhood and the phased infertility of her cycles, is less a sign of death and more a sign of readiness for greater concern with the social good of all at the cultural level.[12]

---

[11] Menopause, like hysterectomy, can seem like a psychic death—but with the tremendous shift toward contraception today these common feelings are often ridiculed. See Helene Deutsch, *The Psychology of Women*, vol. 1, *Girlhood* (New York: Grune and Stratton, 1944) and vol. 2, *Motherhood* (New York: Grune and Stratton, 1945).

[12] The loss of one's hormonal cycle can translate into a more even emotional state, especially for those who have had strong mood swings prior to menopause. Premature menopause, whether due to surgical removal of the ovaries, or from medical causes and the resultant loss of the ovarian hormones, frequently leads women to experience de-

When considered more deeply yet, a woman's seasons of periodic fertility can be rightly read as signs of God's fidelity to all people, to those who know him and to those who do not. It is his faithfulness that provides new children, the new lives that are the ever renewed hope of the race, the new shoots of ever recurring spring in the midst of this life's apparently endless winter. Not every peak of fertility will result in a child; but each peak is capable of this. Each is a pledge and promise of God's further great work of creation by bringing into being each marvelous creature that a new infant is.

We have been speaking here about the seasons of the year, but it is not the annual cycles of the seasons that are most important in human fertility so much as the monthly cycles that parallel the waxing and waning of the moon. What exact connections there may be between the light sensitivity of the endocrine system and the phases of the moon is not clear.[13] In our great cities the nights are far less dark than a field under a full moon. Yet neither is it possible to disregard out of hand the fact that a woman's cycle is more or less the length of a lunar month.

One way in which to understand the meaning of the menstrual cycles is by considering what would happen were a woman continuously fertile. On this hypothesis, nearly every act of intercourse would result in pregnancy. If intercourse occurred more often than every nine months, both the woman's life and those of the infants in her womb would be in grave jeopardy. Fertility does not generally seem to be correlated with the possibility of intercourse but with the conditions that are advantageous for conception. That is, our nature seems to be such that the conditions for possible conception tend to reduce the

---

pression. On the other hand 16 to 56 percent of oral contraceptive users have depressive symptoms. See G. B. Slap, "Oral Contraceptives and Depression: Impact, Prevalence and Cause", *Journal of Adolescent Health Care* 2, no. 1 (1981): 53–56. There may be a biochemical basis for this, for some 60 percent of adolescents who begin using the pill discontinue in less than one year. According to Hanna Klaus, M.D., the pill tends to wipe out the hormonal cycle; the release of endorphins is simply prevented, and this brings on the depression; see her "Positive Woman or Negative Man?" in *Linacre Quarterly* 43, no. 4 (1976): 244–48.

[13] Joy DeFelice has studied the perception of some light by parts of the body other than the eye and on the relation of artificial lighting to melatonin production and the pineal gland. Joy DeFelice, *The Effects of Light on the Menstrual Cycle: Also Infertility* (Spokane, Wash.: Sacred Heart Medical Center, 1996). See also R. J. Wurtman, "The Effects of Light on the Human Body", *Scientific American* 227 (1975): 69–77.

absolute number of conceptions that do occur, precisely so that those that do occur will be more likely to continue in good health and without harm to the mother.

Continuous fertility, on the other hand, would require a quasi-continuous release of fertile ova. If this were the case for human beings, women would be like hens, whose eggs appear daily. Given the longevity of sperm, even fairly infrequent intercourse would then result not merely in more frequent children but in what would amount to multiple conceptions, that is, one each day over the period of sperm vitality. Unlike the conceptions of a chicken, whose eggs leave her body long before the young develop, multiple human conceptions would take place independently. If they were to implant in the uterine wall, it would seem likely that it would notably increase the risks of pregnancy for both mother and children, were frequent coitus to bring about conceptions of high multiplicity.

Were a woman continuously fertile throughout her childbearing years except for the interruptions due to the carrying or nursing of a child, then every act of intercourse outside such periods would result in another child. A normal family would number fifteen to twenty. How many women are physically strong enough to bear so many children without loss of their own life or permanent debility?[14]

Thus, fertility, even considered biologically, is fundamentally at the service of the family. The rhythms of fertility cycles exist to preserve the health and the physical strength of the mother as well as to guarantee a suitable spacing of the siblings.[15] Human fertility in its integral sense belongs only to a couple and is realized only through their sexual union. The range of meaning for this type of union is far more intimate than among animals and characterized by penetration face-to-face.

The ovulatory cycle serves both to decrease the number of multiple conceptions and to diminish the multiplicity of those that occur. This

---

[14] Birth intervals of two to three years have been shown to correlate with optimal child survival as well as with maternal health. Thus, a woman who begins childbearing at eighteen and has adequate nutrition and prenatal care could have nine to twelve children. Sadly, even in optimal circumstances, many women suffer from hypertensive cardiovascular disease after multiple pregnancies.

[15] The spacing between siblings has its own importance for their psychological growth as well as for their physical health. See Herbert Ratner, M.D., "Child Spacing" in *Child and Family* 8 (1969): 290–91 and 9 (1970): 2–3 and 99–101.

makes it easier for the newly conceived to survive until birth and for the mother to provide adequately for her offspring both before and after birth. The same purpose is visible in the prolonged postpartum infertility of the nursing mother. Not only does nursing a newborn assist in restoring to the womb its tone and proper strength before another child is conceived, but this special infertility also protects the mother from the physical drain of having to nurse one or more children while carrying others in her womb.[16]

Only through our existence and growth in time is it possible to have the dependencies of the young on the old and of the aged on those younger; these dependencies are among the most powerful of God's chosen instruments to draw us out of our individualism and self-centeredness. The fundamental relationship between parents and their children is one of originators to originated. Basic as this is, it does not make parents different in essence from their children. It is only their displacement from each other in time of origin that makes them seem so. A world in which all the many millions of us had exactly the same age would be notably poorer than our present one, even though it would have vastly greater "equality".

Context

Biologically speaking, all the aspects of sexuality exist only for the sake of the union of the gametes and the nurturing of the children who are conceived. Yet strangely, the act of intercourse, even in a fertile period, does not of itself accomplish the act of fertilization. This vital role of male and female gametes in procreation was unknown until recent times. Such understanding as we have of the special character of the gametes, their genetic properties, and the nature of their activity has come only in the past century. It is, then, only for a short time that

---

[16] Consider the problems that arise when the mother entrusts someone else with the task of nursing. See Howie, "Research on Breastfeeding", pp. 18–19, which tells of Lady Traquair, wife of the fourth Earl of Traquair, who bore him seventeen children, one every ten or eleven months, apart from one gap due to illness, and who lived to be eighty-eight. The secret of such fertility, however, lay in her use of a wet nurse for all her children. Since the situation is not improved by replacing the wet nurse with a bottle, a consistent approach to NFP will require a rethinking of American dependence on the bottle.

people have been able to distinguish between *conception* (the union of gametes by which a new human person comes into being), *implantation* (the blastocyst's taking root in the mother's womb, at which time the newly conceived child begins to control some of the mother's vital processes and to direct them to his own benefit as he grows), and *impregnation* by her husband's seed (the condition of being made pregnant, which begins with coitus).[17] Therefore, in speaking of the natural symbolisms of the various aspects of fertility, it is necessary to note the different types and levels of activity about whose meanings we are interested, while focusing on the gametic level as the most basic one, albeit the most mysterious.

All that was known of fertility until recent times was its observable effects and certain other phenomena indirectly correlated with it. Thus, conception came to be known by a woman's missing of her periods. It was then experienced in other ways during an actual pregnancy. The most obvious of correlated phenomena was the menstrual cycle. The menstrual cycle, however, was often incorrectly interpreted in its relations to fertility. Even as late as the early years of the past century, physicians commonly thought a menstruating woman to be fertile.[18] Other correlates, for the most part unrecognized in the West until recently, include the infertility of women who were either pregnant or nursing.

The sterility of old age was easily recognized, but otherwise sterility was known only by inference from a complete failure of a woman to conceive (despite many opportunities) or the complete failure of a man to beget (even though having many wives and concubines). The infertility of childhood was known, of course, but its limits were not, except for menarche. Indeed, the onset of presumed fertility can be easily recognized from various physiological signs of ovulation, and these signs form the basis for the practice of natural family planning.

---

[17] See X.G. Fan and Z.Q. Zheng, "A Study of Early Pregnancy Factor Activity in Pre-Implantation", *American Journal of Reproductive Immunology* 37, no. 5 (1997): 359–64. Even prior to implantation the blastocyst emits several steroids, among them early pregnancy factor, an immunosuppressor detectable within forty-eight hours of fertilization, and hCG (human chorionic gonadotropin), which appears a few days later. It directs the corpus luteum to make the changes necessary for the continued support of the pregnancy.

[18] This is true in the case of a woman who has a short follicular phase.

Hence, one can rightly say that fertility as such was largely unknown and unknowable through most of history. A woman's cycles of fertility, often surmised from such correlated signs as menstruation, could not be identified with any precision or known in truth. Thus, for the first time, natural family planning offers a way of entry into the symbolism of the fertility cycle as such, as distinguished from, say, the menstrual cycle.

This difference in symbolism (with regard to what intercourse means) would seem to be one of the most significant differences between natural family planning and contraception. In the latter case, the woman (or, less commonly, her partner) is rendered sterile; neither sort of sterility occurs through natural family planning. The symbolic difference is considerable. In natural family planning there remains the promise and even the hope of conception and of new life that can develop. This consideration is made not only physiologically but also in terms of the family needs that serve as the motivation for the use of natural family planning. By contrast, in cases of contraception, one has as a result only death—dead ova or dead sperm—or, when an interoceptive drug is used, the suppression of growth and the suspension of life.

The natural symbolism of the general dependence of fertility on age (that is, that procreation is something proper only for the mature and that maternity is a duty proper to younger women) has been known for so long that it is hard even to imagine the fact without thinking of its meaning. Yet there are problems in connection with this meaning, especially in our current situation as the age of menarche drops while psychic maturity seems to occur at later and later ages in the same populations. Yet even in this country the basic symbolism is confirmed, for instance, when one hears such remarks as that a thirteen-year-old is simply too young to have a baby, even though she is physically quite ready.

The natural symbolism of the menstrual cycle has also been known for countless ages. For example, the menses were seen in some cultures as a ritual uncleanness, since marked by a physically repellent flow of blood and tissue that, especially in hot climes, calls for quick cleansing if further unpleasantness is to be avoided.[19] It was also seen as a danger,

---

[19] See M. Morofushi et al., "Positive Relationship between Menstrual Synchrony and Ability to Smell 5α-androst-16-en-3α-ol", *Chemical Senses* 25, no. 4 (August 2000): 407–11.

since it is a flowing away of the blood that gives life, and as a threat to men, whose blood is not so expendable in the ordinary course of nature. But in fact menstruation has no direct connection to fertility, convinced though many were of some hidden link. Strictly speaking, menstruation is a sign of failed fertility—it is what happens when one has not conceived.

Nonetheless, the menstrual cycle offers a symbolic bond to the other cycles (especially the lunar cycle) of the natural world. By association, the fertility cycle inherits this bond to the cycles of the world, but with a great intensification of the cyclic meaning and in some respects a strong alteration of the rest of the symbolism. The natural meaning of the cycle of fertility, for instance, makes it a cycle of life. Better understanding of the fertility cycle makes possible the distinction between infertility and sterility, as well as appreciating the symbolism of an aging woman's sterility.

The symbolism of a woman nursing a child is as ancient as the others mentioned above. But its connections with postpartum infertility seem not to have been as widely known. Since a woman often simply stops nursing a child if she becomes pregnant again, it is not clear just how well understood this matter is. The question then arises as to what symbolic value can be given to our current understanding of fertility.

The Independence of Gametes

A first point of interest lies in the strange relationship of the dependence and the independence of the gametes to be found at all levels of reproduction. The gametes are formed by and in the bodies of adults, and they depend on these bodies for the conditions that enable them to live. Yet the gametes, as long as they remain in a hospitable environment, are independent organisms. Each lives with a life of its own, not with the life of the person within whose body it has been formed. The fact that the gametes are living beings that are distinct from the spouses in which they live and that act independently of the will of the parents of any child conceived through the process of fertilization has its own symbolic importance.

Whether a couple's gametes unite is not a matter of anyone's volition. The possibility for the gametes to unite is wholly dependent on when the couple chooses to have coitus. Only when the time chosen for intercourse and the ejaculation of sperm-laden semen coincides with the presence of a viable ovum is the union of gametes possible. All the more so, the child is an independent entity, but considered symbolically he is the most dependent of all, for he must grow to maturity within the womb for long months, and even after birth he remains dependent on the care of his parents, and especially his mother, for a long time.

At least this much seems solid: first, that the union of gametes is independent of the act of coitus, even though this union requires coitus as a necessary condition (if one may neglect, for the moment, laboratory fertilizations) and, second, that genetic diversity between parents and offspring or between siblings can range from exceedingly little to very great.

Suppose that there are a thousand gene pairs that allow for individual variation within the species. Suppose also that each parent has some gametes with one member of each pair and some with the other (for simplicity, say that there is a fifty-fifty distribution). It is at least possible, then, that two siblings could be conceived that have none of these genes in common. Hence, too, it is possible for one of the siblings to be genetically closer to someone from a different family who has some of the same genes and is adopted into his family than to his own blood brother.

Coitus during a fertile time is necessary but insufficient for gametic union and conception. The gametes act independently of the knowledge and will of the couple. Their fusion occurs sometime after coitus. It is brought about by whatever biological attraction draws the ovum to attract the sperm or the spermatozoa to seek out and penetrate the ovum.

A child's every trait and his genetic endowment as a whole comes from his parents, half from his father and half from his mother. The strange combination of similarity and dissimilarity of each child with respect to his parents and his ancestors constitutes as well as symbolizes the social bonding of the child with his family, most strongly with his parents. Although God has given the world for us to know by studying it through physics and biology, he keeps his mysteries to himself. As human persons, new children are in some respects like brothers and sisters to their parents, but displaced from them in time. There is a sort of equality between those of different generations; otherwise one generation could not take the place of another even approximately. Hence, we need to admit that the essential good of human sexuality lies beyond all human determination.

The parents of each newly conceived child also received their traits from the genetic structures of their parents. These genetic relationships with prior generations were always dimly recognized in the notions of one's "lineage" or "blood" or "family". Likewise, the dangers of inbreeding, of producing "degeneration", or of "weakening" the line, as well as the need for "fresh blood" were of deep concern to people millennia before gametes were discovered.

Yet, whenever the union of the gametes results in a healthy zygote, a new genetic type is formed, one that was hitherto nonexistent.[20] Even though a child's physical qualities may be familiar on either or both sides of the family, they are in aggregate wholly new. But more, this person is, in a far stronger sense, wholly new. Although sharing in the personal properties of his family lineage, the child remains an individual and has a distinct destiny. The child is not the exact genetic replica of any of his forebears but constitutes a new human type. Those of his problems that are rooted in his genes (whether the standard types of genetic disease, or the genetic predispositions to other diseases or to certain traits of temperament, or patterns and intensities of feeling and emotion) may be unique to him, or at least not shared with anyone in his family. Conversely, in the many ways in which the new child is like one or the other parent or a sibling, a bond of potential attachment is created. The parents and siblings have a more than ordinary moral responsibility to cultivate this bond. It is something that they can understand well from within themselves. Further, that this particular new genetic type is formed rather than some other one out of the incredible number that are theoretically possible is determined

---

[20] In principle (though utterly improbable in fact) there could be parents of such a genetic structure that a child might have exactly the same set of genes as one of his parents. (It would, of course, still be the case that half the genes would come from one parent and half from the other.) This is in strong contrast to the relation between siblings, whose genetic structures (though occasionally almost identical, as in the case of identical twins who still have different gaps in their genomes) usually range over a quasi infinity of combinations and may even share no genes at all (if one speaks only of those freely varying traits that do not alter the basic life processes).

by factors that lie wholly beyond the knowledge and control of the couple.

Once conceived, the child (throughout the stages of his development as zygote, embryo, and fetus) is wholly dependent on his mother's body for his sustenance and protection—indeed, for seemingly everything —if he is to continue to live and grow. Despite the fact that each parent contributes a single gamete (a symbol of the fact that each parent gives the gift of a numerically equal genetic component to the constitution of this organism), there is a great difference in size and structure between male and female gametes. This indicates that, once constituted, everything else of a material nature that the child needs for his growth and development is supplied by the mother: love, food, elimination of waste, warmth, physical protection, suitable environment, and so on. Yet, from his conception the child is an organism that is radically distinct from the mother in whose womb he lives. He can, in principle, be separated from her completely and still survive insofar as it proves possible to substitute artificially for her nurturing activities. But bonding begins in utero, and separation can mean the stunting of psychological development, for the child in the womb is already responding to various sorts of stimuli. At sixteen weeks his ears are sufficiently developed to hear his mother's voice, and he can feel his mother's movements.

The newborn, too, is profoundly dependent on others for his life and development (physical and intellectual). He becomes part of a family, a clan, a tribe, a people. From them he must learn a language and a culture. Otherwise, like a wolf child, he will be unable ever to think at all, or, at best, only on a level hardly distinguishable from that of animals. Yet, this new human being has his own destiny as an individual, under God's grace, independent of his own destiny of the others on whom he depends and whom he may have to resist, or oppose, or even fight. Further, his participation in society will invariably change the language and the culture, modifying them for children yet unborn.

In sum, at every level of human life one can speak of the normal growth and development of an individual only insofar as he exists, both in radical dependence on others and in radical independence of those others—the ancient dialectical relation between the individual and the community. Only by total self-gift to others can the individual develop fully his potentialities, and only by living in proper independence from others will he have character enough to be able to give anything.[21]

Even at the prepersonal level of the gametes, the symbolism is writ large. Each individual, whether gamete or person, lives well only insofar as it is in continuous transition from a state of nearly total dependency to a state of nearly total independence, which latter state brings it into a new dependency at a higher level. And at all intermediate stages, too, this same dialectical duality that makes further growth essential occurs.

The Scriptures show the full range of this dialectic as it is manifested in the interaction of the individual and the people to which he belongs. In revelation we also find a general awareness of the dialectic of dependence and independence as it is found in the infant, even before his birth, still living in the womb,[22] and a somewhat dimmer appreciation of the transmission of genetic traits and the independence of coitus and conception. What is new today is that for the first time we are able to see clearly this entire dialectic as symbolized at the hitherto unsuspected level of the prepersonal life of the gametes.

It follows, then, that if a child is conceived, we can see more clearly than prior generations could that his parents have not "created" him, even unconsciously. Neither has it been brought about technically by their will as an object that they have made and thus not something that is therefore owned by them.[23] His actualization, even biologically, is not their doing.[24] Children are begotten through the creative act

---

[21] There is a parallel here to the inner life of the Trinity. The Father gives the Son everything except his fatherhood, yet loses nothing of his essential Being by this giving. The Son receives all that he is from the Father without in any way diminishing the Father. The Glory that the Father bestows on the Son and the Glory that the Son spires forth to the Father is the Holy Spirit. Yet the love of the Father, the Son, and the Holy Spirit is not a self-contained love but spills onto all creatures until they too can dwell in that love. See Paul M. Quay, S.J., *The Mystery Hidden for Ages in God* (New York: Peter Lang, 1995), pp. 44–53.

[22] See, e.g., Wis 7:1–6 and Job 10:8–12. How compatible these passages and such others as Jer 1:4–5 are with a later Jewish notion that life begins only with the first breath taken at birth is not immediately clear. See Wis 8:19–20 for what seems still another approach.

[23] See William E. May, "The Laboratory Generation of Human Life, Part I", *Fellowship of Catholic Scholars Newsletter* 3 (June 1986): 9.

[24] The evil of in vitro fertilization (IVF) consists in its rejection and attempted denial of this latter fact. IVF ignores and tramples upon one pole of this dialectic. It treats the

of God, not made as items of property desired or designed by their parents.[25]

Nevertheless, in spite of the independent existence and behavior of the gametes, when all proceeds normally, coitus does provide the necessary conditions for fertilization. Sexual intercourse is not only directed to the actual union of gametes but can in a sense be said to bring it about. Just as a person who pulls the trigger on a gun initiates a causal chain that results in the firing of the bullet, its particular trajectory, and its entry into the target, so coitus initiates a sequence of nonfree actions that, if all else is ready, results in conception. Once ejaculation has taken place, all that is needed for the fusion of the gametes (if, in fact, this occurs) follows by strictly necessary causality.

Thus, the fusion of the gametes is morally attributable to the couple, even though it is not directly caused by them. The process of their union is not perceptible to them, nor is it under their direction or immediate control, save in the merely negative sense that such fusion can be prevented by means of barriers or drugs. Coitus permits the gametes to unite by a process that is in accord with their own natures; but the coitus does not actualize their union.

The meaning of the marital act is not, therefore, contingent upon an actual fusion of gametes.[26] Provided that the couple has not intrinsically altered the nature of their act through contraceptive interventions

---

gametes (and implicitly the child who results) as parts of the parents or as totally belonging to the parents for their existence and for their goals. Contraception treats the gametes as some sort of foreign bodies, alien to each of the couple (or as totally dependent, since they can be blocked and disposed of at will). IVF reflects symbolically a clear technological will to make a child, regardless of what happens to the marital union in the context of which it takes place, regardless of what happens to the zygote if "things do not work out", regardless of the implied grounds for ownership and consequent expectations laid upon the child who has been so made, and, above all, regardless of the radically altered understanding of what it is to be human that is implicit in the making process.

[25] See William May, " 'Begotten, Not Made': Reflections on the Laboratory Generation of Human Life", Pope John Paul II Lecture Series in Bioethics, vol 1, ed. by Francis J. Lescoe and David Lipak (Cromwell, Conn.: Pope John Paul II Bioethics Center, 1983). See also 1 Sam 1:28, where Hannah treats Samuel as "on loan" (but to God) for his entire lifetime.

[26] Conversely, the fact that the fusion of gametes can take place on occasion through masturbatory genital contacts does nothing to change the evil nature of these modes of "togetherness".

of poisoning or blockage, the act continues to symbolize the fullness of spousal love, even should fusion not follow.

The generation of children is the essential or constitutive end of marriage, and in this sense its primary end. Without this orientation of marriage to children, there would be no need for sexual differentiation or for sexual union. As Pope John Paul II has so well shown, the personal union involved in spousal coitus cannot be properly conceived without an openness to the generation of children. But it is important to bear in mind that the personal union involved in spousal coitus is also an intrinsic end of marriage, and the desire for such union may well be what is more in the mind of a given couple on any particular occasion.

It is crucial here to understand that one's fertility is an essential component of one's life as a person, for the earthly life of a human person is not something other than one's existence as a living human body. In intercourse, to give oneself to another (or to receive the other) is to give one's own fertile substance (or to receive the other's) if fertility is physically present at the time of coitus. To say "I wish to be one with you totally" and yet to act in such a way as (in effect) to say "But I do not wish the consequences of total union" is to beget not children but frustration, depression, and anger.[27]

The intrinsic meaning of coitus, therefore, includes the procreation of children, but in a different and less direct way than it includes love and personal union between the spouses. The act means marriage, the union between the spouses themselves at all levels of their being. It does not mean the actual union of gametes but only the possibility of their union. To state it a little differently, the "self" of each spouse contains his fertility, such as it is, strong or weak, healthy or impaired, or even nonexistent. So each spouse's fertility, such as it is, must be included without reserve in the gift of self that constitutes

---

[27] But there are limits here on what such language can express, for in the world children are a greater good (they exist independently), even if not necessarily thought to be a greater good in the concrete motivation of a specific couple. A good deal more finesse is needed in any discussion of this topic if we are to make this matter clearer than any of the formulations that have been offered thus far regarding the ends of marriage. The conscious and deliberate reason for doing or allowing something need not be its intrinsic end, where both are present, i.e., the natural, intrinsic end and the purpose intended by the persons involved.

each act of coitus. But this gift will often fail to bring about conception.

In the procreative act, a sort of adoptive aspect can also be discerned. For in the case of an offspring whom they have generated, the parents are called upon freely to accept the child who, though coming from them, is not theirs but God's. Even though begotten and borne by them from their own substance, the child is genetically different from each of them and, hence, to some degree a stranger at birth. In some cultures one sees a recognition of the need for adopting the child in the way that a child is given a name related to his father. In these sad days when abortion and infanticide make clear that what is natural to us is not always acknowledged or accepted, we see parents refusing and killing an infant who is not what they wanted. If God sends them a child whom they regard as "damaged goods", or even just not the "model" they wanted, they return him at once to his Maker.

On the other hand, the fact that the genetic inheritance of the child comes entirely and in equal measure from both parents, with all that this implies of sympathetic and spontaneous understanding between child and parents, along with the entire dialectical relationship that we have just examined, means that the child belongs within his family until ready to leave home and begin a family of his own. Nothing in this "adoptive" aspect can be a legitimate basis of an argument for the legal independence of the child from his parents.

The similarity that a child shows to both lineages is the physical basis for the sad practice of one parent's using the child against the other, manipulating the youngster through some adult's grasp of these similarities of temperament. And how often today a child is abused in the presence of his own mother by her new husband or boyfriend, something that is possible only through her contempt or hatred of the child's father, to whom the child is fatally similar.

There is a certain mystery here, however. Although physical maturation in bodily growth and in fertility seems always to be closely linked in development, yet changes in the age of their onset does not seem well correlated with psychic maturity. Teenage boys are not ordinarily ready for the responsibilities of fatherhood and tend to shirk them disastrously. The full range of powers associated with physical maturity are needed, or at least highly advantageous, for the proper begetting of a child and his healthy social incorporation. Yet, to an increasing degree, in the industrialized parts of the world, fertility often begins several years before many of the other aspects of physical maturity.

On the other hand, careful demographic studies at least suggest that in a truly "normal" situation (biologically speaking) the correlation between maturity in its fullest sense and sexual fertility may be much closer than is usually observed in most of the world's cultures.[28] First menstruation can occur as late as nineteen to twenty-one years of age in young women living physically vigorous lives in undisturbed and isolated country surroundings.[29] But among girls living in urbanized environments, there has been an increasingly early onset of menstruation (one year earlier every thirty years or so over the past two hundred years).[30] Although less easy to document, an apparently similar, ever earlier onset of nocturnal emission has been occurring among urbanized young men. Here the chief importance of these observations is to suggest that what is regarded as normal in our culture—and, it seems, in many others—may not prove to be what is truly natural for the race at large and may not necessarily be easily incorporated into the natural symbolism of sexuality. What is occurring here may be the result of various changes in the psychological environment of young people, especially an increased exposure to erotic stimuli, and at the same time changes in diet that improve nourishment in ways that produce marked changes in fertility.[31]

At a still more basic level, the mere fact that human reproduction takes place by sexual union at all—that is, by a union of gametes rather than by a division of the organism and thereby the mere multiplication

---

[28] See Howie, "Research on Breastfeeding", p. 16 for the !Kung people, among whom menarche occurs at about sixteen years, menopause at forty. He gives references to other cultures also. All this stands in strong contrast to the current average for cities of highly industrialized societies, where menarche occurs at eleven, menopause at fifty-one. See also J. M. Tanner, "Growing Up", *Scientific American* 229, no. 3 (September 1973): 35–43 for a fuller survey of the situation.

[29] Thus, among the Bundi of New Guinea, the average comes to 18.8 years. See *International Review of Natural Family Planning* 10, no. 4 (Winter 1986): 327.

[30] Tanner, "Growing Up", pp. 42–43.

[31] In most animals fertility is strongly conditioned by seasonal changes, especially among mammals. Calving, foaling, and lambing take place in spring, when there is grass. Lions, tigers, and other carnivores also have their young in the spring. It seems that the longer winter nights enhance melatonin secretion, which is involved in ovulation. See Joy DeFelice, "Effects of Light".

of the individual, as it does with many lower organisms—is heavily charged with symbolic content. For the new individuals arising from sexual union are new also in the sense seen above. They are genetically unique and have siblings who differ from each other over a range from near genetic identity to complete dissimilarity.

This sort of differentiation has brought about the extraordinary variety of living forms within one species, rarely duplicating exactly any individuals yet on earth. Sexual reproduction continually stirs up and activates the genetic pool for the conception of ever new types of individuals, capable of new adjustments to the changes in the world around them. On the other hand, when a sexed individual dies, his unique genetic type dies, never to be replicated materially, still less in mind and will. This dying out of genetic types serves to clear away worn-out generations and to enable the new types to manifest their powers.

Sexual reproduction, then, permits the continuation and continuous adaptation of a species, despite the deaths of the individual genetic types.[32] As a result, there is a sort of shadow to sexual symbolism. Although fruitful coitus snatches ever new life out of our continual dying, grounding hope for a future that the parents can never themselves see, yet there is also an element of sadness present that we shall have to consider in its place.

Indeed, parents will not live forever. They may see their children to the third and fourth generations, but rarely beyond that. They will see the results of the new combinations of genes and the similarities as well as the striking differences in the generations of their progeny. If the sadness is indeed symbolic, it is yet preceded and overcome by the joy of love, and followed, before long, by the further joy of new life.

---

[32] The individual genetically defined amoeba, for instance, never dies, save by accident. Such accidents are indeed effective. Without them amoebas would live forever, and the earth would long since have had no room for other life. Yet, in asexual reproduction, the genetic type continues indefinitely. The individual's substance divides into two identical parts, each going its own way. There are no offspring, but only endless sets of identical twins.

Hiddenness

We have adverted a number of times without comment to a crucially important fact about the gametes, to which we must now return. The discovery of the spermatozoa, visible only under the microscope, took place less than four centuries ago; the ovum, though much larger, was not found until just under two centuries ago.[33] The nature and activity of the gametes are in large measure even now hidden from us, even from our science. Perhaps, then, the physical hiddenness of human fertility has its own symbolic value. What, then, is the human meaning of these facts? What is their symbolic signification?

As many couples who have longed for children know, mutual love and coitus are insufficient to guarantee offspring. Begetting and conceiving require more than good intentions and bodily action. A couple's generative powers must be "well disposed" for procreation in some way that thus far escapes human awareness and control. Hidden and mysterious is the activity of gametes that, for reasons no one knows, sometimes results in conception and sometimes does not.

Other aspects of sexuality are not so deeply hidden. In both man and woman the signs of sexual maturity are obvious to all the world. Even though menopause is not as evident, it is not long before it is possible for anyone to recognize that a woman has lived beyond her power to conceive.[34]

The fertility cycles, however, are hidden. The signs that indicate where a woman may be in her cycle—the fertile mucus, the slight rise in body temperature, the relaxation of the cervix, changes in electrolytes, magnesium, and hormonal levels, perhaps some shadow of estrus—are mostly private and largely invisible to any woman not trained to notice them. Even when noticed, their connection with fertility is also most obscure and can be overlooked or misinterpreted by entire cultures for centuries. This has happened in our own culture, which even now is largely ignorant of this connection.

Although a woman can detect the temporal patterns of her fertil-

---

[33] Karl Ernst von Baer discovered the ovum within the follicle in 1828.

[34] Various modern surgical techniques, including artificial reconstructive plastic surgery try to mask these signs.

ity with sufficient skill and attention, and although this detection is sufficient to render natural family planning as effective as the pill (or more so) for the avoidance of conception, yet certitude is not possible, whatever one's choice of means.[35] There are no signs that are sufficient if one's concern is with the union of the gametes. Not only the intrinsic viability and biogenetic match between ovum and sperm but their time of survival within the particular woman in a particular cycle is unknown and, save on some sort of average, unknowable. The fact that useful details of both joint and individual fertility have escaped the notice of most cultures over most of human history does not legitimate ignoring our present knowledge so as to act out of cultivated ignorance. But it does say something about the degree of hiddenness involved.

Thus, we know of nothing in a man that indicates that his sperm will penetrate his wife's ova. Likewise, we know of nothing in her that tells whether her ova will be receptive to his sperm. Why gametes form in the first place, why they unite as they do, which ones will unite —these are mysteries still. Millions upon millions of spermatozoa are required, for example, for the ovum to be penetrated by any one of them. Between one thousand and six thousand, on average, enter the cervix. Yet only one of all that horde can in fact penetrate. Genetically, we know only that each ovum ripens in its turn, with its own set of genes, randomly allotted so far as we can tell. We have no way of knowing in advance the genetic content of any one of them. A fortiori is this true of the sperm. Yet from all this randomness and intense but hidden activity comes a determinate infant, one of ourselves.

The question is not simply one of science. I am not arguing that we will not eventually find answers to many of our questions. But it does not seem likely, even should a whole gametic physiology and medicine be developed, that the mystery will have dissolved. The perennial mystery of human existence remains: What is the connection between

---

[35] Even surgical excision of large sections of the fallopian tubes and other modes of sterilization have turned out not to prevent all conceptions. They do, however, greatly increase the likelihood that the conceptions that do take place will be ectopic or defective. See *Contraceptive Technology Update* 19, no. 1 (January 1998): 5–6. Although natural family planning is highly effective for avoidance of children, it is less so when used for the sake of conception. In any event, it is not possible to see each act of coitus as directly tied to conception.

the free human person and the biochemical necessities of the body? More importantly for our present purposes, however, it is evident that, even were we to find a description of conception solely in biochemical terms, the natural symbolism would not be altered, except perhaps by some enrichment and gain in detail, even as (at a higher level) coitus does not have its meaning altered by knowing the biology of fertility, except for greater specification and clarity.

What the Scriptures see symbolized by the hiddenness of fertility is that conception is not of human doing but divine. Well aware that a man's seed must act within a woman to beget a child, the patriarchs, and all Israel after them, saw conception as effected by divine power, however dependent on human action. It is still so for us today, in spite of our increased knowledge and technology. Recall the account of the promise that God gave to Abraham, namely, that through carnal union with his sterile wife, Sarah, he would have an heir in whom all the world would be blessed. The generation of Isaac resulted from ordinary coitus between Abraham and Sarah. Yet this conception, more than others, was God's doing.[36]

The cases of various barren heroines of the Old Testament, however, show something about the symbolism of intercourse, namely, that the union of the spouses is a primary good of marriage, which can prevail over the sadness of infertility, even as love can conquer death. Yet, precisely here we see that the woman is much more than just one who bears children. It is clear that adult life, for the man as well as for the woman, includes the strengths and abilities needed for generating and raising children, and yet is meant to contain much more than the raising of children. One meaning of the fertility cycles, then, is that reproduction is not the sole purpose of life, indeed, not the sole purpose of sexual activity, even though sexual activity would not exist were it not for reproduction.

It is God who acts in the darkness of every human conception: "You [the Lord] formed my inward parts. You knitted me together in my mother's womb. . . . You know me right well; my frame was not hidden from you, when I was being made in secret, intricately wrought in the depths of the earth. Your eyes beheld my unformed substance" (Ps

---

[36] Gen 15—18 and 21:1–7. See Heb 11:11 and also the analogous case of the conceptions of Samson, of Samuel, and (in the New Testament) of John the Baptist.

139:13–16). Or, as Job said: "Your hands fashioned and made me . . . Remember that you have made me of clay. . . . Did you not pour me out like milk and curdle me like cheese? You clothed me with skin and flesh, and knit me together with bones and sinews. You have granted me life and mercy" (Job 10:8–12). It is he also who can cause sterility, as when he closed all the wombs in the household of Abimelech (Gen 20:17–18), and it is he who alternately opened and shut the wombs of Leah and Rachel.[37]

Indeed, almost all religions recognize the hidden mystery involved in procreation. They respond to it by acknowledging the divine activity. The awe that the nature religions felt before the mysteries of conception was not misplaced, even though they wrongly directed that awe to nonexistent deities. The hiddenness of the gametes is the sign that makes us appreciate most concretely the mystery involved in every human conception. Some aspects of that mystery can be delineated, but it is not given over in fullness to human understanding. Further, as we saw earlier, the activity of the gametes escapes our control as well as our understanding. The procreation of new human generations is ultimately God's doing, not ours. This is evidently a sign that is not merely ignored by in vitro fertilization but is wholly destroyed thereby.

The natural symbolism of conception is that of hidden divine power. The profound secrecy and still far-from-resolved mysteries concerning the biological bases of human conception point beyond themselves to the greater mystery of God's direct act of creation of every human being. The philosophical necessity that God create each human person (though not argued for here, and perhaps not arguable, on this ground) nonetheless is symbolized by this hiddenness. The converse—non-age-related sterility—may also be seen as the operation of divine power or else a simple withholding of that power.[38] In either case, coitus is

---

[37] See Gen 29:31–32; 30:1–2, 14–24. God's intervention is not needed for the conception of animals. His action as reported in Gen 30:31–43 is confined to overriding ordinary genetics in favor of Jacob's plans and prosperity.

[38] Sterility can also be a consequence of human acts. According to a 1989 report by the World Health Organization, in sub-Saharan Africa, some 60 percent of female sterility is due to sexually transmitted diseases (STDs). In the rest of the world, between twenty and forty percent of female sterility is linked to STDs. Phenomena such as mucus hostility is frequent in prostitutes and in women with several sexual partners. On the exceedingly low pregnancy rate among the sexually hyperactive youth of the Muria people in

necessary but not sufficient for conception. It is therefore not directly symbolic of conception, even though requiring total openness to it.

In sum, the hiddenness of the tremendous power of generation symbolizes what the race has always known, that fertile intercourse is a procreative act only. Unless God also acts to create, no child comes into being. Each parent contributes a material but living element, drawn from his own biological substance and self, which may, if God so chooses, enter into a life-giving union of sperm and egg.[39]

The parents of a child cannot be said strictly even to prepare the matter for a child, for there is a randomness to the particular genetic endowments of the gametes that are used in natural generation. For this reason, even natural generation is in a sense adoptive. Natural intercourse is adoptively oriented toward the children who are conceived as the result of that intercourse. Although adoption is generally thought of as one couple's taking the infant from another couple's union and treating him as if he were their own, something similar takes place when a father or mother remarries after the death of a spouse. Then the children are adopted by the new spouse, and the natural children of the second union are half brothers and half sisters to those who have been adopted.

In the various challenges that daily life presents, one may consider not only conception and birth but the rearing of children in its symbolic meaning. Part of the natural symbolism of conception, considered as the union of gametes, is the fact of parental difficulties with children. I am not referring here to any particular type of conflict—in many families, nothing worthy of so strong a designation as "conflict" ever takes place. But parents often, if not invariably, feel a general responsibility for the child's virtue or vices. How often they wonder, "What did we do wrong?", and many times they stand amazed at the strong virtue of a child that exceeds anything they have taught or even encouraged. Yet they also know the child to be a free agent. In some sense, a child is a kind of temporally displaced brother or sister.

India, see George Maloof, "The Psychology of Fertility Awareness and Natural Family Planning", *Marriage and Family Newsletter* 8 (October–December 1977): 4n3.

[39] Obviously, God acts no less when a child is conceived by in vitro fertilization. He cooperates with the world that he has created according to the natures that he has given to creatures within it, save when he wishes to act miraculously. Sin does not ordinarily provoke him to a gesture of withdrawal and disgust but to anger and punishment.

Children are begotten through the creative act of God, not made as items of property desired by their parents. They are left with their parents as "a heritage from the LORD" and "a reward" (Ps 127:3). "On loan" from God, they are to be returned to him with interest. Their ultimate destiny is, under God, their own free choice.

Fertility and Estrus—an Inadequate Signal

In subhuman animals, fertility makes itself manifest by means of the special smells, sights, and sounds of estrus—all the physical signs that the female is in heat. The cycles of fertility are automatic and automatically respected by the animals. For estrus is not only the external sign of fertility but is normally the sole inducement to copulation. When the female is in heat, the males respond to this time-limited condition with sexual interest and arousal; when she is not, the males show no desire to copulate. Thus, sexual desire is the clear sign of fertility.

Human sexual desire, however, shows very different patterns. In human beings, even though there are some remnants of the estrus cycle, they are sufficiently dim and obscure, so that only with proper training is a woman able to know her fertile days; still less is her husband able to do so.[40]

This decoupling of fertility from what is among lower animals its principal signal reflects itself in the fact that the ovulatory cycle (and, also, the postpartum interruption of fertility) is, in the ordinary course of nature, unperceived. Although the menstrual cycle is evident, its relation to the woman's fertility has been only slowly elucidated. More than eighty years ago Kyusaku Ogino and Hermann Knaus first demonstrated for Western medicine the nature of the woman's fertility cycle.[41] Even though careful observation can tell a woman when she is fertile, the very need to have such fertility awareness taught by one

---

[40] Some men, it seems, can tell by smell when their wives are fertile, and they find it harder to abstain from intercourse in natural family planning because of her "fertile scent". See T. N. Moore, "Male Fertility and Sperm Survival", *Proceedings*, First International Meeting, Ovulation Method Teachers at Saint Margaret's Hospital of Sydney, Australia (July 1973), mimeograph.

[41] Hanna Klaus, M.D. "History and Methodology of Natural Family Planning" in *Natural Family Planning: A Review*, 2nd ed. (Bethesda, Md.: NFP Center of Washington, D.C., 1995), p. 9.

woman to another shows that the matter does not impose itself on consciousness.

Even should a woman's fertility be perceived, it remains inaccessible to direct regulation or control by the couple, despite its sensitivity to the woman's emotions. Further, whatever pertains to fertility yet somehow escapes its proper hiddenness so as to be perceptible to the human eye, defiles both man and woman till ritual purification has taken place. At the supernatural level, the cycles and histories of fertility are correspondingly hidden.[42]

Not only are the signs of fertility obscure enough to pass without notice in many women not sensitized to the signs of their fertility, but desire can as easily be aroused in both partners at times of infertility as at the fertile times. Pathological infertility does not ordinarily show itself in any lack of sexual desire. This lack of correlation between fertility and what is in other animals the principal sign of fertility and the stimulus to copulation exists in man not only with regard to individual cycles of fertility but with regard to the whole of his life.

To begin with, the patterns associated with maturation, sexual interest, and desire (for example, for genital stimulation) are present in the infant and the prelatency child. Naturally repressed during latency by the child's intense interest in the world around him, much fuller desires arise rapidly in adolescence, then slowly decrease over the rest of his life without, ordinarily, being extinguished, no matter how old the individual. Thus, human sexual appetite precedes fertility in a complex way, remains more or less continuously during the cyclic absences of fertility, and lasts well beyond its total disappearance. Yet, although the pattern of desires is conscious enough, the pattern of fertility is not detectable through it.

Yet a postmenopausal woman's pleasure in coitus, as well as her husband's, can well remain as intense as ever. For some women, at least, the pleasure becomes greater as the sometimes quite unconscious fears of another conception are definitively allayed. Satisfying sexual activity remains possible, in any case, for many years more for men and women both.

This continuation of sexual desire and the power of enjoyment into old age, long outlasting fertility, symbolizes clearly that personal union

---

[42] This point will be developed further in the next chapter on pp. 195–200.

is a good that may be sought through coitus indefinitely, even when children cannot be expected. This realization is an element in the decoupling of love and union from the procreation of children.

Indeed, as physical beauty fades and as the possibility of having children ceases, as the home empties out and as physical strength and ability to work diminish slowly, the couple—but especially the wife—feels increased need of reassurance, of confirmation that each of them is loved by the other, even though less and less remains of the charms that first attracted them to each other. Hence, the significance of coitus' remaining a part of life well beyond all these diminishments.

Human sexual desire is, moreover, largely free with regard to estrus in spite of the existence of the ovulatory cycle (and perhaps even a cycle of some sort in the male). Although both sexes experience fluctuations in sexual appetite, no universal pattern seems to be discernible in either sex. In any case, the variations in the intensity of sexual desire that are rooted in the cycles of the body are largely masked or obscured by the much stronger psychic variations that arise from the individuals' emotional reactions to the varied circumstances of their lives. Men and women are drawn spontaneously to sexual intercourse at almost any time when external or psychological circumstances are favorable. There is no need to depend on "being in heat" to trigger their sexual activity.[43]

Thus, there is in human life a considerable decoupling between sexual desire and fertility. There is a loosening, if not an uncoupling, of a woman's fertile times from her times of maximal desire. There is the still greater decoupling of a man's desire from the constraints of estrus; that is, he requires no signal that the woman is fertile (or even desirous of his advances) to be filled with desires for sexual union. Obviously, as with the animals, both male and female can be completely occupied with nonsexual matters, even in periods of maximal desire. But human

---

[43] At least this is true in our fallen condition. Some people speak as if we (men especially) were in rut permanently. And indeed, if chastity is not taught and learned, something close to that seems to become the ordinary condition of our race. But, by the grace of Christ, the truly natural condition of man, including perfect chastity according to his state, can be restored. What might have been true before the Fall seems unclear, but I see nothing in the lives of Jesus or Mary that would indicate in them anything resembling estrus. It would be better to describe the state of integrity as a still greater freedom from such compulsions. See Quay, *The Christian Meaning of Human Sexuality*, pp. 123ff.

beings are quite unlike animals, in which fertility is in total control of
desire, since our desires and psychic states are at least largely independent of our fertility.

Evidently, there can be no expectation that every act of coitus should
result in conception.[44] The existence of a regular "fertility cycle" does
not guarantee actual fertility. It does signify, however, that conception
is not always in order, that it is not always to be desired—since one
cannot truly desire what is not possible—and that it is not connected
in any biologically obvious way to the desire for sexual intercourse.

Desire for physical union, as something expressive of other levels of
desire for union, is not, at least in our fallen condition, tied in any
evident way to fertility. Hence, one may argue to a certain priority of
mutual love (defined by the natural and supernatural symbolism of sexuality) over procreation. This is not to argue in any way that it might
be licit to separate the two, seeking one while blocking the other. It
is not. But it will be important in later discussion of the moral arguments concerning natural family planning to know whether there are
adequate grounds for coitus even should fertility be absent.

Freeing Sexuality from Death

Part of the symbolism of coitus derives from the state that follows
shortly upon it. The matter is summed up by the observation *post
coitum, omne animal triste est* (after intercourse, every animal is sad).[45]
This suggests at least one ground for a natural spacing between the
acts of intercourse and, possibly, between children. Why *triste*? This
sadness following intercourse is a sort of "letdown" and a depression
of physical tone in reaction to the high and often sustained level of
physical excitement needed for coitus.

This tremendous excitement, tension, release, and exhaustion are
proportioned to the importance of what is taking place: the possible

---

[44] This is not a discussion of whether coitus should be limited in such fashion as never
to take place except when conception is likely—a moral question that we shall consider
later. Here the topic is simply the meaning of the cyclicity for the couple at the psychic
level.

[45] Often attributed to Galen and sometimes to Aristotle. For a related point, see Aristotle, *Problems* 877b.

procreation of the species.[46] One may consider the letdown, then, as a part of the symbolic shadow mentioned above that is the necessary concomitant of gametic reproduction: the very success of the couple in generating offspring indicates that the older generation has decreased in importance, that new genetic types are at hand to take its place.

Hence, such sadness would seem to point, not only symbolically but even physically, to the biological linkage between sexual reproduction and the eventual death of the procreating individuals. Interestingly enough, this linkage seems everywhere stronger wherever the link between coitus and fertility is the tighter. The males in many lower species often die almost at once after impregnating the female; the females, very soon after laying their eggs. The closeness of this linkage is less among the higher animals. But there are few that have as long a life span after generation of offspring as is found in man.

This linkage between procreation and the death of the generators is not wholly absent in man, especially given various effects that are deeply rooted in his unconscious. Yet it would seem that such sadness is rather a substitute and a kind of replacement for the death that follows the invariably fertile coitus typical of the lower forms of life —a replacement, however, that is also a *memento mori*. Thus, sexual activity can become in man an integrated part of the lives of individuals, subordinated to other aspects of their lives. It is not meant to be the dominant, all-consuming effort for the survival of the species, in pursuit of which each individual must die.

In man, the link between sexual reproduction and death is thus no more than a shadow to the life-giving process. Sexual union is primarily joyful, filled with the natural hopes for new life and a better future —a point that we saw in looking at the more basic symbolism of the fertility cycle. It is more basic because it is given through coitus itself and not merely a more or less perceptible aftereffect.

---

[46] The fact that this excitement need not correlate with fertility but only with sexual stimulation shows from still another aspect that fertility remains the "hidden variable" throughout our discussion. On the other hand, if such excitement is directly closed off from offspring by contraception, it loses an essential part of its natural meaning and its importance.

Words as Sexual Acts

What largely takes the place of estrus in man is human speech. The expression of love and passion through words is a far more potent stimulus to copulate than estral pheromones or even provocative glances or touches. And couples whose sexual union finds its sole pleasure in the mere physical act cannot stay long together.

Further, in man, the use of language relates male and female mutually and reciprocally with regard to the sexual stimulation of one another. Words give a woman great power to draw and stir a man, quite apart from estrus. And a man's verbal language of love stirs desire in a woman more intensely and makes her more receptive to further action than any merely biological factors. Every genuine seduction of a woman by a man takes place through his words.

One might think at first that a man is aroused much more by the sight of a woman's body and by whatever physical signs she gives that she is interested in him than by any words she utters. At the very least, however, should she choose to speak, the additional element that her words provide can arouse the man more strongly than any merely bodily signs, lifting his attention to a level all the stronger, precisely for being more than mere lust.[47]

This dominance of speech in arousing sexual desire makes still deeper the separation between desire and fertility. Given his rational nature, it seems most suitable that actions as important as coitus be principally subordinated to his mind, not merely as to the ultimate choice to copulate or not but also as to feeling the desire to do so. Admittedly, this rational control of sexual passion is imperfect. But, as explained earlier,[48] a condition of integrity like that of Adam before the fall can be approximated in this life—and God intends for us to do so. Whatever his sexual desires may be, they have to be rationally understood,

---

[47] It is, in fact, characteristic of perversion that one's principal interest is focused on the body. The infantile adults who masturbate over the pictures in *Playboy* or other erotica or those who abuse children or who torture women or who go very far into homosexual activities show little or no interest in the inner life of their "partners". It is the body or its parts that rivets their interest and is the focus of their desire, however much personal converse may precede action in less depraved cases.

[48] See pp. 124–25.

brought under moral control, and made subject to the demands of faith.

Man's freedom with regard to the cycles of estrus both symbolizes the basic freedom given by his nature as an intellectual being and makes more complex and difficult the rational control that he must exercise over his sexual desires. His mind must govern not simply his passions but the entire range of his feelings and emotions. In our present condition, the mind cannot control these directly, nor should it seek to do so. But it can exercise control indirectly by finding and choosing what is reasonable and by the gift of continual attention to meaning and circumstance, however one may be impelled by one's feelings.

One meaning of the pattern of our fertility cycles is that reproduction is not the sole purpose of life. The implications of fertility need to be dealt with only part of the time (when the fertility cycle is known) or dealt with in random fashion (when it is not known). The seeming randomization of conception with respect to coitus that is produced by the relative hiddenness of the fertile times shows clearly enough that coitus itself has functions other than the procreation of children.

The length of the fertility cycle is highly species-specific, varying widely even among closely related species, although each species has its own characteristic length. Why the length of each species' fertility cycle should be exactly as it is does not yet seem to be well understood. In any case, it would be a matter of much more detailed biology than can be indicated here. As already noted, too, the length of the cycle is often conditioned by the natural environment, even, it seems, among human beings.

Further, the decoupling of man's sexual desire from fertility and the subjection of both to the control of his mind in faith, seem to indicate something that is only gradually being rediscovered in our culture. Through Marriage Encounter and similar movements, people are learning once more that the primary means among men and women for the expression of love is not coitus or foreplay but words.

A major block to having a happy marriage today is a surprising lack of communication between the spouses. In part, this comes from shyness, awkwardness, fear of speaking out. In part, it comes through thinking of coitus as a substitute for all other expressions and words of love. The puritanism in the roots of our culture gave the physical aspects of marriage too great an emphasis, albeit a negative one. I have known couples who have raised a half dozen children and yet are ashamed to speak to each other about what they experience, desire, suffer, or dislike in sexual intercourse. Indeed, "engaging in sexual intercourse" often means nothing more than "having sex", with no thought being given to making coitus a form of truly human intercourse.

Words can be the supreme expressions of love if not separated from the reality of our life or from sacrifice for those we claim to love. For proof of this statement, which today sounds strange in the ears of many, consider the unmatchable power of words to destroy. Even an adultery or a murder, if wordless, seems not as brutal or destructive as the cruel choice of words, carefully chosen to enter at the weakest spot, so as to annihilate the other person. Although we are perhaps not used to doing it because of our own weakness in love and charity, words can be used just as powerfully, even more so, in fact, to build up and to give life.

Hence, there is need to make sexual intercourse fully human, not as a substitute for words but as a word that sums up and gives bodily expression to all other words of love. Recall the role of words in a couple's mutual acceptance of one another in physical and, still more, in spiritual nakedness. Where beauty or power are deficient, words can supply what is wanting. To be seen noticing a deficiency in cold silence can crush, especially if it also indicates an inability deliberately to rise above it.

To sum up what we have seen, one aspect of coitus is that it takes place between adults endowed with human fertility, that is, with a limited fertility. Their fertility is limited temporally, in its onset and in its ending. It is limited by the menstrual cycles, as well as by conditions of psychological and physical stress. It is further limited by the gametes' independence of the couple's will and control. It is limited also by its lack of obvious external signal, especially of any close linkage with sexual desire. From all these points of view, it is clear that, symbolically, there is more to sexual activity than procreation.

II

THE SUPERNATURAL MEANING

Maturation and Decline

Limits to fertility are connatural to every creature, but in God there is no such limitation. The Father's fertility is infinite, eternally begetting a Son who is in all respects his equal and eternally breathing forth, with the Son, the Spirit of their love. But on the created order God shows and shares his life-giving power in ways that are compatible with beings that are circumscribed in space and time. Even though made in God's image, man perdures only through a fertility that extends the race across the world and through the centuries. As a result, God activates in us his supernatural life, our share in God's own inner life, only gradually and in due season, by giving many of his gifts only when the creature has been readied and has come to a certain maturity.

All things were created in, through, and for the Word (Col 1:16). Yet it was only many hundreds of millions of years after the physical universe was created that man was created in his image. Man subsequently fell, and only after ages of seeming forgetfulness of this wretched creature did God speak to Enoch, Noah, and Abraham. Nineteen centuries more had to pass before, in the fullness of time, at the end of the ages, the Word became flesh among his chosen people. He grew physically, at the same rate as all other men, spending most of his life on earth as a woodworker in Nazareth. Although he completed his mission on earth some two thousand years ago, yet even now hundreds of millions of people have not so much as heard of him. It is scarcely possible to think that great lapses of time are unimportant to God, however much we may dislike them.

God is always Master and Lord. He has set and still sets the requirements and conditions for conversion and rebirth, whether of an individual or of a people to whom he appeals through the Church. The pattern that the individual Christian must follow in spiritual growth is, in accord with the doctrine of recapitulation that is laid out in the Scriptures, properly understood. To grasp the relevance of the persons and events of the Old Testament, we need to look at the mystery of Christ.[1] The development of an entire people follows one roughly like that of Israel. Like the maturation process of the individual, this pattern of growth is aimed at spiritual fertility, so as to bring still other peoples to life in Christ.

The uniquely slow pattern of human growth to adult fertility symbolizes the life history of peoples and cultures. Like almost every ancient people, Israel bore the name of her eponymous ancestor, thereby showing forth God's relations to her as if to a single individual rather than to a mere collectivity. Through the prophets God kept directing the long, slow growth of Israel toward full maturity. She was, first, to bear children who became his by adoption. Then she was to be sent to the nations, so that these children of strangers could be made her own through faith in the word of God that she would preach to them and, thus, be adopted by God.

But Israel according to the flesh tore loose as a great branch from its trunk, so that there were two Israels. Israel according to the flesh proved unfaithful, being unwilling to become mother to those not of her own flesh and blood. Israel according to the Spirit (the Church) was a smaller branch at the beginning, though larger now. Holding firm to the trunk of the patriarchs and the prophets through Christ and his apostles, she went as the true and faithful Israel to the nations as well as to the Jews, in order to make all of them her children and to offer them back to the Lord.

Even as Israel grew through long years of not yet fertile infancy and childhood, to reach womanhood at the time of the covenant at Sinai (see Hos 2:15; Ezek 16:8, 23:3–4), so the Church in each culture must grow through her own seasons, lifting the people from their pagan infancy to adolescence when brought within the Church, until they too reach adult fertility.[2]

---

[1] For a more complete discussion of the doctrine of recapitulation, see Paul M. Quay, S.J., *The Mystery Hidden for Ages in God* (New York: Peter Lang, 1995).

[2] Israel became fertile at Sinai by being able to offer God her natural children for his adoption. Her fertility with respect to the Gentiles comes only with Christ. All this has a bearing on the conflict between Calvinists, who see the Church as simply continuous with Israel, and Baptists, who see her as wholly distinct. God's fidelity requires, it

The Church is the ever growing domain of Christ's reign upon earth, yet at no time has she included among her children all the children of men. Further, her own children, who become by this fact part of the Church herself, grow but slowly, and often rebelliously, so that her fertility is often compromised by the actions of her members.

As Judaism was a religion of waiting for the Christ to come, so Christianity is a religion of waiting for him to return, a wait that is seemingly conditioned on the spread and growth of the Church among all peoples. Thus, one must pray for the coming of the kingdom, but one cannot in any strong sense labor to bring it about. Rather, one labors and works for the King himself, as a witness to his reigning through the Holy Spirit until he comes in glory. As Christians, we should be especially sensitive to our obligation to shorten this long delay and to work so that the nations may sooner be gathered in. Although the Church bears scattered individuals in any given period to full adulthood, she is not always ready, in a given people, to bear children for the Lord. She begins among each people as she did among the patriarchs, typified in this case by Sarah.[3]

Further, this maturing toward fertility symbolizes that even when the Church has been introduced into a given people or culture, the latter is not always ready for Christ, not always ready to respond, save in very primitive fashion, to the graces proffered by the preaching of the gospel. Missionary activity may be limited by the resistance of a given people. One need think only of the effective hostility of Muslims to Christian evangelization, or the growing opposition of Hindus, or of the mission in A.D. 860 of Saints Cyril and Methodius to the Khazars, who seemed impervious to the gospel but shortly afterward embraced Judaism.

But there are also the times of nurturing those newly born, when the Church is infertile, not currently conceiving other children for the Father and showing scant interest in missionary effort until those already

---

seems to me, that there be a greater continuity than the Baptists allow; yet it is clear too that the Church does not exist as such until the New Testament, for she is the Bride of Christ, his Body, and all the many things that cannot be predicated of the old Israel. Birth into the New Israel is by baptism, not as in the Old, where it takes place by carnal generation.

[3] Cf. Augustine, *City of God* 15, 2 and 16, 26; Cyril of Jerusalem, *Catechesis* 18 (*PG* 33:1048b).

hers have begun to mature.[4] Before long, the basic conflict between
the gospel and any human culture begins to manifest itself, and a movement of quiet deepening and enrichment of the Church and her newly
born begins.

I know of no scriptural allusion to the Church as aged, or as sterile
as a result of age. Yet very early one finds patristic texts that do speak
in this fashion.[5] It remains to be decided whether, in context, this is an
appropriate symbolization of the Church as the transmitter of culture
(and especially the good news) to all men and not merely to her own
children, or whether this is an implied rebuke: that at a given time she
is not bearing new children for her Spouse. Yet any such symbolism
seems essentially secondary, since the Church does not grow old but
enters heaven as a Bride, prepared for the wedding feast.

As noted in the previous chapter, the cyclic aspect of fertility taken
together with the gametic independence means that sexual intercourse
need not always issue in the birth of a new individual. Similarly, a person naturally born is not always ready psychologically and culturally, or
even always enabled by grace, to be reborn. Although the grace of God
can be fully efficacious whenever he gives it—and is thus efficacious
whenever it is given to an infant by baptism—it is not so in general.
The human will is ordinarily left free to accept or reject what grace
makes possible. And the natural pattern of childhood, adulthood, and
old age makes conversion possible only at certain times, apart from
miraculous interventions of grace.

The individual who as an infant receives the life implanted at baptism is not yet able to act in accordance with the Word of God until
he gradually recapitulates the early seasons of the race. The individual soul through its sinfulness and willed deafness may not be able to
receive the word that the Spirit breathes. This condition is a kind of
evil, a sort of spiritual sterility, permanent or temporary. It can hardly
be considered an aspect of cyclic infertility, which is not evil.

Human fertility and divine fertility are similar in that male fertility
is constant; female fertility (here, that of the Church) is cyclic. The

[4] Needless to say, this in no way conflicts with the insight that one of the best ways
for a young church to mature in faith is to become interested in the missions at an adult
level. But a precocious interest is unavailing or even damaging, since it is conducted by
those too young to understand what the Lord truly desires of them.
[5] See Hermas, *The Shepherd*, Vision 2, 4, 1 (*PG* 2:898–99).

Holy Spirit, indeed, and the word of God that is preached are always powerful, as the gift of the Spouse (the Son) and the Father. So too for all the gifts that God has given the Church in custody only (for example, the sacraments, the Mass, the Scriptures). They differ indeed in that God makes all the Church's children to become his by adoption (though they may eventually break away from him and even from her).

Before discussing the relations between God and creatures under the aspect of the giving of life and fertility, we should note several preliminary points. First, in God there is nothing corresponding to male or female as such. Each sex denotes a radical limitation of being, just as, say, walking or eating does. God has nothing corresponding to these latter, even though he has the perfections that they adumbrate in his omnipresence and fullness of being. That which in us is sexual, for the sake of the propagation of the race—its strengthening through the mixing of genes, mutual love and support, and so on—exists in him simply as the Creator, the sole and single Source of created being. Hence, he can speak of himself as both Begetter and Bearer, that is, he brings his people into being as a people—not as individual beings —totally and entirely of and by himself (see Deut 32).

The powers of procreation, split asunder in the creature in order to help the creature go beyond itself, are reflections of the power of creation that in God is simply one and not a composite of male and female. Thus, we can use such metaphors as these: God goes and comes, stretches out his arm to save, begets a people, bears them, speaks to them and threatens them, and so on. Now, all this use of human language about God remains merely metaphor. On the other hand, he has revealed himself as Father in a very different way, one that is, with the imperfections and limitations that come from our poor understanding removed, directly applicable to him in the Trinity, so that the Word is Son (not the daughter) of the Father (not his mother).

There is an intermediate sort of usage that is indeed metaphorical but that differs from the first one mentioned. It uses in the comparison only those aspects of human sexuality that symbolize perfections. Hence, if taken eminently, it can be predicated truthfully of God. It is in this last sense that the creature is always feminine with respect to the Creator's infinite masculinity, here taken in its symbolization of freedom and initiative in the process of giving life. It is in this respect that the Fathers saw a woman's sexual growth and maturation as symbolizing the Church's growth to maturity and spiritual fertility within a given culture. The symbolism of a woman's cycles of fertility is less obvious, but this also is to be found in revelation, as we shall see shortly.

Cycles

The question here is whether one may see any analogue to a woman's fertility cycles, either in the individual's relations with the Lord and his Word or in those of the Church.

To learn how revelation makes use of the natural meaning of cyclic fertility to signify symbolically something of supernatural mysteries, we first note how the Bible deals with cycles of nature. Setting the tone for all that follows in Scripture is the passage in which God establishes his covenant with Noah: "While the earth remains, seedtime and harvest, cold and heat, summer and winter, day and night, shall not cease. . . . I set my bow in the cloud, and it shall be a sign of the covenant between me and the earth" (Gen 8:22; 9:13).

The context is one of beneficence: God's reconciliation with sinful man and his promise never again to destroy the world because of man's perversity. Here God consecrates the cycles of nature as abiding goods, excellent for man and for all other creatures. The text thus reconfirms what was made clear in Genesis 1:14–19, that the cycles of sun and moon, begun on the fourth day of creation, are good with a goodness given them by God from the beginning.

The cycles of the world are good, established ultimately for man's good (see Acts 14:15–17) precisely as a firm framework on which man can rely in his labors (see Ps 104:19–23). But God corrected the misunderstandings of the more sophisticated pagans who often saw the cycles of nature as wheels of fate, ineluctable, and ultimately without intrinsic sense or meaning (at times not far from Nietzsche's eternal recurrences). Thereby his people were able to see them in truth, as abiding signs of God's fidelity and tolerance for the sinful people who so defiled his image in themselves: "Let God be true though every man be false" (Rom 3:4). Like the breath of life itself, the cycles of the earth and the world maintain life and draw man ever again toward peace with God, who is faithful.

At the level of the covenant with Noah—hence, with all mankind, for all are descended from him—the menstrual cycle, though not mentioned as such, seems to indicate in this context of begetting and multiplying and filling the earth (see Gen 8:17; 9:7) a similar promise of God's abiding favor and willingness that the race of men, in spite of sin, be propagated and multiplied (Gen 4:1–2, 17; 5:1–3; 9:1–7).

Fertility, like the other rhythms of nature, comes and fades and comes again, in the life of the couple and in the lives of the successive generations as young people mature. Life continues, not in an unremitting and ever sustained activity but in cycles of action and remission. It would be blasphemous to attempt the former sort of life in an effort to replicate in time the intensity of God's eternal life (in which the Father eternally begets the Son), for the true pattern for man, the material creature most like God, is cyclic.

The cycles of the solar year and the lunar month are prominent in the liturgy. This is not, however, something with any special religious significance that belongs to these periods as such. Rather, these cycles exist and Israel is required to acknowledge that God's gifts are given in and through them, for by them Israel once again has the wherewithal to sow and, through his blessing, to begin and to end the harvesting of crops as well as to see the increase of flocks and herds.

More prominent in these cycles than the seasonal feasts of thanksgiving for the harvest are various anniversaries: the Passover, the Day of Atonement, the feast of Tabernacles, and such later festivals as Purim and Hanukkah. All these are commemorations, in the circle of months and years, of the great historical interventions of the Lord in the life of Israel for the salvation of his people. Indeed, even the feast of the first fruits of the harvest (see Ex 23:14–17) was converted in time to a commemoration of the first entry into the land flowing with milk and honey that the Lord had sworn to give to their fathers (see Deut 26). The cycles themselves are but frameworks.[6]

The cycle of fertility is one among the many cycles of nature. As these are the result of the Lord's creating the world and are declared to be still good even for fallen man by the covenant with Noah, so a couple's cycle is good. It is a sign not merely of natural hope for

---

[6] See also Ex 23:14–17 and Lev 23 in relation to what is said about the firstborn in Ex 13. As the day of conception is not known, the birthday is therefore considered wholly the act of the Lord.

the continuation of the race but also of God's fidelity. It signifies our grounds for hope in him in spite of the havoc that our sins work.

The couple's cycle, like those of the moon and the sun, is not itself religious. It serves as the framework within which God acts, first by the creation of new and immortal beings; then, in symbol, by his great interventions. They are divine acts that are wholly beyond the natural order: His deeds of redemption and salvation that bring his Church to be, and those further deeds of grace that constitute her the fertile mother of children (Ps 113:9).

Thus, through the fertility of one woman, from whose womb was born our Savior, he has created a new order of the world. His redemptive actions are commemorated in their human concreteness. Because his birth is celebrated each year, Christians can celebrate their birthdays, even though baptismal days and name days (that is, the feasts of their patron saints) seem to have greater reason for commemoration. It is not, then, fanciful to see as symbolized by a woman's ovulatory cycle not merely the goodness of God's world but also his gift to his Bride of saving fertility. This gift is recalled in the Church's liturgical cycle, which runs annually through the seasons of grace.[7]

As in ancient Israel, the years and months are not intrinsically religious. They provide the cyclic framework for ever again recalling and giving thanks for God's great deeds on behalf of his people. These events are not brought back to mind in their historical sequence and spacing but as linked to the cycles of months and seasons of the year, or even, as with jubilees and holy years, to the passage of the years within the centuries and millennia. The links are those of metaphoric association. Christmas comes just after the winter solstice, thereby reminding us that the Sun of Justice will rise out of the darkness of our world to illumine and to warm us by his light and love. So, also, the high point of the liturgical year, the Easter Vigil, comes in the springtime when all nature can join with the Church by bursting out into new life as she gives birth through baptism to those prepared and growing

---

[7] "Quando autem, dilectissimi, opportunius ad remedia divina decurrimus, quam cum ipsa nobis sacramenta redemptionis nostrae temporum lege referuntur?" Sermon 42, no. 3, ll. 67ff. by Pope Leo the Great, *Tractatus septem et nonaginta* (Turnhout: Brepols, 1991), p. 254. Translation: "But when, my beloved, do we more suitably hasten to the divine remedies than when we are directed by the law to the very sacraments of our redemption?"

within her, nurtured by her instruction in faith during her months of pregnancy.

In this way the Church makes manifest endlessly and without interruption, in unceasing variety, the different ways in which God's fidelity has been manifested in history. His "great works" were proclaimed first in their fullness on Pentecost, but they are never allowed to die away and are now "fixed" in the cycle of the Church year. The purpose of the liturgical cycle, of course, is not mere recollection. Rather, as on Pentecost, Christians remember God's great deeds the better to touch his promises and fidelity in order to make actual now in their own lives the fullness of the power of God's promises.

Although its particular forms are conventional and man-made constructions, the whole Christian life of devotion lives with such rhythms. For a life rooted in basic and natural rhythms does not spontaneously choose to act arrhythmically. Such liturgical practices as novenas and forty hours devotions either have a breathing rhythm in themselves or occur only at a breathing frequency during the year. There are also such practices as the annual retreat, the special collections taken at different times, designed ideally to provide the maximum boost to the people's charity. And like coitus or abstention in marriage, they are frequently adapted to special needs and exigencies, of either joy or sorrow.

The cycles of the Church show us also that times of hidden and imperceptible spiritual growth need not be times of sterility. Thus, all are required to attend Mass once each week, but not more often, even though the same graces are available at every Mass. Confession, if needed, and Communion are required of each person once a year during the Easter season, although they are no weaker as instruments of grace at other times of the year.[8]

Most Christians have much need to be often reminded of this lesson about imperceptibly slow but regular growth in the area of the spiritual, where we so easily become disheartened because we do not perceive better progress. God is the one "who sees in secret" those praying quietly within their rooms, who give alms secretly, whose good deeds remain hidden from the public gaze (Mt 6:5–6). As a hallmark of Christian life, this emphasis on acting (if not in secret, then at least

---

[8] These regulations about frequency seem parallel in certain ways to the Church's prudence with regard to the "rendering of the debt" in marriage when asked.

without calling attention to what one does, even in one's own mind) bears a close analogy to the infertile times in a woman's cycle.

But, more generally, God's action within those who are growing spiritually can be well hidden from the eyes of those around them, and even more from their own view. His actions within the soul to bring someone to faith and to conversion of heart, to grow as a catechumen, until made his adopted child in Christ at the moment of baptism, is not only hidden but a far deeper mystery than natural conception. Trent's decree on justification[9] makes clear enough that one is here dealing with a mystery essentially beyond human comprehension.

The Espousals

Spousal union should always be open to fertilization and procreation, but this does not, of course, mean that actual fertilization or procreation will result. Rather, these take place only by God's creative action, and then there is need for an adoptive relationship. Parents receive their child from God and need to accept any child whom he sends. The child is formed from the parents' own substance, genetically determined by the genes of their own bodies and nurtured within the mother's body. Yet the child has not come to be simply by the power of the parents but by God's power. The complex dialectical relation that we saw in the previous chapter between the parents and the child symbolizes, in turn, our adoption by God as his sons and daughters in Christ.

As the symbol itself is complex, so too—far more so—is the divine reality. Rather than try to parallel the symbolism trait by trait, I shall, to begin with, try to present in unitary fashion what is symbolized by our procreative adoption and only then refer back to the symbol itself in order to manifest the parallels.

Only those sexual relations that occur between husband and wife when they act so as to reflect symbolically the love between Christ and his Church are legitimate; all others are wrong.[10] But in pondering this truth, we might well find that the Scriptures themselves seem to offer

---

[9] Council of Trent, Decree on Justification, session 6, January 13, 1547, in *Documents of the Ecumenical Councils*, vol. 2, *Trent to Vatican II*, ed. Norman A. Tanner, S.J. (Washington, D.C.: Sheed and Ward and Georgetown University Press, 1990), pp. 671–81.

[10] See chap. 6, "Christ on the Cross: Sexual Lies and Counterfeits".

a serious problem for this whole symbolic approach. For the scriptural passages that deal with the marital relations between Christ and his Church (or, in the Old Testament, between God and his people) usually say nothing at all about children, even when children are talked about in the verses immediately following (see, for example, Eph 5:22–33; Is 54:1–13). Further, where children *are* mentioned, they seem not to have been begotten through the supernatural relations symbolized by Christian marriage.

Christ and the Church delight in each other through their common love of the Father, and thus in a union that is not directed to children but to love for the Father.[11] Those who become God's children by baptism are made so by the action of the Holy Spirit. As our Lord explains in response to a dilemma posed to him by the Sadducees, those who rise will be like the angels of God (Mk 12:25). In heaven the union of husband and wife (and, for that matter, all other bonds of human union) will be like that of the angels. So the union of Christ and the Church is in the Holy Spirit, to whom the angels are specially related by their natures.

Thus, Christ is nowhere said in the course of revelation to beget children of his Church. The Scriptures present the relationships between Christ and the Church not as those between husband and wife but as those between bridegroom and bride. Our Lord identifies himself as the Bridegroom, but one who will in some mysterious way be snatched away from the wedding party, so that the festivities are changed into fasting and mourning till he returns.[12]

In the Old Testament, all aspects and stages of the marital relationship are utilized to show the relations between the Lord and Israel: God's first interest in this wild girl, the espousals, the wedding, their relation as Husband and wife, her adulteries, her repudiation and divorce, and even widowhood. Although carefully wrought over the centuries into

---

[11] See Lk 20:35–36: "Those who are accounted worthy to attain to that age and to the resurrection from the dead neither marry nor are given in marriage. . . . They . . . are sons of God, being sons of the resurrection." This seems to confirm "from below" (so to speak) that procreation and generation of new children is solely a matter of this life. That is, the marriage of individuals passes away with the coming of that which it signifies; its primary purpose is to prepare for eternal life numerically and to manifest it.

[12] See Mk 2:19–20, with its parallels in Mt 9:15 and Lk 5:34–35, and the echoes found in Jn 16:16–19, 28–33.

a major theme of God's revelation of himself to Israel, it is not clear that all elements of these elaborate analogies and complex imagery are to be treated as consistent and mutually compatible parts of a single eight-hundred-year-long allegory.[13]

But the New Testament is completely consistent in its marital symbolism. Betrothal alone is used to symbolize the relations between Christ and the Church. Christ's mission requires his absence as King on campaign until the final victory is won (see 1 Cor 15:24-28; Rev 17:14; 19:11-21). His coming in triumph and the wedding itself are deferred until all the guests have had a chance to accept his invitation or to refuse. He awaits the Gentiles, who must recapitulate in each culture and people the Old Testament's plan of preparation for their proper relation to Christ.

Likewise Saint Paul says, "I betrothed you to Christ to present you as a pure bride to her one husband" (2 Cor 11:2). And he speaks of baptism as the nuptial bath that prepares the fiancée for her wedding on the morrow (Eph 5:26-27; see also Jn 3:29). Jewish marriage in our Lord's day took place in two steps: espousal (see Mt 1:18-19 and Lk 2:5) and permanent cohabitation. Espousal was binding enough that sexual intercourse with someone other than one's spouse-to-be was considered adulterous.[14] Yet the couple did not come together in physical union until the wedding itself had taken place.

On the Cross, Christ wrested his Bride from the enemy and affianced her to himself. Now espoused but separated from the sight and sound of one another, their marriage is to be solemnized only in heaven. Only there will we share the wedding banquet prepared by the King for his Son.[15] The book of Revelation makes explicit what is only implied in Matthew 22: the feast begins when the bride, who has been long pleading with her Lord to return (Rev 22:17), herself at

---

[13] For a consideration of these images in greater detail, in ways that try to respect the typological meaning of the Scriptures but without reducing it to a unidimensional allegory, see Quay, *Mystery Hidden*, esp. pp. 292-311.

[14] See Gen 19:14 and Deut 22:13-21. Also, see Pope Siricius, *Epistola I ad Himerium* 4 (*PL* 13:1136-37), in which he condemns a man's marrying a woman who has been espoused *but not married* to someone else, commenting that a violation of espousal is seen by the faithful as something very like a sacrilege.

[15] See Mt 22:1-14 and parallels. Also cf. Mt 25:1-13; Mk 13:34; Lk 12:16-24, 35-38.

long last suitably appareled (Rev 19:7–9), is brought to him, entering in glory.[16] Nothing more is said of the final union—but clearly new children are not envisaged. None are missing who are her children, but she will bear no more.[17]

Indeed, the imagery shifts and the emphasis is strongly altered. Rather than speaking of the Bride as bringing all her children with her, the language now is not of children but of guests invited to a wedding banquet (Rev 19:9) and of inhabitants of a city of gold and precious stones (Rev 21:9–22:5). Although still called Bride, the glorious Church is now identified as the Jerusalem on high (Rev 21:2–3). She is indeed our mother (Gal 4:26). This Jerusalem is the dwelling place of God with men, his people, the sons of God (Rev 21:7), the servants of God and of the Lamb, who will reign with him forever.[18]

It is not immediately clear how the symbolism of the espousal and marriage of Christ to the Church accords with any of the aspects of human fruitfulness, of the actual begetting and bearing of children. If Christ and the Church are now only espoused and not husband and wife, the arguments based on sexual symbolism would seem to fail. And if this symbolism does not extend to procreation, then is it possible to maintain it as a basis for *all* sexual morality among those whose intercourse is intended of its nature to result in children?

On the other hand, if we suppose that an adequate response to this difficulty can be given, as we shall shortly seek to do, there remains yet another one that we need to consider. If we suppose that the natural meaning of coitus between spouses provides the most adequate symbolism of the love between Christ and his Church, then the practice of natural family planning for the avoidance of children would seem to be morally evil.

For surely, during her earthly pilgrimage, the Church is to bring as many people to life in Christ as possible, to become the mother of as many children as possible, without other limitations than those

---

[16] Note especially Rev 21:2, 9–10 and 22:17 where, as in the Old Testament, the Bride is the city, the heavenly Jerusalem.

[17] The fundamental teaching of the Church concerning the decisiveness of one's state at death is a doctrinal reflection of this.

[18] The return in such strength of this Old Testament theme of God's wedding to the holy city Jerusalem, (see, e.g., Is 54:11–17 and Jer 25:29) is especially noteworthy, coming at the very end of the New Testament as its climax.

imposed by the mysteries of the divine decrees and human freedom. How could Christ refrain from giving her more children? If more children are possible through Christ's gift of the Holy Spirit, how could the Church refuse to bear them? Would not natural family planning, if used to avoid children, always be illicit, precisely as a violation of the basic meaning of sexual activity? Would not couples be obliged to use natural family planning, if they use it at all, precisely in order to have as many children as possible?

To respond to this difficulty, we will have to consider, on the one hand, the structures of human fertility and their meanings, natural and supernatural; and within this framework, we shall need to ponder in the next chapter the moral rightness or wrongness of the particular patterns of sexual activity that make use of such knowledge by governing one's sexual activity according to the ways of natural family planning.

As the understanding of typology weakened in the course of history, a certain misunderstanding of this sexual symbolism appeared.[19] One finds traces, even among the Fathers,[20] of an interpretation of the union between Christ and the Church that would treat this union as that of husband and wife.[21] As we shall see in detail shortly, there is no correct

---

[19] Allegory is, fundamentally, a sort of elaborated and extended metaphor. But the genuinely symbolic relationship is much closer to typology, but a sort of typology in reverse, for the Antitype has already come. See p. 13.

[20] Saint Pacian of Barcelona, most notably, seems to see the relations between Christ and the Church in just this imaginative or allegorical fashion. Although clearly uncomfortable with it, he tries, through complex qualifications, both to honor the Tradition as he has misunderstood it and yet to preserve solidity of doctrine. Part of his difficulty probably arose from conjoining this symbolism with the metaphor, deeply rooted in Tradition and of considerable theological importance, of the marriage of the Word with mankind in his Incarnation, a metaphor based especially on Psalm 45. Yet metaphor it remains. See the texts of Pacian in *Iberian Fathers*, trans. Claude W. Barlow (Washington, D.C.: Catholic University of America Press, 1999).

[21] Methodius of Olympus, *The Symposium: A Treatise on Chastity*, Ancient Christian Writers, vol. 27, trans. Herbert Musurillo, S.J. (Westminster, Md.: Newman Press, 1958) speaks in a manner that some have taken in a contrary sense. Despite his evident Platonic inspiration, he writes clumsily and expresses his ideas poorly. Yet, from the totality of his thought it is clear that he is no exception to the principle given above. Indeed, he takes the virginity of Christ with respect to the Church in so strong a sense that, at times, it seems almost to annihilate marital intercourse. Further, the climactic hymn of Thecla, the victor in the contest, is unambiguous in referring to Christ as the Bridegroom, the Church as the Bride. Also, the *ekstasis* of Christ on the Cross should be taken in its proper Greek sense of "trance" or "suspension of the powers of the mind" and not at all as our English cognate "ecstasy" might suggest.

way to speak of Christ as our Father, begetting children of the Church through the Seed that is the Holy Spirit. He is the Son of the Father, but he is not the Father of anyone. He enters into no generative union with his Bride. The children of the Bride are not the children of Christ but of the Father, being brothers and sisters of Christ.[22]

As we will see, there is no problem in dealing with matters of sexual activity and fertility by means of the symbolism of the relations between Christ and the Church. The desirability for Christ and the Church to have as many children as possible remains. But the goodness of bringing as many children to the Father as possible does not imply any need to bring the largest possible number of children into this world of sin and death. It is, rather, a question of bringing all those naturally born (or at least, as many as possible), whether those who belong to his chosen people or others, to be reborn of water and the Holy Spirit from the womb of the Church by baptism. Likewise, even the vast number of possibilities that can occur by genetic combination and recombination can only dimly indicate the infinite number of aspects of Christ's human nature as they are endlessly conceived and brought to birth by the Church.

Response

The core of the difficulty lies in seeing the affiance of Christ and his Church as if it were the sole biblical symbolism pertaining to human sexuality. It is true that children are not mentioned in the biblical symbolism that we have seen thus far. The passages at which we have so far looked pertain rather to the *kind of love* that exists between Christ and the Church. The love between those engaged has a visible tenderness, delicacy, generosity, and beauty that seem rarely to be found later on. Hence, this first blossoming of love is sensed as a sort of model for the love that all couples would like to preserve, no matter how much it might have to be deepened subsequently. The Scriptures seem to validate this and yet to remind us that it goes far beyond the ordinary limits of romantic love.

While children are not mentioned in the symbolism that discloses the kind of love that exists between Christ and the Church, they are

---

[22] See Quay, *Mystery Hidden*, pp. 344–45.

often mentioned in two other scriptural symbolisms of a sexual character: maternity and adoptive paternity. God's adoptive paternity is mentioned, with increasing emphasis, from at least the time of the prophet
Hosea. A few examples will suffice.[23]

Of particular clarity and poignancy is a passage at the beginning of
Isaiah. "The LORD has spoken: 'Sons have I reared and brought up. . . .'
Ah, sinful nation, a people laden with iniquity, offspring of evildoers,
sons who deal corruptly!" (Is 1:2, 4). Within three verses, God speaks
of the people of Judah as sons whom he has reared and yet also as
the sinful offspring of evildoers. Already from this we see that God's
children are his by adoption. Their natural birth as human individuals
is attributed to their human parents. Likewise, further on, "When [Ja-
cob] sees his children, the work of my hands, in his midst, they will
sanctify my name" (Is 29:23). The children of Jacob were begotten by
him, but God considers them his children because they are the work
of his hands as the people that he has formed for himself.

Much later, the Lord speaks to Isaiah in similar terms and with the
same contrast between his holiness and the sinfulness of the parents of
his children: "your offspring . . . my sons . . . and my daughters . . .
every one who is called by my name, whom I created for my glory,
whom I formed and made" (Is 43:5–7), "the people whom I formed
for myself" (Is 43:21); "your first father sinned" (Is 43:27); "I formed
you, you are my servant" (Is 44:21). Concerning those who found it
hard to understand that the pagan king Cyrus could be God's chosen instrument for his people, he says: "Will you question me about
my children, or command me concerning the work of my hands?" (Is
45:11). And again, concerning the sins of both parents and children, he
speaks of "your mother's bill of divorce. . . . For your transgressions
your mother was put away" (Is 50:1).

Correlative to God's adoptive paternity, of course, is the maternity
of Israel. That God's people bear children for him is, as discernible
from the passages already cited and many others, at least as strongly
emphasized as his adoptive paternity.[24]

---

[23] For fuller exposition and more texts, see pp. 81–82.

[24] Note, for example, how Isaiah speaks of Abraham and Sarah as parents, made fruitful by the Lord (Is 51:1–2); how God carries Israel's children from birth to old age (Is
46:3–4), prophesying that "All your sons shall be taught by the LORD" (Is 54:13).

As early even as Hosea one finds a hint of a link between the symbolism of fatherhood and that of husband and wife (2:2, 4, 5; 1:10). The link is clearer still in Ezekiel, though even here it is given only indirectly, by way of the symbolism of the motherhood of Jerusalem. Through the prophet the Lord says, "You took your sons and your daughters, whom you had borne to me, and these you sacrificed to them [to idols] to be devoured" (16:20–21; see also 23:4, 37).

Nowhere, however, is God said to have begotten these children of his spouse, or she to have borne them by him. The basic relationship, even though the word is not used, is that of adoption. Born naturally of human parents, the people become God's children because he has espoused Jerusalem, their mother. She has borne them for him and to him, but not by him.

With the coming of our Lord, these relationships (though similar sexual symbolisms are used) become much more complex, for God is revealed to be not only Father but Son and Holy Spirit, only one Being yet three distinct Persons. For example, the marriage of God with man was said to have taken place when the Word of God took unto himself our nature. The union of his two natures in the one flesh (that is, in the one incarnate Person of the Word) was early seen as in many ways like a human marriage.[25] Yet this "marriage" is only metaphorical, not symbolic, and thus is not given to us in the Scriptures as symbolized by natural marriage.

There is only one Father, the sole source of all. There is only one Son naturally begotten by him, his eternal Word, Jesus Christ (Jn 1:1–5, 18). All other children of the Father are made his only by being born to the Church. Just as the first adoption took place when God took Israel as his bride by the Mosaic covenant at Sinai, so all children of the Church were adopted by the Father as his own when Christ died for his Church on the Cross, thereby espousing her by the sacrifice that initiates the New Covenant (Eph 5:25–27). So also a couple offers to the Father through the Church the child whom they have procreated as a gift that he can make his own child by adopting him, having first created him.

We are children born to the Church through reception of the word of God by faith. Believing his word, we are received into Christ the

---

[25] See Methodius of Olympus, *Symposium.*

Word and given to live by his life. The Jerusalem on high is our mother (Gal 4:26). Not only does Christ not beget children of his Church, but she is intrinsically sterile (Gal 4:26–27; Is 54:1). Her fruitfulness is miraculous. She cannot give us life by natural generation but only by gift of the Holy Spirit, by the adoption into Christ of those who are the Father's creation (Rom 8:15).[26] As Isaac was born of the promise when Sarah was made fertile by the promise and power of God and not by Abraham (although he had to act for her to become pregnant),[27] so we are born to a Church made fertile by "the Promise of the Father" that is announced through his Word (Acts 1:4; 2:33).

How, then, do we become her children since she is without spot or wrinkle but we are already born into the world, outside of her and in sin? Natural birth does not suffice, as it did among the Israelites, to make us members of his people. To this variant of Nicodemus' question, the answer is the same as the one that was given him: we are to be *reborn*, of water and the Holy Spirit. Our birth as Christians is from the womb of the Church, the baptismal font.[28] Since she is not

---

[26] *Augustine's Commentary on Galatians*. trans. Eric Plumer (Oxford: Oxford University Press, 2003), pp. 194–96: "(7) Isaac enim mirabiliter natus est per repromissionem, cum ambo parentes senuissent. . . . (9) Nec ipsi [haeretici et schismatici] ad haereditatem inveniuntur pertinere, id est, ad caelestem Hierusalem, quam sterilem vocat scriptura, quia diu filios in terra non genuit. (10) Quae deserta etiam dicta est caelestem iustitiam deserentibus hominibus terrena sectantibus tamquam virum habente illa terrena Hierusalem, quia legem acceperat. (11) Et ideo caelestem Hierusalem Sara significat. . . . (13) Accesserat autem sterilitati etiam senectus, ut ex omni desperatione divina promissio magnum meritum credentibus daret." Translation: "(7) For Isaac was born miraculously through the promise, since both his parents had grown old. . . . (9) For they [heretics and schismatics] are also found not to belong to the inheritance, that is, to the heavenly Jerusalem, which Scripture calls 'sterile', because for a long time she did not bear sons on earth. (10) She is also called 'deserted' because men desert heavenly righteousness when they follow earthly things, just as that earthly Jerusalem 'has the husband' because it had received the law. (11) And thus Sarah signifies the heavenly Jerusalem. . . . (13) Now in his old age [Abraham] has also approached sterility, so that the divine promise might bestow great merit upon those believing in the face of utter despair."

[27] See Henri de Lubac, S.J., *The Motherhood of the Church*, trans. A. Englund (San Francisco: Ignatius Press, 1982), p. 41.

[28] "Non enim potestis non esse fratres, quos iisdem sacramentorum visceribus una mater Ecclesia genuit, quos eodem modo adoptivos filios Deus pater excepit." Optatus of Milevis, *De schismate Donatistarum*, 4, 5, in *Corpus Scriptorum Ecclesiasticorum Latinorum*, vol. 26, ed. C. Ziwsa (Vienna: Tempsky, 1893), pp. 103–4. Translation: "For you

only the Body of Christ and his Bride but also the people of God, the newly born Christian becomes part of her as one of God's people.

A final aspect of human generation will make it easier to understand a supernatural paradox. Children are born from the bosom of the family, from the physical union of their parents. Yet they are born into that family and help to constitute it. This seemingly paradoxical movement symbolizes the fact that each child is born from a culture (from its marriage customs, religious attitudes, etc.) and is also born into the culture. A similar paradox takes place in the Church, in which each new brother and sister of Christ is brought forth from her precisely by being incorporated into her.[29] Those who are borne by her become part of her—naturally in the old Israel, supernaturally through baptism and through faith in the new Israel.

Christ respects his Bride-to-Be and leaves her still a virgin. Remaining a virgin like Mary, she brings forth virginally, as Mary did, the members of Christ's Body. Hence, she who bore Christ has borne his Church; and Mary is, therefore, the Mother of the Church, as Pope Paul VI declared during the Second Vatican Council.[30] The mother of Christ's physical body is mother of his Mystical Body, and conversely. But as the Church *is* his Mystical Body and thus not its mother, in this respect, so Mary in this respect *is* a member of his Mystical Body rather than its mother.[31]

The Church bears us by the power of the Promise, the Holy Spirit who has been given to her. Just as the Holy Spirit was the agent of the Father's begetting of the human nature of the Son of the virginal Mary, so he is the agent of the Father's regenerating us of the virginal Church into the life of Christ. Thus, we can be truly said to be born of the Spirit (Jn 3:5).

---

cannot be brothers whom the one mother Church has brought forth by the same womb of the sacraments, whom God the Father has accepted the members of Christ's Body as adoptive sons in the same way."

[29] "In carnal marriage, the mother and child are distinct; in the Church, on the contrary, mother and child are one." Augustine, *Enarrationes in Psalmos*, commentary on Psalm 127, no. 12 (*PL* 37:1684), quoted in de Lubac, *Motherhood of the Church*, 77.

[30] Pope Paul VI, "Solemn Profession of Faith", June 30, 1968, in *Acta Apostolicae Sedis* 60 (1968), 438f.

[31] See de Lubac, *Motherhood of the Church*, p. 57, quoting Augustine.

Jesus spoke of his disciples as his brothers only after his Resurrection (see Mt 28:10; Jn 20:17). If we are his brothers, and no longer slaves, servants, or even friends, it is because of his triumph on the Cross, where he won the Church as his bride. The disciples became her first-born on Pentecost. We are, then, the brothers of Jesus, not as if the Father has begotten sons other than Jesus but because he has given us a share in the life of his Only-Begotten (see Gal 3:26–27). Thus, with the sole exception of Jesus, all the children of God are adopted.[32]

This adoption, however, unlike all human adoption, gives a share in the very life of the One who adopts. We are given a new principle of life, the Holy Spirit.[33] The Holy Spirit is the Spirit of the Father, who has given him to Jesus because of his triumph, in order to give him to us. The Spirit, then, who is the Spirit of Jesus no less than the Spirit of the Father, cries out "Abba! Father!" within our hearts as he did in Christ's heart (see Rom 8:13–17). The Spirit turns us toward the Father as Christ is turned toward him. It is the Spirit who makes us sons of God by making us one with Christ, the only Son (see Jn 3:3–8).

Hence, we are in Christ not simply as his brothers but by a oneness of life and identity, a true deification. Men and women alike, we are, in him, adopted children of the Father, who has "destined us in love to be his sons through Jesus Christ, according to the purpose of his will" (see Eph 1:5). We are turned toward the Father as he himself is and led as he himself was by the Spirit that is both his and the Father's. The Spirit anoints us so that we live by Christ's life.

The Spirit makes the Church fertile (no longer sterile or infertile) but does not make her fruitful (that is, actually having conceived). Recall the case with Sarah, to whom Saint Paul compares the Church, where Abraham's action was also needed in addition to the Lord's healing of Sarah's sterility. As was the case with Mary, who conceived Christ first in her heart before conceiving him in her womb, the Spirit acts upon one who is fertile to make her open to God's word addressed to

---

[32] See Gal 4:5; Rom 8:23, 29–30. As to Gal 4:6, note that God sends the Spirit of his Son into our hearts *because* we are sons, not to make us sons. But see also Rom 8:14. And Rom 8:16 seems closer to Gal 4:6. In Heb 2:10–17 note the steady insistence on our being the brothers of Christ and the sons of God.

[33] Hence, John (especially in 1 Jn 3:1) speaks of our adoption as our being born or begotten of God, a phrase he never applies to our Lord.

her faith. She conceives then by the power of the word when this is received and recognized by the Spirit acting within her.

When the Church is fertile, she is made so by the Holy Spirit. Those to be joined to her, as adults, are first conceived through their hearing and assenting, by his power, to the revealed word of God. But although Christ gives her the Spirit, Christ does not become father of her children. His gift of the Spirit is not an act of paternity but of "breathing forth" that the Son does with the Father without being thereby any less the Son, distinct from the Father. The Spirit is both the Spirit of the Father and the Spirit of the Son. Because he proceeds from both Father and Son as from a single principle, the Spirit can be given by the Son without making him our father.[34]

Let us turn now to yet another aspect of the mystery of our spiritual regeneration.

The Independence of the Gametes

The strange independence of coitus from the being and acting of the gametes gives a deeper insight into the mystery of a child's coming to be. This in turn symbolizes aspects of man's spiritual rebirth that we tend otherwise not to see.

In both cases, though in different ways, there is simultaneous activity of beings with different natures. Just as the bodily lives and activities of the couple who produce the gametes is independent of the lives and activities of these gametes, the supernatural life given by God is independent of the lives and activities of unconverted "natural" men. Even as Scripture describes the divine "adoption of sons" as our being begotten by God the Father, so the parents who beget and conceive us must, in one aspect, "adopt" us. Indeed, the whole freedom of the children of God is here symbolized. Each person belongs ultimately to God alone, not to the parents, still less to the state or to society or to the people.

This adoptive quality of the acceptance of a child by his parents (whether they wanted him or not) points to the awesome freedom that God has given to his children. The freedom under discussion here

---

[34] See Jn 1:12. There is mystery here but no contradiction in his making someone to be son of the Father while yet being the anointing of the Son that he sends upon the Church to make her children his brothers.

is not the natural freedom of the will but precisely that sort of freedom that comes from the charity by which Christians (hence, the Church) receive those whom God gives, whatever their preferences or missionary efforts may have been. They may have labored long for certain conversions without any having come about. They may have felt little attraction for having others join, and yet they may be born to the Church in great numbers.

Hiddenness

At the supernatural level, the cycles and histories of fertility are correspondingly hidden. As mentioned in the previous chapter, this applies not only to the cycles but to the entire process, especially the mode and manner of conception.[35] Already in the nature religions, this hiddenness was seen as a sign of divine activity. Coitus was a sacred act for them because it was an invocation of a deity.[36]

This natural symbolism has been taken up in Scripture as pointing beyond itself. The Lord is not merely one who acts in secret when there is question of new life. He is, by essence, a hidden God,[37] who "dwells in unapproachable light, whom no man has ever seen or can see" (1 Tim 6:16).[38]

Further, there are important lessons here in ways that might not be expected. In the Old Testament, whatever pertains to fertility yet somehow escapes its proper hiddenness so as to be perceptible to the human eye, is regarded in the Old testament as something that defiles both man and woman until ritual purification has taken place. Thus, a man's seed, insofar as it escapes his body but not in a way that is effective for fertility renders him unclean. So too a woman's menses render her unclean since it is the result of a fertility that was not fulfilled. Even the seed that results from fertile coitus (see Lev 15:1–18, 31–32; Deut 23:10–11) and the blood that accompanies birth render the person unclean since in some fashion it is excessive (otherwise they

---

[35] See H. P. Dunn, "Semen Examination", *Linacre Quarterly*, 54, no. 1 (February 1987): 88–91.

[36] One recalls the caustic satire of Saint Augustine on the Romans' postulation of minor gods for every aspect of the sexual act. See *The City of God*, 6, 9.

[37] "Truly, you are a God who hide yourself, O God of Israel, the Savior" (Is 45:15).

[38] See also Jn 1:18: "No one has ever seen God."

would not be noticed). The Law deals with the menstrual cycle not as a mystery but as a religious defilement, not because it is evil, but because blood is shed.[39]

One can profit from seeing the action of the sperm on the ovum as reflecting the initiating activity of the word of God as it is moved by the grace of the Holy Spirit toward that spiritual "fertilization" that is conversion to the Lord. It leads to the Church's conceiving this person and nurturing the child newly conceived in faith within her catechumenate until she can give birth to the new Catholic at baptism. In like vein, there is a genetic similarity of all children (genetically speaking) to their parents, and yet their frequent dissimilarity with their siblings.

The symbolism involving the hiddenness of the divine action and the freedom of the human persons who are thereby aided to salvation under God's action leads to further consideration of the divine adoption. This action by God lifts us to a new level of supernatural life that is at once an adoption by the Father and regeneration. The consideration of the divine act of regeneration offers some difficulties that could have been raised earlier but can no longer be avoided here.

We have spoken of the supernatural meanings of the physical determinants of fertility. Now we wish to see the supernatural meanings associated with the weakening, if not the total loss, of the signs of fertility in man—in this respect we are so different from all other forms of life. Desire for coitus may be found before and after the fertile times as well as during them, and yet it is also possible that there need be no trace of desire during the fertile times, whether these times be considered in terms of the maturation of the individual or of the cycles of the couple.

Here it is crucial to call to mind the "shadow" that I spoke of earlier: reproduction by gametes makes possible the death of the genetically unique individuals who are the parents. Its correlation is found here in the Crucifixion, the death of the Only Begotten, the One who is wholly unique. Yet the shadow is followed by the Lord's rising on Easter, his entry into the newness of life, firstborn from the dead.

We began to consider this question in the previous chapter. To the

---

[39] "You shall not approach a woman to uncover her nakedness while she is in her menstrual uncleanness" (Lev 18:19); also Lev 15:19–30 and 20:18. See also Gen 9:4: "You shall not eat flesh with its life, that is, its blood."

extent that coitus is disconnected from the death of the couple, it becomes something subject to choice rather than being controlled by the processes of estrus. It is no longer the goal of the entire life of each individual. To this same extent estrus subsides as the sole control of coitus. In man, estrus is not merely replaced but is spiritualized by language. For rational beings, words replace estrus as the dominant influence in bringing about coitus. One's love is manifested, as distinct from one's passion, chiefly by words.

So it has been with God, who spoke so often and in so many ways to Israel in the past. So it has been with Christ, who by his words has called all men to himself and to the Father. So, too, the Father has showed the fullness of his love in this, that he sent his Word as propitiation for our sins. And Jesus, the Word, showed the meaning of this Word most fully when his heart was pierced on the Cross.

The spiritualization of the natural order and of the Old Testament life of Israel is not, then, to be thought of as a separation from the body or from materiality—often as this oversimplification of the doctrine has occurred. Rather, it refers to receiving the key to the meaning of the body and of the whole material order. For coitus becomes far more profoundly pleasurable and prolonged and repeated in man, for whom, nonetheless, it is only a part of his life, than, say, in the mantis, where mating and egg laying are fatal. A man's love for his wife, whether she be fertile at the moment or not, symbolizes Christ's love for his Church, which never fails, whether she is bearing new children for the Father at that time or not.

Sterility does not signify the death of the individual, but (as seen in Romans 4:19)[40] there is a dying or partial death implicit in any sterility. Recall, too, in chapter 1 of Genesis that the reason given for woman's creation is not to bear children but to be a companion and helpmate for man. Scripture lays considerable emphasis on the sterility of many great women from Sarah to Elizabeth. Though sterile, Sarah was to be regarded as at least the equal of her husband's other wives and concubines, to be loved and cherished by her husband even more than if she were fertile. God gave offspring to these women for their trust in

---

[40] The Greek text reads: "ten necrosin tes metras Sarras", which could be translated as "the deadness of Sarah's womb". It is not clear that this has anything to do with age, since she was sterile from the first, as was Elizabeth much later.

him, precisely through her husband's continued cherishing of them. Though often cut off from giving new lives to Israel, by a double sterility, that of bodily defect as well as that of age, yet they were not cut off from maintaining that life already given to Israel by its religion and, in some weaker sense, its culture. Further, it is the word of love that actuates the merely potential fertility of the couple. So it is the word spoken by the Word that is received through the power of the Spirit that makes the Church fertile in act.

In what way did Christ express his love most intensely and most strikingly for the Church? And how does he wish her to express hers for him? The Word did so by words. In God, the Father eternally utters his Word, in an act of perfect and mutual love that is the Holy Spirit. The Word came to speak the words of God to men, to preach and teach the way of salvation. Still more, he came as the Word, God's own, united to our human flesh. And just as a human word, if it is to be understood as part of a message, must sound and then fall to silence and disappear, so too for Christ. Once uttered into this world, he sounded in time by his life and then fell into the silence of death through his sacrifice of himself on the Cross in order for his meaning to be made manifest to us in the Resurrection.[41]

The Church herself lives by words. Words are needed for the bringing about of each sacrament. Words are the normal medium of prayer, of law, of preaching, and above all, of worship in and through Christ's sacrifice, into which she is incorporated constantly by the words of the priest. For it is not sufficient to speak of the Church who is our mother. Christ is made present to his people through the fatherhood of the clergy.[42] It is they who preach the word, as did Paul and the other apostles. It is they who receive the children, begotten by the Father through his giving of the Holy Spirit.

---

[41] With respect to the Church's perpetual fertility by means of words, one must note that any image of "seed" that is used refers to the revealed word spoken to men (in the parable of the sower, for instance, in which the seed is the seed of plants). Here is the intrinsic periodicity of the Church's fertility, received from Christ. Christ is not yet her husband, but he gives the Spirit, who makes her fertile by opening her to be receptive to Christ's words, which are not his but the Father's.

[42] See de Lubac's striking phrase: "The motherhood of the Church, the privileged expression of which is the fatherhood of her spiritual leaders". Henri de Lubac, S.J., *The Motherhood of the Church* (San Francisco: Ignatius Press, 1982), p. 113. See especially chapter 5: "Fatherhood of the Clergy", and chapter 6, "Ecclesia de Trinitate".

That which renders the individual soul fertile so that Christ can be born within it, that which makes the Church fertile so as to receive into her womb the one to be reborn is the word that God has revealed to her, "living and active, sharper than any two-edged sword" (Heb 4:12). This word is always fertile and powerful. This word is Christ's word. Yet it is the power of the Holy Spirit that acts within the hearer that he may accept the word that he hears, the Spirit of the Son recognizing the word heard as the word revealed by the Son. So he makes the word active in the Church to make her fertile.

The Holy Spirit is the Breath of God by which the Word of God was uttered into the world in our flesh, the Breath that gave him life in the womb of Mary. By this same Breath, God's word is preached to the nations, a word that is always powerful, the gift of the Spouse and his Father.

Thus, too, words are required in the bringing about of all the sacraments. We are baptized "in the name of the Father and of the Son and of the Holy Spirit",[43] once we have professed aloud our faith in Christ (Rom 10:9). The Church gives life again to the dead by words, renewing the divine life given in baptism, should it be lost by sin: the penitent's words of confession and repentance, her priest's words of absolution. The solemnity of the words of consecration that make Christ's Body and Blood present upon the altar, the words of the exchange of vows that unite husband and wife, and the words used in all the other sacraments make clear that the Church does not act without words.

Ultimately it is to Christ and the Father that each of us must talk —not only to gain the easing of frustrations, doubts, suspicions, and the like but to raise up children for the Father and brethren for Christ. Finally, we must do so because we need to mature in Christ as we grow in inner knowledge of the Lord and recapitulate his life in ours.

With these points in mind about the natural and supernatural meanings of natural family planning, let us now turn to various moral questions.

---

[43] Mt 28:19. See also 1 Pet 3:21: "Baptism, which corresponds to this, now saves you, not as a removal of dirt from the body but as an appeal to God for a clear conscience, through the resurrection of Jesus Christ."

MORAL ASPECTS OF NFP USAGE

Natural family planning can be used when trying to achieve pregnancy or to avoid it. But the avoidance of pregnancy (the use to which NFP is most often put) is not a property of any physical action by those who practice it. If they are using NFP well, their actions in preparation for and during the act of coitus need not be different in those cases in which they are seeking to avoid children and those in which they seek to have them. The difference between the two cases lies rather in the pattern of coitus and abstention that the couple chooses, a pattern that, as such, exists only in their minds as part of their intention.

The moral quality of natural family planning is determined, then, not by the nature of one's acts (as in contraception) but by the ends and goals that motivate one's free choice of a particular pattern of intermittent coitus. If one's motivation is good, then the practice of NFP is good; if the motivation is bad, then its use is bad also. Thus, when analyzing the moral quality of a choice to use NFP, we presume that the coitus itself is integral so that it retains its integral meaning. For the symbolic meanings of the body and its natural activities must be preserved and respected, whatever one's motivation or one's patterns of intercourse may be. The moral question is whether the intent to use NFP violates these symbolic meanings, and if so, to what extent.

Given, then, that one is speaking only of acts of integral coitus between spouses, it is the human goals and intentions that govern the moral judgment to be made on the use of any method. What we must ask is whether the human goals and intentions in using a certain pattern of intercourse are compatible with the beings and processes in question.

A pattern, in the sense used here, is an intended and regulated sequence of activity. For the purpose of this analysis, the activity is assumed to be morally legitimate in itself, that is, legitimate when considered in independence of its position in the pattern. If a pattern of coitus and abstention is to have a moral value, good or bad, *precisely as a pattern*, we must speak of the meaning of this pattern itself. At the natural level, the meaning of NFP will be precisely that it can be reasonably judged to be an effective way to engage in sexual activity without having a child as a result or, conversely, to make conception more likely. Now, from what we have seen above concerning the biological values of the cycles of fertility, surely one of the most obvious regulative goods in this domain is this natural spacing of pregnancies.

The essential moral questions, then, concern the moral quality of coitus when the couple know themselves to be infertile, of abstention when they know that they are fertile, and of the intentions and good ends that would seem to justify the choice of a particular pattern of coitus and abstention. It will be noted, however, that the operative and effective aspect of NFP lies entirely in the fact of abstinence throughout all fertile times, whether the couple engage in coitus during the infertile times or not.

The moral quality of NFP is determined entirely by the couple's motives and the relations of these to the meaning of coitus itself and to the particular pattern of coitus that they are choosing. For the cycle of fertility is good, the practical acknowledgment of its existence is good, and the employment of the natural activities of the body for good ends is good. Properly practiced, NFP is one manifestation of the spouses' love, for it acknowledges in action the intrinsic limits to fertility. In this particular way, we shall now see, it can symbolize the love of Christ for his Church and hers for him. But it remains always a love that expresses itself in full truth through the bodies of the couple, in active consideration of the cyclic nature of human fertility.

Nevertheless, what we have just said does not exempt a couple from their obligation to maintain a complete openness to children in every act of coitus, especially during the fertile times, since coitus at such times is, ordinarily, the necessary and sufficient condition for fertilization. What lies at the end of a causal chain is morally the responsibility of those who initiate the chain if they know (or ought to know) of its nature in advance. Thus, the basic moral questions that we need to answer in order to decide the moral quality of NFP can be put in the words that a couple might well use when considering the issue:

Are we obligated to have all the children possible for us with our current understanding of the operation of the natural cycles of fertility?

Are we obligated to refrain from intercourse when we know as a couple that we are infertile?

The questions can be put a bit more abstractly:

Can abstention from coitus be morally right during times known to be fertile?

Can coitus be morally right during times known to be infertile?

Put yet another way:

Given our current knowledge of the cycles of nature and the purposes of sexual activity, are we not morally obligated to have all the children we can? To have intercourse as often as possible?

Hidden in this last question, however, are some unintended presuppositions and a certain confusion. How many children are possible? Is one assuming something concerning the frequency, if not the ordering, of the acts of coitus? Is physical exhaustion the only limit to the frequency of intercourse during the fertile times? If not, then what other principles are operative?

Although the love between the spouses can be expressed positively by coitus, it can also be expressed negatively, by refraining from intercourse for the good of the other. It seems evident that a couple must seek many goods during their fertile times that will simultaneously exclude engaging in coitus. Presumably these many other goods may be so sought.

There is the good of life itself. The couple—and any children for whom they may already be responsible—must eat and sleep. They must work to earn what is needed for the family, to keep the home in order, to prepare meals, to take care of the sick—not only each other and their children, but their own parents and various relatives and sometimes also their neighbors.

Abstention from sexual intercourse may be needed for the sake of the common good, not only of the family but of the community and the country, for civic duties are real. Even though such duties are not always as demanding as they are, say, in time of war, they may well take much time and energy from one or both of the spouses, leaving them little opportunity to schedule their relations in accord with the fertility cycles.

The love between the spouses can call for abstinence from coitus for the sake of each of the traditional "goods of marriage" (permanence, fidelity, children). For example, when one's spouse is sick or absent, no licit sexual activity is possible. Abstinence is then undertaken for the sake of the basic good of mutual fidelity. Likewise, the indissolubility of their union could be threatened if they should engage in the marital act in certain circumstances, for example, when the husband is drunk or seeking to force contraceptive intercourse upon his wife. Perhaps most importantly, abstinence may be called for by the third good of marriage, their children, those they already have or even, in some circumstances, those for whom they hope.

Think also how often a couple rightly forgo intercourse when they are very tired, when forced in traveling to spend the night without private accommodations, when the woman is emotionally upset, say, by a death among her kin or by a quarrel with her husband, and in countless other cases. Evidently, no particular relation to fertility enters into any of these decisions.

Marital love can impose intermittent abstinence not only for the sake of permanence, fidelity, and children but also for prayer (so Saint Paul says in 1 Corinthians 7:5–6), even to the point, in very exceptional cases, of permanent abstinence for the sake of some extraordinary spiritual good, as in the case of virginal marriages. Since virginal marriages are, in principle, acceptable to the Church,[1] it seems clear that abstention from coitus during fertile periods for the sake of a great spiritual good can, in general, be morally acceptable.

Yet this language leaves something to be desired, for it would seem, through the analysis given above, that NFP is not merely something that is morally tolerable but something that is positively good and to be actively chosen for the sake of a proper spacing of the children within the total framework of the couple's life and the overall good of the marriage. But it is a legitimate method only if the intentions are truly adequate.

---

[1] The reasons are far from clear to most people—but most people are not called to such a life. What is involved is, in traditional language, the conceding of a right to coitus to one another, supplemented with a solemn agreement and pledge that neither party will make use of this right.

Clearly, then, a couple may, and at times must, abstain from coitus even when they are reasonably certain that coitus at this time would result in a child. Other goods exist—some optional, some necessary —that may rightly be sought through sexual abstinence.

Let us consider another pressing question: "Would we not be obliged to refrain from intercourse when we have advance knowledge of joint infertility?" What factors, over and above the natural orientation and openness toward the union of gametes, are legitimately operative as goods that are intrinsically symbolized by sexual activity and that therefore can justify such activity even in the absence (but not in the exclusion of) possible conception?

The natural meaning of coitus is composite. It signifies and symbolizes natural marriage, with all that this implies both of mutual love and of openness to children. Hence, neither element in this meaning may rightly be suppressed or contradicted by any choice that the couple may make. On the other hand, either element may be sought without positively seeking the other, provided the act remains open to children.

In more traditional language, there exist, as mentioned above, at least three ends, or "goods", of marriage, each of which can provide an adequate reason for coitus.[2] Having children is one of these ends; indeed, children are the primordial end that may never be repudiated since having children constitutes part of the very definition of sexuality as such. But having children is not the sole end of sexual activity.

Even during fertile periods, sexual intercourse does not symbolically require that a couple intend to generate a child with this act. No one can intend what he has no power to effect, however much he may desire it. At the level, then, of the union involved in natural marriage, the couple are not required to intend conception in every act of

---

[2] These are the "good of offspring", the "good of fidelity", and the "good of the mystery", a terminology introduced by Saint Augustine and handed on by Saint Thomas Aquinas (see *Summa theologica*, Suppl. q. 49, arts. 2, 4). The good of offspring includes the begetting and the raising of children and the community of life forged by the parents' care for the children. The good of fidelity includes both the "rendering of the debt" (the willingness to engage in coitus for the good of one's spouse) and the refraining from coitus with anyone else. The good of the mystery includes not only the indissolubility of the marriage but all the other goods that are implied by the marriage's being the symbol of Christ's union with his Church. For their being able singly to justify coitus (remember, there was then no knowledge of fertile or infertile times), see *Summa theologica*, Suppl. q. 49, arts. 4, 5.

intercourse, if for no other reason than simply because such intending is in itself ineffective.[3] Such "intentions" are in fact mere velleities or desires.

Nothing in the natural symbolism of the body restricts sexual activity to that which guarantees the generation of a child. The independence of fertilization from coitus and the freeing of man from estrus both indicate that intercourse may be rightly desired for many reasons that are not directly tied to having more children, even though it remains oriented toward children and open by its structure to conception. The reason here is that coitus brings about many goods that are not made obligatory by circumstance or by the couple's intentions and yet that are rightfully sought in marriage even when the couple is not fertile.

As we saw in chapter 10, the replacement of estrus in man by loving speech symbolizes not only the freedom that is proper to genuine love but also much of the mystery of the Lord's Incarnation and of our redemption. Thus, a man is required, for his spiritual good, to sustain his wife by his affection and physical interest in her, whether she is fertile or not. Obviously, too, a wife can be called on to support her husband by her interest in his physical intimacy (say, when he has lost his job). So, too, after menopause, when a couple has become sterile, their intercourse can no longer signify concretely the possibility of children. Yet the good of mutual support and affection remains and can rightly be made a goal of their activity. In addition, the Church has long spoken of the easing of concupiscence as part of the good of fidelity. This is a good of coitus that is constituted by the desire in charity to help one's partner to the rightful release of sexual tensions.

The number of aspects of marriage that are symbolically expressed by coitus is very great, as I explained earlier.[4] Many of these a couple needs to learn by direct experience, very deliberately and thoughtfully entered into. But they must learn to go further still so as to enter into their proper function of manifesting to the world the mystery of Christ's union with his Church.

---

[3] Indeed, an intention not to conceive when having intercourse is also, of itself, ineffective, and hence not immoral or contrary to the symbolism unless it results in an action at least thought to be effective that would change the internal nature of the act so that conception could not take place.

[4] See part 1, esp. pp. 65ff.

Coitus simply to express their desire for children, even though none seem likely, on a "just in case" basis, would seem to be of value to the marriage and to having children. Such expression of mutual love in the context of desire for children can be of genuine help to conception by making the cycle's contribution to fertility concur with the biochemical and bodily fertility that brings about the union of gametes.

Finally, it is important to note that most, if not all, of these goods are of long-range advantage both to fertility and to the raising of the couple's children, those already present and those still to be conceived. Thus, intercourse can be good independently of actual fertility (assuming that the spouses' intentions are good), as they approach ever more closely that sexual integrity that was the condition of Adam and Eve before the Fall.

A further question deserves discussion here as well. For assessing the morality of a couple's actions, what is the effect of increased and more accurate knowledge about the internal structure of their acts and their intrinsic consequences?

Simple knowledge of their joint fertility and infertility does not change the nature of their act of intercourse or alter its intrinsic meaning. Their intentions and the meanings that they personally impose upon the act through their use of it as a kind of language, of course, can vary greatly. The bodily cycles are known to be part of human nature. A couple should acknowledge them and act in accord with this knowledge, in reverence, with reason and faith, for the purposes of familial love. Properly practiced, NFP is meant to be the activity of the love that acknowledges in action the intrinsic limits to fertility and thus symbolizes the love of Christ for his Church and hers for him.

It belongs to neither spouse to deny their fertility when it is present or to suppress it. Rather, they are both called on to act with their knowledge of it, so far as this is available to them, in such manner as to take that joint fertility into account, just as they do with any other aspects of their sexuality, that is, they should act with understanding and prudence and all the virtues. Thus, the couple are required in any act of intercourse to maintain its integrity of meaning and not to exclude conception.

The use of NFP for the sake of having more children or to overcome a seeming sterility shows clearly enough that the moral quality at the natural level of such a pattern of intercourse is, *of itself*, good.

Note, however, that when used for achieving pregnancy, coitus is chosen entirely in accord with its inner direction toward children. When used to avoid pregnancy, coitus is chosen only when it is thought to be incapable of its normal effect.

Intention

Let us turn to the question of the goodness of the spouses' intention, especially in its relation to the intrinsic meaning of coitus and to the structure of NFP. It is important to keep in mind that natural family planning is not an entity or a natural process but a humanly devised and chosen method. In fact, NFP refers to any of a number of consciously chosen patterns of intermittent coitus, a particular pattern chosen from among many possible patterns, for the purpose of either achieving pregnancy or avoiding it. As a method, NFP directs sexual activity, already fully constituted as to its intrinsic structure and meaning, to ends and goals that are determined by the individuals employing the method. Evidently these ends and goals may or may not be in harmony with the natural and supernatural meanings of the activity in question.

Since, physically, NFP is nothing other than intermittent intercourse, the act of coitus can remain intact at the level of its own meaning, saying all that it ever says, by speaking principally of the love of the spouses and of their openness to children. Precisely because NFP does not poison the germ cells or block their union or expel the child newly conceived, this openness to children remains intact, whatever the desires of the couple may be at the moment. If this openness did not matter to them enough to affect the moral quality of their decisions, they would ordinarily be using the less demanding method for avoiding pregnancy that is provided by contraception. Whatever their intentions, the coitus of husband and wife remains integral and sound so long as it is able to express rightly the love between Christ and the Church.

As in any human action, a bad intention can vitiate the best of deeds. Sin can be involved in a couple's use of natural family planning. But if so, it would arise from an intention that is already bad, without reference to NFP—for example, if a seemingly sterile couple sought to have a child by means of NFP in order to make money from forcing it into prostitution—or from some direct contradiction between the couple's intentions and the intrinsic structure and meaning of their intercourse.

An intention is morally good if it is an orientation toward something that is good in itself, something that can be rationally sought by means of the action under consideration, and something that other circumstances do not make unsuitable for the one choosing. An intrinsically good intention for (intermittent) intercourse will be any of the goods arising from coitus that might be lost or harmed if one were not to pattern one's actions in this particular way.

Hence, the principal moral question in regard to the motivation for using NFP concerns the desire for children. We have tended to lose sight of the fact that children are a gift from God (see Ps 127) and a great good both for the couple and for our whole race. Children do bring problems. They misbehave, sometimes seriously. They require economic support until they begin to work on their own. They can bring about family conflicts. They increase the population and consume some portion of the world's resources. But at least as important as any of these is the fact that children also help to solve these problems. They have the resilience, vigor, and freshness of thought to deal with them well. They also have the motivation to do so—it is their world that will be improved. Finally, the efforts to deal with these problems are of great help in growing toward Christian maturity.

What constitutes the proper size of a family often underlies discussion concerning NFP. Families of more than three or four children are sometimes regarded as impossibly large and as an undue strain on the parents, especially on the mother. Yet, as is evident from looking at families of eight to fourteen children, large families have much to commend them despite the obvious difficulties under which the parents must toil in our country at present. But such toil itself is not necessarily evil and may lead to far greater personal growth on their part, with benefits for the younger children particularly as a result.

Further, the Church has steadily insisted that a grave reason is needed if one is to set about limiting the size of one's family by any method other than total abstinence. If the sexual powers are exercised, then that which is their most fundamental aspect cannot be avoided without true and serious cause. As mentioned earlier, these reasons, insofar as they are genuine and interiorly consistent, are to be found among the goods of marriage.

Ordinarily, then, NFP is not morally permissible early in a marriage. Quite apart from the danger to the stability of the marriage, for which in most circumstances a child acts as a cement, there is the fact that those who are not ready for children are not ready for marriage. Openness to children is a constitutive element in marriage; it is too important a factor to be subordinated to other goods before any children arrive. For many, even those not trying to delay family building, the deliberate choice of intercourse during the time of fertility represents a conscious desire to join with the Lord in procreating a child, rather than simply "letting it happen".

It remains true, nonetheless, that NFP differs fundamentally from all use of contraceptives. It is not self-indulgent or automatic but requires some sacrifice from the couple, since the temporal pattern of intercourse and abstention rarely fits the spontaneous desires of both. Hence, it is not nearly as likely to be abused as contraceptives, even if there were no more serious problem with these latter than the intention aimed at. This pattern is deliberately chosen in order that more or fewer children may come about than from unpatterned acts of union. But in all cases, sexual union is morally allowable only within the framework of true love of God and of one's spouse.

Nor should it be overlooked that NFP will almost always involve sacrifice on the part of at least one of the spouses for the sake of the other and of their children, actual or future. The husband's continence can be very difficult for him; he may find even more difficult the "need" to be "ready" when intercourse is to be desired. A man can rather easily get into a condition of mind and emotion in which he feels that he must "perform" on these certain days, with a resultant risk of psychological impotence.

A woman will ordinarily have less trouble with abstinence as such, but she is if anything more likely to have emotional repercussions from her husband's need to distance himself physically from her at night— a distancing that she may well understand and yet feel in her emotions as rejection or coldness. Good initial instruction and eventually some counseling, if needed, can go far to prevent such painful situations or at least to alleviate them should they occur. But the sacrificial nature of the pattern of abstinence and intercourse remains. Accepted from love and for the motives of love, such sacrifice can only strengthen love in the long run, although a couple may well wonder in the short run how to deal with the unfamiliar emotional terrain on which they find themselves.

If one is to speak of the "symbolic meaning" of NFP or other patterns of intermittent coitus, it is crucial to focus on the intelligible purpose and structure of the method itself. This meaning is not, however, to be taken as one that inheres naturally in one's actions as such but one that constitutes the method as a human artifact.

To understand the supernatural symbolism of NFP, it will be necessary to consider what is analogous in the relations of Christ and his Church. What is it that is parallel in the ways of ordering and directing supernatural goods and processes so as to obtain or avoid more children for God and the Church? There are, as we shall see, supernatural methods that are, albeit weakly, analogous to NFP.

The pope and bishops, who are fathers within the Church, as we saw earlier, have the authority and even the obligation, for the good of the whole Church, to set up patterns of abstention from particular graces. This occurs by virtue of authority that is usually exercised through the priests and deacons under them. As fathers, priests must always act as the instruments of the love of Christ for his Church that is symbolized by coitus, a love that remains active even when these fathers in the Church impose abstention from some ordinary means of grace.

The Church does not always act so as to maximize the number of children supernaturally born to her or to increase the percentage of those born to her among all those naturally born. But neither does she ever regard more children for herself as an evil. If she, as it were, avoids special focus on the sort of missionary work that would raise up new children for a time, it is only in hope of a greater number eventually. There is no pattern of withholding grace in order to avoid a larger number of children. But she may legitimately seek to maximize her own love for Christ in all her children, and their greater health and vigor in the Lord. Insofar as this is achieved, it will indeed be the best means to bring more of the children of Adam to become also the children of God.

The Church does at times refuse to accept new children. She may, for example, refuse to accept converts in a certain region in order to be able to remain present and active in readying the populace at large to be more receptive to the gospel. She did this, to give one example, through the Franciscan Guardians of the Holy Places in Palestine at the time of Saint Ignatius Loyola. He wanted desperately to preach the gospel to the Muslims who ruled there then. But Ignatius acknowledged peacefully in the Lord the authority of the Guardians to forbid him to do so at that time. Something similar was the practice some years ago at Al-Hikma University in Baghdad, where any Muslim student or teacher who wished to become a Christian was told that he would have to go to some non-Muslim country before he could be baptized. In other ways, too, the Church fails to have as many children as she might. For example, she may dedicate some of her priests to works other than the ministry of the word and the sacraments, even though this would slow down the spread of the good news.

At a different level, the Church withholds certain graces that she could give, where the grace withheld is not that of baptism but, say, that of forgiveness of sin and the raising up of a person from spiritual death. Thus, she refuses absolution, for a time, to those who have been excommunicated, until the appeals and penances prescribed are carried out. So, too, it seems clearly an abuse of the sacrament of reconciliation to allow those who are habitual sinners or who are scrupulous to go to confession except at predetermined intervals, say, once a week, whatever their state of soul in the interim. They must learn to turn to the Lord more personally and come to trust his word and his mercy. Thus, in order that Christ may again be rightly loved and served by her children, even if spiritually dead, she can make them wait "on schedule", even though always herself seeking union with her Spouse in and through the Eucharist.

As a final example, the Church has always refused to let certain graces be hurried. There are, for instance, the special seasons of penance, Lent and Advent, each with its own special character of penitence and preparation for what is to come. They are commemorative of the Lord's mysteries, but inasmuch as they are penitential, they are a sort of abstinence for the sake of greater or better fertility. In the early Church, and once again in our day following upon the renewal initiated by Vatican II, baptism is administered to adults (apart from imminent danger of death) only at Easter. She may also delay the reception of those to be baptized by requiring a longer catechesis or moral preparation. Properly, she is pregnant with her catechumens, bringing them to birth, in the ordinary course of events, only at Easter, and while bearing those quite able to conceive others who will be born a year or two later. So too she is infertile for those to be married during the Lenten season. All this, of course, is infertility, not sterility, being sought solely for the sake of the spiritual health of her children, those already born or those still in her womb or yet to be conceived.

The story is told of a young couple who were teaching NFP to junior and senior girls at a parochial high school when the husband likened the period of abstinence in NFP to the anticipation of Christmas: "Class ended shortly afterward, and as the girls left for their next class, one smiled at the couple and wished them 'Merry Christmas.' Every child will tolerate the wait for Christmas and during Advent imagines the presents which he would like to receive. The greatest gift of all is Christ himself, a new life giving us new life."[5] This seems similar to abstinence during fertile times for the sake of coitus later, in the sense that feast days—apart from Easter, the day of maximum fertility—are not directly ordered to the procreation of new children but only indirectly, through the building up of the inner union between the individual in the Church and Christ.

There is, however, one obvious difficulty still to be dealt with. If we suppose that the natural meaning of coitus between spouses provides the most adequate symbolism of the love between Christ and his Church, then the practice of NFP for the avoidance of children would seem to be morally evil. For surely, during her earthly pilgrimage, the Church is to bring as many people to life in Christ as possible, to become the mother of as many children as possible, without other limitations than those imposed by the mysteries of the divine decrees and human freedom. How could Christ refrain from giving her more children? If more children are possible through Christ's gift of the Holy Spirit, how could the Church refuse to bear them? Would not NFP, if used to avoid children, be illicit, precisely as a violation of the basic meaning of sexual activity? Would not couples be obliged to use NFP precisely in order to have as many children as possible?

To respond, we need to keep firmly in mind that the symbolism with which we are concerned is not imagery, even though using images, nor is it allegory, which is the elaboration of metaphor into anecdote or

---

[5] George Maloof, *The Psychology of Fertility Awareness and Natural Family Planning: Psychology of Sexual Relations and Natural Family Planning* (Peterborough, Ont.: John E. Harrington, 1977), p. 10.

story. Thus, although fire is a multicultural symbol of human love, it is not an image of it. So, sexual activity symbolizes the natural goods of marriage. It is this natural meaning of sexuality that God has ordered toward a particular, supernatural fullness of meaning.[6]

Hence, the concrete actions of a couple in their sexual relations are not ordinarily predicable of Christ and the Church. Coitus does not picture or image the relations between Christ and the Church, nor do fertility and the other aspects of human marriage. There is, then, no problem in dealing with matters of sexual activity and fertility by means of the symbolism of the relations between Christ and the Church. The need for Christ and the Church to have as many children as possible remains. But this need cannot be directly translated into a need to bring the largest possible number of children into this world of sin and death. It is the need to bring all those naturally born, whether to those who are already his people or to others—and, where possible, to bring all those begotten though not yet born—to be reborn of water and the Holy Spirit from the womb of the Church by baptism.

In the next section we will consider more directly the questions that have arisen about the difference between natural family planning and contraception.

---

[6] For fuller development of this point, see chapter 4.

13

NFP AND CONTRACEPTION

A detailed comparison between NFP and contraception would need to be done more carefully than is often the case. Without attempting here to undertake that project, perhaps a brief reflection on some of the differences can provide some help in understanding this subject. Failing to put the comparison on the right basis would obscure some crucial differences between them.

In any moral system where *intentions alone* are allowed to count toward the goodness or badness of an action, there could be no awareness of the crucial differences between any form of contraception by chemical or barrier means and any use of NFP for the sake of not having children. From this point of view, both practices would be seen as treating the gametes as if they were irrelevant to the moral evaluation of any form of contraceptive practice. An approach to moral evaluation based only on intentions so discounts their relevance for the ethical analysis that (even if it does not make any explicit mention of them) it in effect treats the gametes as if they were some sort of foreign bodies, alien to the individuals who constitute the couple, or as totally dependent on their choices since they can be blocked and disposed of at will. But this sort of approach would miss considering most of what we have been discussing about the real role of the gametes in human fertility and the distinctive nature of human sexuality, let alone the supernatural meaning and dimensions of our sexuality.

It is, of course, important to include considerations of *intention* in one's moral analysis, so long as we do not reduce moral analysis to considerations of intention *alone*. It is important to consider the character of the act (for some types of action are wrong always and everywhere) as well as the circumstances, including the consequences. Sexual immorality (and contraception in particular) has its evil effects directly on the love between the spouses and within them. The question of children (their number, the spacing of them, the timing of new children, etc.) does certainly concern the couple's motives, but not only their motives. Contraception destroys the very meaning of their action. Their language of love is damaged and defective in its capacity for meaning anything at all.

Perhaps the most significant difference between NFP and contraception is this: The use of contraceptives renders the woman or (less commonly) her partner effectively sterile, whereas neither sort of sterility occurs through NFP. The symbolic difference is considerable. In NFP there remains the promise and hope of conception and thus of new life developing, not only physiologically but in terms of the family needs that serve as the motivation for its use. In contraception, one has only death—dead ova or dead sperm or dead zygotes—or, in the least bad scenario, the suppression of growth and the suspension of life.

Upon deeper reflection, however, we find that death is present in another way as well. To see the point, let us recall something that Christopher Dawson observed concerning the early nature religions, and as we consider this, we will do well to remember, too, the tendency of the technological to become magical:

> In so far as these ceremonies take the form of a mimicry or imitation of the processes of nature, they afford an opportunity for men to acquire a knowledge and control over nature which is substantial and real, not merely an illusion of magical art. When, for example, the Australian native collects the grass seed and blows a little of it in all directions in order to make it grow plentifully, it is easy to see in the ceremony the germ of a development which might eventually lead to the discovery of agriculture.[1]
>
> For the first development of the higher culture in the Near East, the beginnings of agriculture, irrigation, and city life were profoundly religious in their conception. Men did not learn to control the forces of nature to make the earth fruitful, and to raise flocks and herds, as a practical task of economic organization in which they relied on their own enterprise and hard work. They viewed it rather as a religious

---

[1] Christopher Dawson, *Progress and Religion* (Garden City, N.Y.: Doubleday Image, 1960), pp. 89–90.

rite by which they co-operated as priests and hierophants in the great cosmic mystery of the fertilization and growth of nature.[2]

Magic seeks to perform feats of control and dominion from without, with no necessary bond or inner linkage with what is being controlled and dominated. It is simply manipulation. Technology too often moves in the same direction. By contrast, religion enters into the natural constitution of the world, with reverence and respect (not with simple esteem or mere valuing) so as to lead nature from within to subserve human purposes, without doing damage to its intrinsic being and purposes. It is, thus, a sort of education of the natural world. It is this same aspect of being "from within" that characterizes natural family planning in contrast to the quasi-magical means of contraception.

One can see this point in more detail by reflecting on the fact that many treat the body as if it were a machine, albeit a biochemical one, with parts that are able to be regulated and replaced. Each of these parts is considered to have assignable functions that can be used, should we so choose, for one function only, with all others simply suppressed or eliminated. Indeed, the whole machine can, in consequence, be replaced if similar functions are available from elsewhere. But the truth is quite different: the body is an organism, in which every part is affected by every other. Each part is unique, yet with none having simply independent functions.

The magical, technological attitude insists that we should value our bodies rather than revere them, that we should use them rather than treat them with reverence, that we should own them rather than be merely the steward of their powers and custodians of their being, that we should control them totally rather than submit them to the Holy Spirit. We fail to see that total control of any living being means its death; and that only animation by the Spirit can give eternal life. In sum, the body is sacred, holy, and has sanctity, a sanctity that is not wholly lost even when it is dead.

Considered in this way, it becomes ever clearer that contraception results from a view of persons as machines and fails to see the body as the temple of the Holy Spirit, at least in anticipation, and to see ourselves as children of God. To understand this would be to acknowledge that we are profoundly dependent on structures that reflect his

[2] Ibid., p. 95.

mystery in the world and not primarily on our own powers. Hence, contraception is a basic violation of the sanctity of innocent human life, even when not involving any abortifacient—a rare situation today, with the pill and the IUD. For the actions that generate what is sacred are themselves sacred; those that generate what is good are themselves good; those that bring about the valuable are themselves valuable.

A fortiori is this true when God himself must act in conjunction with his creatures to effect new life. His intervention each time a child is conceived is in strong analogy with his intervention to change the bread and wine into the Body and Blood of his Son in each Mass at the words of the priest. In both cases, we are forced to see that he acts within this world to effect something beyond the powers of nature, and that he does so in seeming total subordination to the often sinful will of his creatures.

Is There an Obligation to
Have as Many Children as Possible?

What we have said above tries to show the vast difference between NFP, even when practiced with the intention of not having children, and any form of contraception. But now we must ask about the permissibility of this intention. One way in which to begin that consideration is to ask whether there is an obligation to have as many children as possible.

The obligation of Christians to have children as a result of their marital union is not the same as was Israel's when still looking forward to the coming of the Messiah. In Israel there was a greater obligation than that which rests on all married couples in general to contribute to the good of their people by bringing forth children to replace and to augment the population.[3] As members of the people God had chosen to be his own, they looked forward in expectation and sought to make possible, as far as they could, the coming of the Messiah.

Interestingly, the Law proscribed intercourse for seven days after the cessation of menstrual flow (see Lev 15:19). Thus coitus, when

---

[3] Whatever the proponents of Zero Population Growth may say, a growing population of young people provides both the pressure for improvement and the ingenuity that makes it possible, despite the problems also created.

resumed with greater desire thereafter, was most likely to occur at a time of fertility, thus maximizing the number of children to be conceived even though decreasing the frequency of intercourse. This is perhaps the first recorded instance of a practice like those involved in natural family planning that we know about, and here it is used not for avoidance but for the generation of children. This prescription of the Law was among the large set of directives that were abrogated with our Lord's coming. It could be abrogated because of the change that occurred with the coming of the Messiah. Fertility always remained a good thereafter, but one at a lower level of urgency.

Scripture lays considerable emphasis on the sterility of many great women from Sarah to Elizabeth—all of them, we should note, before the coming of the Christ. There were probably as many sterile women proportionately among those mentioned in the New Testament after his coming. If nothing is said about their condition, it is that with the coming of the Lord, sterility had ceased to have religious significance.

Since the Messiah, the Christ of the Lord, has come, the pressing need to maximize the number of one's children is gone.[4] Apart from the new demands that arise after conditions such as all-out war, pestilence, widespread famine, and so on, Christians seem to be free of any intrinsic obligations to maximize the number of their children. There are, however, lesser social obligations also to consider. There is, of course, the obvious need to maintain the race. A couple owes, at the least, a replacement for themselves to their people and country. All the good that comes from the mobilization of energy and culture and from personal development that is brought about by the needs of one's children is not a merely familial good. Since it is made possible beyond the most primitive level only by society, it is owed in gratitude to society for its hope and continuation into the future.

It is worth recalling that in at least one major Jewish tradition, there is no thought of personal immortality, of none at least worth having, for the individual. Through his posterity the individual is made "immortal", or, as an alternative, he may labor to leave behind him a good name and a blessed memory of his virtue and his benefactions to his

---

[4] Cf. Karl Barth, *Church Dogmatics*, vol. 3, *The Doctrine of Creation*, pt. 4, as discussed in John C. Wakefield, *Artificial Childmaking* (Saint Louis, Mo.: Pope John XXIII Medical-Moral Research and Education Center, 1978), pp. 161, 188.

people and so to mankind (see Ps 102:24–28). But Christians, looking forward in hope to the glorious resurrection of the body in Christ, need no substitute form of immortality. Hence, they can engage themselves without ultimate loss in a wholly celibate existence as a priest or a religious. They can afford to suffer loss of reputation, fame, and even a blessed memory, with and for Christ, who suffered the same for them in a mode of humility without equal on earth.

Since our true citizenship is in heaven and our hope is directed toward the life to come (Phil 3:20–21), our social duty to procreate is greatly qualified and limited. For no indication is given us of the optimal size of earth's population. What matters most for Christians is not the number of new children to be naturally begotten but the universality of the conversion to Christ of all who are born. In the next section we will turn to the question of the use of fertility pills for the sake of increasing the number of children begotten, but here we must focus first on the question of the salvation of those who are conceived. Everyone who is conceived has an eternal destiny. What matters, then, is the eternal salvation of those who *are* brought into this world.

It is not clear that having more children necessarily provides more children for the Church. Human freedom of the will, to say nothing of the mysteries of God's distribution of his graces, makes clear that parents do not have the ultimate say about the eternal destiny of their children. On the other hand, the greatness of God's gifts to us in Christ lays a greater obligation on Catholic couples to have children who will receive their share in such spiritual riches, in comparison with those couples who can offer their children little or no human hope of a blessed eternity.

None of this gives us direct answers to questions concerning number or spacing of children. But it does give us a framework in which to think about such questions. At the natural level the maximum number of children is not required of each couple, but God does desire all who are naturally born to be born supernaturally as well. Yet for those who do not die as infants or as the equivalents of small children, he waits on their cooperation and free choice.

The Moral Quality of Fertility Pills

Since the various sorts of fertility pills are as fully artificial as contraceptive pills, many argue that the moral characters of the two varieties of pill must be roughly at least the same. As mentioned earlier, the obligation of Christians to have children as a result of their marital union is not now what it was for the Jews who still looked forward to the coming of the Messiah. It would seem particularly difficult, then, to show that a couple lies under any obligation to use fertility pills, most especially if there be any doubt about the risk of multiple births or of dangerous side effects.

But *may* they be used? Such use does not stand in violation of the basic principle that those created in the image of God must, like that image, be "begotten, not made". For what is brought about by fertility pills is a biological change in the mother-to-be that of itself does not "make" a child. On the other hand, just as contraceptive pills render a woman's body inept for the full meaning of sexual union, so fertility pills would seem to render it insensitive to one of the key elements in the procreative meaning of sexual union. For such pills seem very likely to induce multiple conceptions, thus denying those who are conceived the proper physical room and physiological support for proper growth. Thus, they put at hazard the proper development of the children to whose conception they have contributed.

But what if more advanced medicine enables a more refined dosage or a more specific pill, such that what is taken stimulates production of but one egg at a time and does not make that one prone to twinning? If this is but a remedy for a bodily deficiency, and that only, then clearly there would be no moral problem. But if, as it seems, this is a different process, not a direct remedy of the body's normal functioning by a direct stimulating of the normal process, then matters are not so clear. Such use seems to be an intervention "from without" and thus somewhat closer to being "magical". Yet this point is not perfectly clear; perhaps it is merely art and thus something technological, but not magical.

Consider here also the place of the Blessed Virgin Mary, at the boundary between the Testaments. She was naturally fertile, but through her consecration to the Lord as a virgin, she was to be without child of

Joseph. She was made supernaturally fertile, and she came to conceive and bear the Lord supernaturally, by the power of the Holy Spirit. She and Joseph had a virginal marriage and were under no obligation by the use of their natural powers to beget a child. By analogy, a couple is under no obligation to do everything they can to have a child, and thus under no obligation to use fertility pills as a way of trying to do so, even were there no question about their side effects, the risk of multiple births, and so on. What they must do is to remain open to the possibility of children, to welcome them if they come, and to raise them to the Lord.

Natural Family Planning as Part of the Spiritual Life of a Couple

There is great need to see natural family planning in the context of the full dimensions of marital love and of sexual love. Marital love is not solely sexual in its nature or its manifestations, and sexual love is not expressed solely by coitus.

It is essential for the proper use of NFP that husband and wife build up their mutual trust in one another. Only so can they obviate the inevitable misunderstandings of moods and even of words. Such trust is best built through words and by choices and actions that are faithful to the words that they say to one another. A man must be able to trust his wife when she tells him of some bodily condition she is experiencing and not feel that she is just putting him off. A woman must be able to trust her husband and not take his refusal to show physical affection on a given occasion as disinterest in her.

It is not only the virgin and the celibate but also married couples who need to learn how to share even now in the life to come, for our Lord tells us that the life to come will be without the sort of marriage that leads to children (see Lk 20:34–36). Realizing the nature of the life to come can help to free a husband from the constraint of having to be able to "perform" sexually at all times or of having to prove his manhood by the number of his children.[5] Likewise, a wife is freed from the need to prove her fruitfulness by having an unlimited number

---

[5] See Lev 21:17–23: a priest who is ill or sick or deformed cannot approach the altar or the veil, though he can still eat the sacred meats.

of offspring. Nor need she be thought of as frigid or unloving if she does not always desire intercourse. Both must become more deeply free and become better able to give themselves, by a truly free decision, to the other. Intercourse should be not merely a human word that is unthinkingly spoken but a human decision, made in genuine love and charity.

One can summarize what we have been saying here by considering the language that we find in 1 Corinthians 7:3–5: "Render what is owed." Neither owns his own body, but each spouse has a claim on the body of the other. They should not deprive themselves of intercourse except by agreement, perhaps for a time, perhaps to be free for prayer. In prayer, they should understand that they are speaking to God and also speaking to one who is in his image and who is their spouse. Then they can come together again in still greater love and appreciation.

Paul is clear that missionary work is a kind of bringing forth, like a mother's bringing forth a new child: "My little children, with whom I am again in travail until Christ be formed in you!" (Gal 4:19). Now, to be sure, Paul's words refer more directly to the nurturing of the spiritual life in those just beginning and not to their being readied for baptism.

GLOSSARY OF TECHNICAL TERMS

ALLEGORY: a literary form in which the characters and events of a story stand for ideas outside the story itself.

AMENORRHEA: prolonged absence of menstruation.

ANAGOGICAL: within the doctrine of the four senses of Scripture, a level of meaning inspired by the Holy Spirit with reference to eschatology and the sacraments.

ANTITYPE: in the doctrine of recapitulation, a term that refers to Christ as completing, perfecting, and sanctifying the corresponding Type from the Old Testament.

ARTIFICIAL INSEMINATION: the depositing of semen in the vagina by means other than sexual intercourse.

BILLINGS OVULATION METHOD: a method of natural family planning that uses a woman's observation of her cervical mucus at the vulva to identify her periods of fertility and infertility.

BLASTOCYST: the embryo at four days of age; at this time it already possesses an inner cell mass and produces hormones that signal the maternal organism.

BLASTOMERE: one cell of an embryo.

CERVICAL MUCUS: secretions from the cervical crypts that are elicited by the reproductive hormones estrogen and progesterone.

CERVIX: the lower part of the uterus (womb), which projects into the vagina.

CHROMOSOME: one of the forty-six units within each cell that bears the genetic material responsible for inherited characteristics.

COITUS: sexual intercourse.

CONCEPTION: the union of gametes (one spermatozoon with one ovum) by which a woman becomes pregnant and a new human person comes into existence.

CONCEPTUS: the embryo and all the structures that develop from the embryo.

CORPUS LUTEUM: the "yellow body" stage of the ovarian follicle after ovulation, when the lining cells fill in the cavity and now secrete an increased amount of progesterone; in the absence of conception it functions for ten to sixteen days, but will function for at least twelve weeks if there is conception.

EMBRYO: the new organism that results from the fertilization of an ovum; this term applies throughout the first two months of life, from conception until all organs (organogenesis) are formed.

ENDOCRINE SYSTEM: the collection of hormone-producing glands that regulate such things as metabolism, growth and development, reproduction, sleep, and mood, among other things.

ENDOMETRIUM: the mucus membrane that lines the inside of the uterus (womb).

ESTRUS: in subhuman animals, the physical signs (pheromones, reddening of the vulva) that a female is fertile ("in heat") and the inducement to copulation.

FERTILE TIMES: the period during which sexual intercourse can result in a pregnancy.

FERTILITY: the capacity to generate new living beings of the same species; the capacity for reproduction. Properly, fertility belongs to a couple (a male and a female together) but secondarily the term indicates the physical capacity of a person (whether a man or a woman) to contribute all the bodily elements that need to be provided by a person of that gender for a child to be conceived.

FETUS: the stage of development from the end of organogenesis until birth.

GAMETES: the reproductive cells needed for sexual reproduction: the sperm (produced by the male) and the ovum (produced by the female).

GENOME: an organism's complete set of chromosomes.

GONAD: the sexual glands (ovary and testes) that are the source of gametes.

IMPLANTATION: the moment when the blastocyst takes root in the mother's womb.

IMPOTENCE: the inability to engage in sexual relations.

IMPREGNATION: the condition (beginning with coitus) by which a woman becomes pregnant.

INFERTILITY: an inability to conceive that is the result of the temporary absence of a mature ovum. This term stands in contrast with "sterility", for it is a stage of the cycle of fertility and infertility that makes procreation possible.

IN VITRO FERTILIZATION (IVF): a series of procedures for the treatment of infertility problems, involving the collection of oocytes from ovaries and their fertilization in the laboratory.

MEIOSIS: the unique division of oocytes and spermatogonia that produces cells with a haploid (23) rather than a diploid (46) number of chromosomes.

MENARCHE: a woman's first menstrual period.

MENOPAUSE: cessation of menstruation; menopause is established twelve months after the last uterine bleed; ovulation may have ceased years earlier.

MENSES: the monthly flow of blood and cellular debris from the uterus that follows ovulation in the absence of conception.

METAPHOR: a figure of speech that identifies one thing as another, for rhetorical effect.

MITOSIS: ordinary cell-division that results in two cells with forty-six chromosomes each.

MUCUS: see cervical mucus.

NFP: natural family planning

OOCYTE: the germ cell within an ovary.

OVULATION: the release of a mature egg from an ovary.

OVUM: egg cell, oocyte, the female gamete.

PARTHENOGENESIS: the conception of a new organism in a female without any contribution by a male.

POSTPARTUM INFERTILITY: the period after birth in which a woman is not fertile; this period is usually extended for some time while the woman is nursing her child.

PREGNANCY: the state of a woman from the moment of conception.

PUBERTY: the onset of fertility.

SENSES OF SCRIPTURE: according to the traditional understanding of the Church, the levels of meaning to be found in biblical texts, namely, the literal level (the meaning intended by the human author under divine inspiration) and the three spiritual levels intended by the Holy Spirit.

SPERM, SPERMATOZOA: the male gamete.

STERILITY: in a man, the inability to produce or ejaculate sperm; in a woman, either the inability to produce a viable ovum or some condition that prevents its union with the sperm of her husband.

SYMBOL: a sign that stands for something else.

TYPOLOGICAL: within the doctrine of the four senses of scripture, a level of meaning inspired by the Holy Spirit that has reference to the way in which the life of Christ recapitulates the life of God's chosen people by completing what is incomplete, perfecting what is imperfect, and sanctifying what is sinful.

ZYGOTE: the single cell that is produced when the haploid male and female pro-nuclei unite; the one-cell stage of the new being.

SCRIPTURE REFERENCES

TWO IN ONE FLESH: Genesis 2:20–25; 1 Corinthians 6:16–17

ISRAEL, BRIDE OF THE LORD: Hosea 2:4–5, 4:10–15, 9:1, 16–18, 21; Jeremiah 3:1–12; Ezekiel 16; 23; Isaiah 54:4–7; 62:4–5; Song of Solomon

THE CHURCH, BRIDE OF CHRIST: John 3:29; Matthew 22:1–14; Ephesians 5:25–33; Revelation 19:6–9; 21:2, 9

INDIVIDUAL CHRISTIANS WED TO CHRIST: Matthew 9:14–15; 25:1–13; 2 Corinthians 11:2

VIRGINITY: Song of Solomon 4:12; 3:6–11; Jeremiah 18:13; 1 Corinthians 7:1, 7–8, 32–34

EUNUCH SYMBOL: Matthew 19:10–12

READINGS FROM THE FATHERS

Augustine. *Homily 2 on the Letter of John.* In *A Select Library of Nicene and Post-Nicene Fathers of the Christian Church*, vol. 7, edited by Philip Schaff, pp. 469–73. Grand Rapids, Mich.: Eerdmans, 1952.

―――. *Homily 9.* In *A Select Library of Nicene and Post-Nicene Fathers of the Christian Church*, vol. 7, edited by Philip Schaff, pp. 516–19. Grand Rapids, Mich.: Eerdmans, 1952.

―――. *The Literal Meaning of Genesis.* Vol. 2, bk. 9. Translated by John H. Taylor, S.J. Vol. 42 of Ancient Christian Writers. New York: Newman Press, 1982.

―――. *Treatise 8 on John.* In *A Select Library of Nicene and Post-Nicene Fathers of the Christian Church*, vol. 7, edited by Philip Schaff, pp. 58–67. Grand Rapids, Mich.: Eerdmans, 1952.

John Chrysostom. *Commentary on the Letter to the Colossians.* Homily 10. In *A Select Library of Nicene and Post-Nicene Fathers of the Christian Church*, vol. 13. Edited by Philip Schaff and Henry Wace, pp. 303–4. Grand Rapids, Mich.: Eerdmans, 1952.

―――. *Commentary on the Letter to the Colossians.* Homily 12. In *A Select Library of Nicene and Post-Nicene Fathers of the Christian Church*, vol. 13. Edited by Philip Schaff and Henry Wace, pp. 317–21. Grand Rapids, Mich.: Eerdmans, 1952.

―――. *Commentary on the Letter to the Ephesians.* Homily 20. In *A Select Library of Nicene and Post-Nicene Fathers of the Christian Church*, vol. 13. Edited by Philip Schaff and Henry Wace, pp. 143–52. Grand Rapids, Mich.: Eerdmans, 1952.

Methodius of Olympus. *The Symposium: A Treatise on Chastity*. Vol. 27
of Ancient Christian Writers. Translated by Herbert Musurillo, S.J.
Westminster, Md.: Newman Press, 1958.

For further reading in the Fathers, see Johannes Quasten's *Patrology* in
the most recent edition available. Look in the indices in each volume
under "Marriage" and "Church" for references in the text, where
you will find listings of available translations as well as of the original
texts. Note too that Quasten sometimes mentions only in passing
passages of some length and importance for our purpose here.

OTHER READINGS

John Paul II. *Man and Woman He Created Them: A Theology of the Body*, trans. Michael Waldstein. Boston: Pauline Books, 2006.

——. Apostolic Exhortation *Familiaris consortio*, November 22, 1981.

Martelet, Gustave, S.J. *The Church's Holiness and Religious Life*. Saint Louis, Mo.: Review for Religious, 1966.

Quay, Paul M., S.J., "Contraception and Conjugal Love", *Theological Studies* 22 (1961): 18–40.

——. *Contraception and Marital Love*, Washington, D.C.: Family Life Bureau, 1962.

——. "The Theological Position and Role of Ethics", *Listening: Journal of Religion and Culture* 18 (1983): 260–74.

——. "The Theology of Recapitulation: Understanding the Development of Individuals and Cultures". In *The Dynamic Character of Christian Culture*, edited by P. J. Cataldo, pp. 57–95. New York: Society for Christian Culture and University Press of America, 1984.

Vatican Council II, Pastoral Council on the Church in the Modern World *Gaudium et Spes*, December 7, 1965. Nos. 47–52.